The PROPHET M[illegible]AD ﷺ

A ROLE MODEL *for* MUSLIM MINORITIES

Muhammad Yasin Mazhar Siddiqi

Translated by
Abdur Raheem Kidwai

THE ISLAMIC FOUNDATION

Published by

The Islamic Foundation
Markfield Conference Centre
Ratby Lane, Markfield
Leicestershire, LE67 9SY, United Kingdom
Tel: 01530 244944/5, Fax: 01530 244946
E-mail: info@islamic-foundation.org.uk
publications@islamic-foundation.com
Website: www.islamic-foundation.org.uk

Quran House, P.O. Box 30611, Nairobi, Kenya

P.M.B. 3193, Kano, Nigeria

British Library Cataloguing-in-Publication Data
Siddiqi, Muhammad Yasin Mazhar
The Prophet Muhammad: A role model for Muslim minorities
1. Muhammad, Prophet, d.632 – Influence – 2. Muslims – Non-Muslim countries 3. Muslims – Religious life
I.Title II.Islamic Foundation (Great Britain)
297'.09176

ISBN 0 86037 530 7 hb
ISBN 0 86037 535 8 pb

Cover/Book design & typeset: Nasir Cadir
Printed and bound in England by Antony Rowe Ltd, Chippenham, Wiltshire

Contents

Transliteration Table

Arabic Consonants:

Initial, unexpressed medial and final:

ء	ʾ	د	d	ض	ḍ	ك	k
ب	b	ذ	dh	ط	ṭ	ل	l
ت	t	ر	r	ظ	ẓ	م	m
ث	th	ز	z	ع	ʿ	ن	n
ج	j	س	s	غ	gh	هـ	h
ح	ḥ	ش	sh	ف	f	و	w
خ	kh	ص	ṣ	ق	q	ي	y

Vowels, diphthongs, etc.

Short:	ـَ	a	ـِ	i	ـُ	u
Long:	ـَا	ā	ـُو	ū	ـِي	ī
Diphthongs:			ـَوْ	aw		
			ـَيْ	ay		

Dedication

In the name of Allah, Most Compassionate, Most Merciful

Praise be to Allah, Lord of the worlds and peace and blessings be upon the leader of the Messengers and upon his family and his Companions and all those who follow them in an excellent way until the Day of Reckoning.

Preface

In the past eras spanning a few centuries *ʿulamā'* have been projecting Islam as a ruling faith. Islamic *fiqh* underlines only the aspects of Islamic state. It is generally held that Islamic teachings can be implemented and bear fruits only when Islam is the state religion. As a result, the establishment of an Islamic State and gaining power have somehow become the basic goals. Granted that Islam urges its followers to achieve dominance and directs them to somehow not put up with subjugation. However, the notion that Islam must always be dominant and in all circumstances has caused much trouble. Apart from *ʿulamā'*, *fiqh* scholars and thinkers, even the general public seem wedded strongly to the above notion. Little wonder then that rulership has become part of the Muslim psyche.

By the quirks of developments in history, Islam came to be known as a state religion, dictating man's way of life. The Prophet's Islamic state had developed beyond the Arabian Peninsula and during the Muslim Caliphate it had grown into a world-wide Islamic state. Most of the communities, cultures and civilizations and their religions in the Middle Ages pledged their subservience to Islam. It was during this heyday of the rule and domination of Islam that many branches of learning attained progress and were codified. Naturally all the discussion related to these disciplines is in the context of Islam being the state religion.

It must be however, stated that in the same period Muslims led their lives as a minority in many countries. They were under the domination of the adherents of other faiths. After only one and a half centuries of the Abbasid rule, decline and disintegration had set in the Muslim polity. The regions far away from the seat of the Caliphate were constantly exposed to incursion and even defeat. At the fall of the Umayyad Caliphate of Andalusia in the fifth/eleventh century Muslims had lost their dominant position at large. They stood divided and sub-divided and as a subjugated people. By the middle of the thirteenth century CE most of the Muslim lands in the West, particularly Andalusia and Sicily were under non-Muslim rules reducing Muslims to a helpless minority. In some countries and regions Muslim empires, no doubt, flourished. Yet Islam as a faith was no longer ascendant, notwithstanding the political power and rulership enjoyed by Muslims.

Even during this period of trial, loss and subjugation both the *ʿulamāʾ* and the generality of Muslims did not give up their claim to power and rule. Notwithstanding their enviable mental faculties and original thinking, the *ʿulamāʾ* and writers persisted in projecting Islam as a dominant, ruling force. This naturally intoxicated the Muslim masses with illusions about their supremacy. Their thoughts and deeds were dictated by their nostalgic memories about their rule and their glorious accomplishments in the past. Their writings fed the public only on the stories of their political power and domination. It greatly pleased the commoners who dreamt of their return to power. Both the *ʿulamāʾ* and the general public failed to take the ground realities in their stride.

During this period of decline substantial additions were made to the Islamic legacy of sciences and other branches of learning. Some of the achievements recorded in this period are historic and unique. All their disciplines were considerably enriched ranging from *tafsīr*, *ḥadīth* and *fiqh* studies to history, scholasticism, philosophy and other fields of social sciences, arts and sciences. However, these advancements rested on old canons of knowledge. The methodology and line of argumentation adopted in the Middle

Ages was followed strictly even at a much later date. The notions about Islam as state religion persisted in the works on history and *fiqh*. It did not occur to anyone to compile the *fiqh* for Muslim minorities. Nor did anyone analyze the causes of the downfall of the Muslims.

Thanks to this illusion of grandeur, Muslim writers were drawn only towards writing a historical account of their rule and political power. They did so in the face of their own claim that Islam offers the most befitting solution to the problems of every age. Their claim was undoubtedly sound. However, they failed to vindicate it. They could not identify satisfactorily the factors which help a community assume power. By the same token, they were oblivious of the causes of their downfall. As a result they could not offer a way out for the vanquished and subjugated Muslims. I am fully aware of the offence my above statements would cause to many. However, merely getting offended does not change history. Notwithstanding protests, grim facts remain as they are.

The Prophet's exemplary life is regarded as the index to the growth of both Islam and Muslims. It is, no doubt, true. However, the Muslim biographers have followed all along a traditional stance. Following in the footsteps of the earliest biographers of the Prophet, (peace be upon him) namely Ibn Isḥāq and Ibn Hishām they repeat what these great masters have already stated. Some have, at most, added a few more reports. However, there has not been any major change in the methodology or the line of argument. The entire life history of the Prophet (peace be upon him) remains yet to be analyzed. The critical study of his Makkan period is markedly inadequate. No biographer of his has ever given thought to this obvious fact that the Makkan period of his life and of Islamic history represents the phase of subjugation.

The division of the Prophet's life into the Makkan and Madīnan periods, as devised by the Orientalists, is downright pernicious. They were swayed by their ulterior motives in insisting upon this bifurcation. Nonetheless, it is a historical fact. Many Islamic considerations lie at its back as well. Muslim writers have paid little attention to the rationale behind this divine scheme of things, according to which the Prophet's career was split into Makkan and Madīnan. These writers deal only tangentially with this issue while discussing Makkan and Madīnan *sūrahs* and studying important events in the Prophet's life. However, they fall much short of analyzing it in full. They are unable to identify the causes behind this division.

It is hardly recognized that Islam did not enjoy any power in the Makkan period or that Muslims were a minority then. No study has been carried out regarding the divine commands issued to the Prophet (peace be upon him) in the Makkan *sūrahs* in the first thirteen years of Islam. How historical events had their bearings on the Prophet's way has not been explored at all. Nor has any attempt been made so far to study in the light of the above facts the history of Muslims as a minority, the philosophy of history, the way of life and patterns of thought. This is in the face of the fact that in the Makkan period when Muslims were a minority, Islam had a distinctive message, which is adequate for Muslims all over the world, providing them as it does with a comprehensive code of life.

In the present work the Makkan phase of the Prophet's life has been studied from the vantage point of a minority. Obviously the standard material has been sifted. Some additional reports have also been taken into account. More importantly, on placing them in the correct perspective, the entire scenario changes altogether. This brings into sharp relief the character of Islam in a minority context. It might be offensive for some Muslims. However, being a historical truth no one can deny or refute it. On studying the Prophet's life in this perspective, a role model can be gained for the Muslim minorities, scattered in all parts of the world. It might serve as a mirror for them and for deriving guidance from the Prophet's example, which would enable them to lead life in accordance with Islam. It would help them maintain their identity as Muslims. More importantly, it would instruct them how a minority transforms into a majority and how the subjugated ones earn power and rule.

This wisdom underlies the division between Makkan and Madinan phases in the history of Islam.

I have no illusion that it is a perfect, error-free work. As author I am fully conscious of its shortcomings. I frankly acknowledge its defects. A discussion on the evolution of Islamic commands in the Makkan period could not be included in this book. For it would constitute a book in itself. In view of the bulk of the present book, it was not feasible to include this discussion as well. It would form part of another book. In its present form, this book may be regarded, at best, as a pointer to another perspective. Out of His infinite wisdom and power Allah may enable scholars more competent than me to carry forward this work. The present work may inspire and serve as food for thought for more accomplished writers and thinkers. For, it is on record that the wise Solomon picked up his legendary wisdom from the fools among his community.

The subject, the Muslim minority in the Prophet's days, had struck me a long time ago. Owing to my other preoccupations, however, I did not embark upon it. Some twenty years ago my esteemed colleague Professor Muhammad Nejatullah Siddiqi had urged me to write on the Muslim minority of Abyssinia, for it was a timely issue. We had lively discussions on this issue. It brought home the point that there is a pressing need for the Prophetic role model for Muslims as a minority. In my discussions with Professor Siddiqi, however, I insisted that the Muslim minority of Abyssinia constitutes only a peripheral issue. The real issue to be tackled is the Makkan phase of the Prophet's life. For the Prophet (peace be upon him) spent thirteen years in steering the Muslims as a minority. Professor Siddiqi initially stuck to his stance that the Muslim minority of Abyssinia be discussed. Later on, however, he relented, endorsing my priority. I would be failing in my duty if I do not thank him profusely for his inspiring discussion, his suggestions, and his encouragement to take up this study.

I had prepared an outline of this book some time ago. However, without divine help it was not possible to complete this job. Last year I was able to write its first draft. While working on it I managed to identify and consult some new material on the subject. After a year long discussion, reflection and interaction with my friends and colleagues I was able to finish it. It goes without saying that the entire credit goes to Allah who exercises all control over man's mind and heart and directs him to a goal which He desires. Were I to prostrate before Him innumerable times, it would not repay in the least the debt of gratitude I owe to Him for all His favours. He is Most Forgiving and Most Merciful and Oft-Returning and All Wise. For He showers His mercy on one for his single act of prostration. He alone decides one's fate in both the worlds. May Allah accept this humble effort of mine.

Next, I am beholden to the Prophet Muḥammad (peace be upon him). He as a mortal, no doubt, passed away. However, his eternal message would last till the Day of Reckoning. He continues to benefit humanity. Shāh Walīullāh brands it as the inner dimension of caliphate, which manifests the Prophet's favours. Without this mankind would have been poorer. I can offer only my humble presentation in that I do not have anything else to offer. I owe everything to him. It thus constitutes a modest effort for sending benediction upon him.

Among fellow human beings I am grateful to many, both the deceased and living ones. Of them, the favours of my late father Mawlwī al-Ḥājj Inʿām ʿAlī on me are numerous. Apart from being my father, he was my mentor. It is owing to his training and guidance that I have been able to accomplish something. May Allah reward him on account of the present book. I am confident of this, for it is stated in the Qur'ān and *ḥadīth* that good deeds of one's children are owing to the blessings sought by one's parents. I am thankful to all *ʿulamā'*, my teachers and biographers of the Prophet (peace be upon him). I must place on record my debt of thanks to Shāh ʿAbd al-Qādir Dihlawī.

Among my present well-wishers, the pride of place is reserved for my selfless wife who has always assisted in all my good deeds. In addition to being my life partner, she has been my collaborator. Thanks to her, I manage to devote myself fully to academic pursuits.

The same holds true for my children who have assisted me all along. Not only do they love me, they also do everything to make my life comfortable. I must mention, in particular, my son Ahmad Moin who worked hard in the production of this work. Without the help of my student Jamshed Ahmad Nadvi, whom I regard no less than as my own son, many errors would have crept into this work. I owe thanks to Mr. Kabir Ahmad Khan, Librarian, Institute of Islamic Studies Library, Aligarh Muslim University, Aligarh, for all his support. He always obliged me by providing me with the books I needed. I am grateful also to Professor Abdul Ali, Chairman, Dept. of Islamic Studies, AMU and my other colleagues at the Department for their cooperation. I thank my other friends for all their help and support.

I must thank the late Mawlānā Muḥammad Rizwān Qāsimī, Dār al-ʿUlūm, Sabīl al-Salām, Hyderabad, for having organized my series of lectures on *sīrah,* which constitute the bedrock of the present work.

My thanks go also to my colleague, Professor Abdur Raheem Kidwai, Dept. of English, AMU, for having translated this work, from Urdu into English. I am grateful to Dr. M. Manazir Ahsan, Director General of the Islamic Foundation, UK, for the publication of the work.

Muhammad Yasin Mazhar Siddiqi

al-Amin
64 Ahmad Nagar
Aligarh (UP)
INDIA
October 2005

CHAPTER I

Pluralistic Society of Makkah

Makkah is generally taken as the seat of a single faith, inhabited by several families of the Quraysh tribe. This is not a sound view. The Quraysh, no doubt, enjoyed a majority in Makkah. They were at the helm of its affairs and dominated its business and trade. They had a leading role in its political system and economy. They were ranked high in its social life. Yet they were not the only notable tribe in Makkah. Besides them, there were social classes, tribes and groups who enjoyed an influential position in Makkah. The latter would often take decisive steps, changing the course of events.

Even the Quraysh families professed two different sets of social values. In opposition to other Arab tribes they displayed unity at political and military levels. However, they were divided among themselves into numerous political, social, economic, religious and cultural and economic groups beset with rivalry. Their elite had mutual differences, animosity and jealousy. Their social relations, economic ties, trade links and political and cultural alliances were subject to change almost every day. These differences often caused social unrest, economic chaos, religious friction, clash of cultures and commercial and economic tussles.

In their religious life too, there were marked differences and variety. The Quraysh families were essentially the adherents of Abrahamic faith. However, their faith had been vitiated by accretions. They had incorporated many innovations in their original faith. They had deviated much from the original path. Polytheism had become the main article of their faith. Their practices too, had grown intensely polytheistic. Their affiliation with a host of idols had divided them into groups and sub-groups. There was a reform movement against the ancestral faith. Atheism had been entrenched deeply there. Some persons and groups had severed all links with faith. They were under the evil influence of the neighbouring Jews, Christians and Magians. Some had turned into Jews, others into Christians and Magians. Many were influenced in varying degrees by these faiths. By the time of the Prophet Muḥammad's advent Makkah was a truly pluralistic and multi-faith society.

Tribal Divisions in Makkah

The Makkan Quraysh

In the tribal hierarchy and in terms of social status the Quraysh families had different rankings. Quṣayy ibn Kilāb had reorganized the town of Makkah. At the time he settled some leading Quraysh families in the vicinity of the Kaʿbah. They came to be known as 'Quraysh al-Baṭā'iḥ'. This stratification was based on social standing, rank of the family and the distinctions it enjoyed. Even among the Quraysh al-Baṭā'iḥ there were class divisions. The more honourable among them were housed next to the Kaʿbah. The pride of place was annexed by Quṣayy ibn Kilāb, for this family was the custodian of the Kaʿbah and was held in great esteem for its political and social standing. Next to them were Banū Makhzūm, Banū Sahm, Banū ʿAdiyy, Banū Taym and Banū Jumaḥ etc, who were also settled around the Kaʿbah. The settlement was done on all sides of the Kaʿbah. The inner circle was occupied by the Quraysh al-Baṭā'iḥ. Those in the outer circle were regarded as less privileged ones and came to be known as Quraysh al-Ẓawāhir. They were granted land at some distance from the Kaʿbah. Among them were the less powerful families such as of Banū Lu'ayy and Banū Fihr etc.[1]

The Quraysh families held important positions in Makkan political order and administrative set up in relation to their ranking in social life and their financial status. Each family thus occupied some major position while the highest office went to the most distinguished family. The head of the Banū Quṣayy family enjoyed about half of the twelve most important positions, including the provisions for water, flag, hospitality and other offices. These offices were held at a later date by their sons and successors as a hereditary privilege. Anyone outside the Quṣayy family was never granted any of these offices. However, the families belonging to the Quraysh al-Baṭā'iḥ held one or two of these positions. Some of these went to Banū Makhzūm, Banū Taym, Banū ʿAdiyy and Banū Jumaḥ. The Kaʿbah possessions were in the charge of Banū Sahm. None of these positions were ever enjoyed by the Quraysh al-Ẓawāhir.[2]

Around the time of the Prophet Muḥammad's advent, the twelve leading families of the Quraysh al-Baṭā'iḥ dominated the political order, economy and administrative machinery of Makkah. In about two centuries the family of Banū Quṣayy had branched out into five leading families, with each of these controlling some office on hereditary basis. ʿAbd al-Dār, the eldest son of Quṣayy had three positions while the other son ʿAbd Manāf maintained his control over the other three departments. These were later transferred to the three main branches of this family i.e. Banū Hāshim, Banū Nawfal and Banū ʿAbd Shams/Banū Umayyah: Although ʿAbd Manāf's family was divided into four distinct branches they were led by a single head of the family in the encounters with others. The three offices held by Banū ʿAbd al-Dār were assumed by the branches of their family while other positions were retained by successors on a hereditary basis.[3]

Although wealth did not play any major role in the tribal affairs and administrative acumen, its impact was not negligible either. It did have its bearing on retaining or abdicating some positions. As Banū Nawfal belonging to Banū ʿAbd Manāf turned financially weak, their office of providing nursing was bought by another Quraysh family, Banū Asad, who had been earlier entitled only to join consultative meetings. The affluent tradesman Ḥakīm ibn Ḥizām of Banū Asad was able to gain the custodianship of the tribal and community assembly Dār al-Nadwah by dint of his wealth. Banū ʿAbd al-Dār who earlier held this position had to forego it on account of their adverse financial status. The same happened in the case of the leaders of two Banū Hāshim families. In view of his failing financial condition the privilege of offering water to pilgrims passed on from Abū Ṭālib al-Hāshimī to his wealthy younger brother al-ʿAbbās al-Hāshimī and was retained in future by the latter. Wealth and financial condition often played a key role in determining the social status and political power of a tribe and family. The neo-rich aspired for political and social status and this often resulted in mutual hostilities, social disorder, rivalry and jealousy, family feuds, trade war and psychological tension. It often changed the course of events.[4]

Numerical strength, economic resources and social status, it goes without saying, were intertwined. These factors impelled groups and families to lay claim to privileges and rights. Often did two branches of the same family stand against each other, pressing their respective claims for position and office. According to oft-quoted reports, two sub-branches of the Banū Quṣayy family – Banū ʿAbd Manāf and Banū ʿAbd al-Dār turned into foes. Their rivalry could have led to the break out of war. The issue was, however, resolved amicably by dividing power and sharing office.

As the Quraysh families differed on social, community and tribal issues, they were divided into groups and sub-groups. The same social and economic forces accounted for the division of the Quraysh into the two major groups of al-Aḥlāf and al-Muṭayyabūn. It is on record that the Quraysh tribes were in two opposing camps on the issue of the division of offices among Banū ʿAbd Manāf and Banū ʿAbd al-Dār. Al-Muṭayyabūn sided with Banū ʿAbd Manāf. Among them were Banū Taym, Banū Zuhrah, Banū Asad, Banū al-Ḥārith ibn Fihr. As opposed to it, among al-Aḥlāf were Banū ʿAbd al-Dār and their supporters such as Banū Makhzūm, Banū Jumaḥ, Banū Sahm and Banū ʿAdiyy ibn Kaʿb. Then there was another camp of ʿĀmīr ibn Lu'ayy and Muḥārib ibn Fihr, which was not allied with either of the two and acted neutrally all along.[5]

The agreement known as *Ḥilf al-Fuḍūl*, which was contracted for defending the interests of weaker sections and foreigners too, had divided Quraysh families into two main camps. Those who stood for this agreement comprised Banū Hāshim, Banū Muṭṭalib, Banū Taym, Banū Zuhrah and Banū Asad. Even the united family of Banū ʿAbd Manāf was divided on this issue. Among those who kept away from this agreement were Banū Umayyah, Banū Nawfal, Banū Makhzūm, Banū Jumaḥ and Banū Sahm etc. While Banū Hāshim and Banū Muṭṭalib supported the agreement, Banū Nawfal and Banū Umayyah kept aloof from it. Several social, economic and political considerations were at work behind these divisions. This had dealt a severe blow to the ideal of a unified family and united tribe. The same was re-echoed later when Banū Hāshim and Banū Muṭṭalib reacted differently to the social boycott of Muslims. They helped and defended Muslims whereas the two other families of Banū ʿAbd Manāf – Banū Umayyah and Banū Nawfal did support the Quraysh.[6] The Qurayshī stance was dictated by their political and economic interests. In contrast, Banū Hāshim and Banū Muṭṭalib abided by the tribal tradition of protecting their own folk. As a consequence, the leading united family of Banū ʿAbd Manāf was divided.

Other social, economic and political factors too, had sown discord among the Quraysh, dividing them into numerous units at war with one another. These differences existed among families as well. For example, Banū Makhzūm thought of themselves as superior to everyone, especially to Banū ʿAbd Manāf. It caused constant friction among the two. Banū ʿAdiyy was Banū Zuhrah's foe. They were hostile to Banū Taym as well. Many families had strained relations. Often did it surface at the level of the leading families. An instance in point is the serious rift between Banū Hāshim and Banū Umayyah, though they were part of the larger family of Banū ʿAbd Manāf. Essentially it was a clash of interests, without any root in family feuds. Such differences and hostilities were common among the Quraysh.

At the level of individuals too, the issues of property, wealth, politics, business and trade and social relations created tension in tribes. At times, members of the same family with strong blood ties clashed with one another, prompted by their self interest. For example, the chief of Banū ʿAbd al-Muṭṭalib, ʿAbd al-Muṭṭalib al-Hāshimī was hostile to Ḥarb ibn Umayyah, the leader of Banū Umayyah. The former had differences with members of other families. The hostility between Hāshim and Umayyah signified the rift between the uncle and the nephew who were impelled by their economic or social interests.

Apart from the Quraysh, some other Arab tribes were also settled in Makkah. Their details follow in this work. Some leading members of the Quraysh had serious differences with chiefs of the non-Quraysh Arab tribes. ʿAbd al-Muṭṭalib al-Hāshimi differed sharply with several Quraysh and non-Quraysh leaders. This animosity did not rest on any tribal consideration. Rather, he was guided by his economic interests. Muḥammad Ibn Ḥabīb al-Baghdādī has reported at length such hostilities.[7] The Makhzūm chief al-Fakīh ibn Mughīrah developed differences with the chief of Banū ʿAbd Shams, ʿUtbah ibn Rabīʿah. Such hostilities were natural in a multi-tribal and pluralistic polity such as of Makkah. It must be said to the credit of the forbearing Quraysh that they did not let these conflicts flare up into open war and bloodshed. It did not turn them into enemies forever either.[8]

Other Arab Tribes of Makkah

The Quraysh did not always constitute a majority in Makkah. Nor did they ever hold its leadership. In ancient days Banū Jurhum held this position and enjoyed the custodianship of the Kaʿbah. For they were the kin of Prophet Ishmael (peace be upon him) the founder of both Makkah and the Kaʿbah. Banū Khuzāʿah snatched this position from Banū Jurhum: At a later date, it was annexed by the Quraysh chief, Quṣayy ibn Kilāb. In the intervening period some other Arab tribes had their ascendancy. They were however, trounced by some other Arab tribes. Often did the losing tribe leave Makkah. In some cases, however, some of their families managed to settle down in the vicinity of Makkah.[9]

Both Makkan tribes and their opponents secured military and political help from other tribes and with the latter's active support they managed to drive away the enemy. For expelling Banū Khuzāʿah, Quṣayy ibn Kilāb had drawn upon the military strength of Banū Kinānah. Likewise, for putting an end to the interference of the Arab tribe Ṣaufah in the affairs of Makkah, they had sought help from Banū Kinānah and their ancestor Quḍāʿah.[10]

Hāshim ibn ʿAbd Manāf and his illustrious son ʿAbd al-Muṭṭalib of the Quraysh had taken military and financial support from these tribes – Saʿd, Hudhaym and ʿAzrā. This alone had helped them entrench deep into Makkan polity. Muḥammad ibn Ḥabīb al-Baghdādī has recounted at length the agreements carried out by several tribes, families and individuals related to Muṭayyabūn, Aḥlāf, ʿAdiyy, Banū Sahm, Khuzāʿah and other contracts.[11]

There are bits of evidence indicating that at times help was taken from other tribes and foreign rulers. This help was secured for expelling non-local groups from Makkah and for establishing their political power locally. Sources speak of the help taken from the Lakhmī ruler of Iraq, King Mundhir, Yemenī King Zuwayzan and other heads of state by Makkan chiefs.

Besides such help from without, some Arab Bedouin tribes had settled permanently in Makkah. Such non-local elements turned to Makkah in view of the adverse circumstances faced by them. On reaching Makkah they entered into alliance with a Quraysh family which enabled them to settle down in Makkah. Then they formed marital kinship with the same family or its allies. It cemented their position. In the Arab tribal norms both of these relationships were very strong. It was obligatory on a tribe to render help to its son-in-law. It was regarded as sacred as the blood tie. Many Arab tribes moved to Makkah for economic reasons, for being the trade centre it offered them many opportunities and improved their financial conditions. It was common place that these tribes gained wealth and social status in Makkah, which helped them secure political power as well.

A branch of some influential Arab tribe of Makkah was settled there, with some small families living there. They had alliance with some Quraysh family or individual and were reckoned members of their sponsors. The list of the senior most Makkan Muslims, as provided by Ibn Hishām and other classical writers of *sīrah,* includes the names of these allies. Among the allies of Banū Umayyah were Banū Ghanam, Banū Dudan, and around forty members of Asad Khuzaymah. Men, women and children were part of it. A small group of Banū Ghanī was Banū Hishām's ally. The former had close ties with the latter. Among the allies of Banū Zuhrah were influential members of Banū Hudhayl, Kindah and Tamīm tribes. Prominent among them were ʿAbdullāh ibn Masʿūd al-Hudhalī, al-Miqdād ibn ʿAmr al-Kindī, Shuraḥbīl ibn Ḥasanah al-Kindī and his two or three brothers. Their females feature among the earliest Muslims. The same holds true for their children. Among Banū ʿAdiyy's allies were many members of Banū Bukayr of the Layth tribe. They were more than twenty in number. Among the allies of Banū Sahm were ʿAlī Yāsir, Madhḥij and others. Besides these early Muslims of Arab tribes, there were other allies of the Quraysh who embraced Islam at a later date.[12]

The non-Muslim allies of the Quraysh of various Arab tribes outnumbered the Muslim allies. This non-Muslim segment was of much importance in the socio-cultural and economic life of Makkah. Many of them had acquired a status equal to the one enjoyed by the Quraysh elites. By dint of their social standing they influenced Makkan politics, economy and polity. Of them, special mention should be made of the leaders of Banū Thaqīf of Ṭā'if, who lived close to Makkah in Ṭā'if, which was its rival politically and financially. Al-Akhnas ibn Shurayq al-Thaqafī was considered as a peer to the Makkan chiefs such as Abū Jahl al-Makhzūmī and Abū Sufyān. The former played a leading role in Makkan society and politics, especially in the Makkan phase of the Prophet's career. He was merely an ally of Banū Zuhrah yet he was instrumental in important matters. Once along with Abū Sufyān he had tried to oppose the Quraysh hostility against the Prophet (peace be upon him). His move was, however, turned down by the bitterly hostile Quraysh chiefs. It was at his behest that members of the Banū Zuhrah tribe refused to join the battle of Badr. Again, it was he who had urged his tribesmen to insist on the safe return of the Quraysh trade caravan.[13] Ibn Isḥāq speaks of him as one of the elites who had a powerful voice.[14] He was also a member of the delegation comprising Quraysh chiefs that had called on Abū Ṭālib for putting an end to the Prophet's message.[15] Among the Makkan chiefs who had extended protection to the emigrants from Abyssinia, he featured as well. He had extended this privilege to Abū Ṣabrah ibn Abī Ruḥm. According to a variant report, it was done by Suhayl ibn ʿAmr al-ʿĀmirī. Both of them had, however, refused to extend hospitality to the Prophet (peace be upon him) on his return from Ṭā'if.[16] That he occupied an important position is evident from the fact that after his return from Ṭā'if and being deprived of the protection of his own family Banū Hāshim, when the Prophet (peace be upon him) sought help from three Makkan chiefs, al-Akhnas was one of them. However, he excused himself, pleading that he was only an ally. Notwithstanding, being an ally of the Quraysh Abū al-Daghnah, however, provided protection to Abū Bakr and it was recognized by the Quraysh. Ibn Ḥajar correctly states that al-Akhnas was not prepared to do so whereas Abū al-Daghnah was willing.[17] According to Balādhurī, the Prophet (peace be upon him) had sought help from Suhayl ibn ʿAmr al-ʿĀmirī and Muṭʿim ibn ʿAdiyy al-Nawfalī, the Quraysh chiefs and the latter had obliged him while the former refused it.[18] Balādhurī reports also that Akhnas had written to the Prophet (peace be upon him) for returning Abū Baṣīr who had escaped from Makkah and taken refuge in Madinah. In accordance with the clause of the Ḥudaybīyah treaty the Prophet (peace be upon him) made Abū Baṣīr return to Makkah.[19]

According to Ibn Isḥāq, Ḥakīm ibn Umayyah Sulmā, chief of an Arab tribe that was Banū Umayyah's ally, succeeded tried to dissuade his people from opposing the Prophet. He resorted to poetry for the same end. He was a gentleman who was obeyed by his people.[20]

That Ibn al-Daghnah extended protection to Abū Bakr Ṣiddīq is common knowledge. He belonged to Aḥābīsh, the alliance of the following Arab tribes – Banū al-Ḥārith ibn ʿAbd Manāt ibn Kinānah, Banū al-Hawan ibn Khuzaymah ibn Mudrikah and Banū al-Muṣṭaliq/Khuzāʿah. It was named so because the alliance agreement was concluded in the lower valley of Makkah called al-Aḥābīsh. Ibn al-Daghnah was known as being the son of a lady named al-Daghnah while Mālik was his real name. According to Imām Bukhārī, he was a member of Qurrah and according to other chroniclers he hailed from Banū al-Ḥārith/Kinānah tribe and was the chief of al-Aḥābīsh in his day. Abū Bakr's own Quraysh family, Banū Taym had acted cowardly in defending him. Therefore, al-Daghnah, in opposition to the Quraysh chiefs and tribes, extended protection to him. It was recognized by the Quraysh. The latter acted against Abū Bakr only at the expiry of this agreement. Otherwise, they would have to bear the brunt of Aḥābīsh. During the tenure, however, they could not do anything against Abū Bakr.[21]

For Shiblī the only motive which moved the Quraysh army in the battle of Badr was the killing of ʿAmr ibn al-Ḥadramī at Nakhlah at the hands of Wāqib ibn ʿAbdullāh al-Taymī, an associate of ʿAbdullāh ibn Jaḥsh al-Asadī. The Quraysh chiefs took the risk of waging war for avenging the killing of a Kindī ally chief. In contrast, Muslims of Madīnah exulted in the act of their Taymī ally and defended him at every cost. Ibn Isḥāq and others state that the killing of this Quraysh ally had caused the war.[22] Although modern scholars have contested Shiblī's stance, it is nonetheless true that the killing of an Arab ally did play a role in the break out of war.

As opposed to it, an incident of an earlier date underscores the role of the ally in peace. It is indeed a significant event. It was Surāqah ibn Mālik who had pursued the emigrating Prophet (peace be upon him) in order to get the reward money. He was an ally of the Quraysh i.e. Banū Mudlij/Kinānah. According to Suhaylī, he was one of Banū Kinānah elite. The Quraysh and Kinānah had an alliance which was political, military and social. Surāqah came to know of the Prophet's emigration in a meeting of his tribe and he resolved to pursue him tactically. It is reported that Satan had appeared in his guise prior to the battle of Badr.[23] The Prophet's guide during his journey to Madinah was ʿAbdullāh ibn ʿUrayqāt al-Wā'ilī, whose mother came from Banū Sahm, a Quraysh family and he was a resident of Makkah.[24]

The participation of the Quraysh allies in the battles of Uḥud and the Trench is a significant historical event. Some Quraysh allies were influential in concluding the Ḥudaybīyah treaty. Of them, mention must be made of Budayl ibn Waraqah al-Khuzāʿī, Ḥulays ibn ʿAlqamah al-Ḥārithī al-Kinānī, Sayyid al-Aḥābīsh, ʿUrwah ibn Masʿūd al-Thaqafī, whom the Quraysh had deputed as their representative for the negotiations. The Aḥābīsh chief dissuaded the Quraysh from killing the Prophet's emissary, Khirāsh ibn Umayyah al-Khuzāʿī and ensured his safe return to the Prophet (peace be upon him). The treaty was concluded eventually by a Quraysh emissary while these non-Quraysh representatives had paved the way for it. Their role in such a decisive matter for the Quraysh brings out their important social rank.[25]

The above topic may be covered in another independent work. The above brief account points to the presence and role of these Arab tribes in the Makkan society.

Non-Arab Elements in Makkah

Much before the Prophet's advent non-Arabs had made their way into Makkah. They were integrated with Makkan polity. All this was accomplished with reference to the Arab tribal norm of protection and amnesty. Slavery too, played its role in it. Makkah enjoyed greater fame as a place of worship than as a centre of trade and business. Non-Arabs particularly Persians, Abyssinians, Iraqis and Syrians did visit Makkah for pilgrimage. Some of them had settled down there. Some were enslaved and thus became part of its society. As compared to non-Quraysh Arab tribes they were limited in number and position. Yet they lent a special colour to the pluralistic society of Makkah.

In comparison to others, Abyssinians were more in number in Makkah as settlers. Most of them were slaves. Of them, the most prominent is the Prophet's earliest follower, Bilāl ibn Rabāḥ, whose illustrious personality is held dear by every Muslim. His father Rabāḥ and his mother Ḥamāmah were brought to Makkah as slaves. Bilāl and some of his brothers and one sister were born there. They were thus included among Banū Jumaḥ. We would discuss later some other Makkans of Abyssinian descent.[26]

Among early Muslims Ṣuhayb in referred to as a Roman. Some reports suggest that he was an Arab.[27] The Prophet's comment on his Roman descent is significant. ʿAddās was the slave of the Quraysh chiefs – ʿUtbah and Shaybah and hailed from Ninevah. He was settled in Makkah as a slave and was integrated well with Makkans.[28] The Quraysh alleged that someone composed the Qur'ān for the Prophet (peace be upon him). According to the Qur'ān, they gave credit for this to some non-Arabs. Exegetes have identified many on this count such as Yāsir, the slave of al-ʿAlā' ibn al-Ḥadramī, Jābir, the slave of ʿĀmir ibn Rabīʿah and ʿAddās, the slave of ʿUtbah and Shaybah. All three were non-Arabs.[29] There were other non-Arabs in Makkan society. Although they were few and unimportant, their presence did have its bearing on the local traditions, culture and religious life.

Multiplicity of Faith in Makkan Society

The traditional historians and biographers of the Prophet (peace be upon him) merely state that the religious life in Makkah was synonymous with idolatry. Some make the additional observations that the Arab polytheists, especially the Makkan Quraysh were adherents of Abrahamic faith, which they had corrupted beyond recognition owing to their innovations, accretion and deviation. In terms of ideology, faith, rituals and practices they had nothing in common with the original faith. Their thought had degenerated into sheer polytheism. Yet these writers do not analyze their faith and practices. As to the presence of other faiths in Makkah, they pass in silence over it.

Polytheism, unlike monotheism, is not a monolithic, single-dimensional entity. It has numerous varieties. It divides polytheists into several religious groups. With polytheism as the faith a society cannot achieve integration or unity. Along with its divisions and sub-divisions it disintegrates into numerous blocks. Idolatry was the main faith of Arabs and of Makkans. However, they worshipped different idols. Each tribe and family had its own idol and these idols were one another's rivals. All members of a tribe or family were not obliged to worship a single deity. They could turn to any idol. Rather, it was their practice. This pantheon of idols had affected Makkan society and generated many reactions.[30]

Jews and Christians lived in the vicinity of the Quraysh and Makkans held them in awe. Jewish and Christian thought had crept into their faith, rather influenced it. Arabs believed in their superiority in matters of faith. The Arab proximity with Persia had made them thoroughly familiar with Magian thought and practices, though this influence was not wide-spread in Makkah. More importantly, atheism featured in Makkah.[31]

Idolatry in Makkah – A Manifestation of Polytheism

Hubal was the national idol installed at the roof of the Kaʿbah. Around it, however, there were three hundred and sixty idols. Each of these was worshipped on a day of the year. Then there were pictures on the walls of the Kaʿbah. As a result of this abundance of idols and pictures, polytheism was rooted deep in Makkah. Non-Quraysh Arabs who lived in Makkah had their own national idols. Owing to their stay in Makkah, however, they had developed attachment to the Quraysh idols, which had become part of their psyche. Idols of the adjoining area too had their influence on them. Of them, the most important ones were al-Lāt, Manāt and al-ʿUzzā, which are mentioned in the Qur'ān with reference to the socio-religious life of Makkah and Quraysh. Asāf and Nā'ilah were the idols of Banū Jurhum and al-Lāt of the Thaqīf of Ṭā'if. Al-ʿUzzā, the common idol of the Quraysh and Kinānah was installed at Nakhlah. Manāt was worshipped by the Arab tribes – al-Aws and al-Khazraj. Such devotion to a large number of idols had corrupted their religious outlook.[32]

All this had its impact on their religious thought pattern. They had turned into idolaters when ʿAmr ibn Luḥayy Khuzāʿī had imported idols for them. As and when they came across a beautiful stone, they would start worshipping it. By the same token, they would throw away these when they felt tired of these. Reports indicate that they had grown so non-serious on this count that during a journey they carried idols made of flour for being light to carry. They would even devour these when they grew hungry. For them these were without any substance. At most they regarded these as the means to get closer to God. Or they looked upon these as the agents to help them in need, as for example, for rainfall and other needs. ʿAmr ibn Luḥayy had brought for them from Syria the idol Hubal. Visitors to Makkah carried stones of the town for using these as idols back home. Idolatry was, no doubt, their ritual yet it had not crept into their thought pattern or national psyche.[33]

Their non-serious attitude towards idolatry stemmed from their allegiance to the Abrahamic faith. Notwithstanding the corruption in their faith, the spirit of their original faith sustained them. Its remnants were still there in their beliefs and practices. They were, no doubt, polytheists who invoked idols yet they entertained the notion of God being the Lord of the worlds. They did believe in One God but they were guilty of associating others with Him. The Qur'ān cites many instances of this corruption in their faith. These stand out as incontrovertible historical facts.[34]

The Makkans believed in some articles of the Abrahamic faith and practised the same, though their innovations had changed the faith altogether. They had the concept of prayer and offered the same once or twice a day, though in a totally changed form. According to

Balādhurī, the Prophet (peace be upon him) used to visit the Kaʿbah early in the day and offered *ḍuḥā* (mid-morning) prayer there. The Quraysh did not dismiss this prayer.[35] It appears from the Qur'ān and other bits of evidence that their prayer comprised postures such as standing, bowing and prostrating.[36] They believed also in the obligation of fasting and observed it as well. The Makkans and the Quraysh fasted on the 10th of Muḥarram, for it constituted thanksgiving for the beginning of creation by God. They fasted as a token of gratitude for the advent of Prophet Adam and for divine bounties.[37] Spending in God's way, the underlying spirit of charity and *zakāh* was the trait of Arabs in general and of Makkans in particular. It was a synonym for generosity. The Makkans were fully familiar with the practices of pilgrimage and lesser pilgrimage and practised the same. Throughout the year they would perform *ʿumrah* and pilgrimage only on the appointed days. Amid other norms of the Abrahamic faith they were aware of the regard for the Kaʿbah and considered its custodianship as a privilege. Their association with pilgrimage, its rituals and the places linked with it was emotional, ideological, religious, psychological and spiritual. Both the Quraysh and Kinānah chanted the Oneness of God, affirming that He is without any partner. They had, no doubt, introduced some practices in pilgrimage which betrayed their national pride and honour. The alliance of the Quraysh, Kinānah and Khuzāʿah was known as *Ḥims*. They went around the Kaʿbah in a naked state and did not stay at ʿArafāt, dismissing it as the practice of the commoners.[38]

The Qurayshī reaction to their ancestral faith

The point that features in Arab traditions and poetry and which merits the attention of analysts, is that it was a Makkan who had distorted the Abrahamic faith. He was a Khuzāʿī by descent and hence a non-Quraysh. After the expulsion of Banū Khuzāʿah from Makkah, a reaction against their faith was inevitable. The Quraysh Arabs and Makkans were, no doubt, practitioners of idolatry yet they had not drifted completely from their ancestral faith. Idolatry was common. So was the attachment to idols. Yet the community leaders were aware of the roots of polytheism. They were swayed by customs of the day. Their sound psyche and conscience directed them to the Abrahamic faith and caused revulsion against the conventional faith. This spiritual longing, intellectual yearning and emotional urge impelled them to revert to their original faith. This was not restricted to a particular era; in each age this trend was noticeable. However, in the period coinciding with the Prophet's advent this grew into a dynamic movement.

Reports indicate that the Prophet (peace be upon him) was known also as Abū Kabshah. For Abū Kabshah Wajz ibn Ghālib Khuzāʿī had abandoned idolatry and criticized those given to it. He reproached idolaters. While equating the Prophet's denunciation of idolatry with Abū Kabshah's earlier criticism, the Quraysh drew a parallel between the two. Abū Kabshah, it is worth-noting, was the maternal grandfather of the Prophet's maternal grandfather. Some other reports state otherwise. However, the above account is authentic.[39] According to Baghadādī, many persons of the day were known as Abū Kabshah.

It was the Ḥanīf movement, practised by the followers of the Ḥanīf faith who owed their allegiance to their progenitor, Prophet Abraham, in that he was a Muslim and Ḥanīf.[40] According to Ibn Isḥāq, the Quraysh celebrated their annual religious festival near some idol, which they venerated. They would prostrate before it, go around it and offer animal sacrifice to it. Once as the Quraysh assembled for the same purpose, four persons dissociated themselves from them and after mutual consultation declared that their community had turned irreligious for having deserted the Abrahamic faith. The idols were lifeless objects, unable to hear or to see and could not benefit or harm anyone. They resolved to make the quest for true faith. They moved to different places for this purpose of ascertaining the Abrahamic faith. Baghdādī has provided their brief account, stating that they used to keep away from *jāhiliyyah* practices.[41] Some reports put their number at six. It is not, however, confirmed. What is, nonetheless, certain is that a reaction was in the offing against the distorted faith of the day. It manifested their sound beliefs, which were cherished by the Makkans and Quraysh. By the time of the Prophet's advent, the movement had grown strong. There were critics of idolatry in every age. Of them, Abū Kabshah was the most prominent among them. Those opposing idolatry were given the same title. The appellation of the same title on the Prophet (peace be upon him) adduces the point.

Ibn Isḥāq identifies the following allies of the Quraysh and others who made the quest for truth: i) Waraqah ibn Nawfal, ii) ʿUbaidullāh ibn al-Jaḥsh al-Asdī al-Qurashī iii) ʿUthmān Asadī Qurayshī and iv) Zayd ibn ʿAmr ibn Nufayl. Ibn Qutaybah has identified six such persons.

It emerges from the works of Ibn Saʿd and others that some Arab tribes felt uneasy about their ancestral faith. Prior to accepting Islam and during the *jāhiliyyah* period Abū Dharr al-Ghifārī had turned into a monotheist. He did not indulge in idolatry.[42] The early Muslims belonging to Arab tribes abandoned their ancestral faith. On his acceptance of Islam, ʿAmr ibn ʿAbasah of Banū Salīm said that even during his *jāhiliyyah* phase he regarded others as in error and idolatry as something vain.[43] Another report relates at length his disillusion with his earlier faith, affirming as it does his quest for truth. The same had prompted him to draw closer to the Prophet.[44]

In their quest for truth some followed the Abrahamic faith while others opted for other faiths. The Quraysh Ḥunafā' followed the best practices of the Abrahamic faith and adhered firmly to monotheism. Their knowledge about other aspects of faith was little. They acted on their conscience. For example, they meditated, focussed on worship and retired to caves. The significant part, however, of their quest was their abandoning their ancestral faith, particularly idolatry. As Ibn Isḥāq reports, among the four Aḥnāf only Zayd ibn ʿAmr ibn Nufayl stuck to his original faith and died a little before the Prophet's advent. The Prophet (peace be upon him) spoke of him as a community unto himself, for he believed in monotheism, resented dead meat, blood and offerings to idols, opposed child sacrifice and worshipped the Lord of Prophet Abraham.[45] Influenced by his father, Saʿīd ibn Zayd was among the first to embrace Islam.

The other three, namely, Waraqah ibn Nawfal, ʿUthmān ibn Ḥuwayrith and ʿUbaydullāh ibn Jaḥsh opted for Christianity. They found it closer to the truth than their ancestral faith. ʿUthmān settled in the Caesar's court and died there. He wad held in esteem by the Caesar, particularly on account of his Christian faith. The other two accepted Islam later. Waraqah ibn Nawfal turned into a Christian scholar well versed in the Scriptures who wrote books in the Hebrew language. He was familiar with the Bible hence he turned into a supporter of the Prophet Muḥammad (peace be upon him). In view of his endorsement of his Messengership and his pledge to help the cause of Islam, the Prophet (peace be upon him) branded him as a Muslim and monotheist. ʿUbaydullāh accepted Islam. However, on going to Abyssinia he reverted to Christianity and died in the same faith, which was regrettable.[46]

Christianity in Makkah

Apart from the Ḥunafā' and adherents of ancestral faith there were Christians too, in Makkah, though few in number. Their presence lent pluralism to local life and society. Some were Christians by birth and followed the same as the faith of their forefathers while some had accepted it as a result of their quest for truth. The latter comprised several members of various Arab tribes and Quraysh families. Among Arab Christians, mention is already made of Waraqah ibn Nawfal, ʿUthmān ibn Ḥuwayrith and ʿUbaydullāh ibn Jaḥsh. Many Abyssinians have also been referred to above.[47]

Little mention was made in Makkah of Christian dogma. Regarding Waraqah ibn Nawfal there is the oft-quoted report that he identified the revelation sent down to the Prophet Muḥammad (peace be upon him) as the one with which Prophet Moses (peace be upon him) was blessed earlier. He affirmed that the Prophet (peace be upon him) was a genuine Messenger on the ground that his advent is foretold in the Gospels and the Torah. He mentioned in particular the two signs: i) The Prophet (peace be upon him), like every other Messenger, would be forced into emigrating by his own people and ii) as the last resort and by Allah's leave he would have to wage jihād. Bukhārī has cited the above points on the authority of Waraqah ibn Nawfal.[48] Both of these prophecies were very significant. For emigration coupled with jihād and fighting signified the spread of Islam and extirpation of the Quraysh. Balādhurī's report clarifies that Waraqah had stated that the Prophet's advent was foretold by Prophet Jesus (peace be upon him). He was mentioned pointedly in the Gospels. Waraqah had affirmed also that the Prophet (peace be upon him) would be blessed with *Sūrah al-Fātiḥah.*

The report about ʿAddās mentions the Prophet Jonah as the Messenger of God. ʿAddās added that at the time of his departure from Ninevah few people recognized the Prophet Jonah. The Prophet Muḥammad (peace be upon him), however, knew him thanks to the divine revelation to him. He therefore equated the Prophet Muḥammad (peace be upon him) with the Prophet Jonah (peace be upon him) as a genuine Messenger of God who must be obeyed. The above explains why ʿAddās had readily recognized the Prophet as a Messenger of God and professed faith in him.[49]

Balādhurī recounts a report on the Christian dogma about Gabriel that after Gabriel's visit to the Prophet Muḥammad (peace be upon him) Khadījah enquired two Christian scholars in Makkah. Waraqah ibn Nawfal readily affirmed that Gabriel is God's angel who calls on the Messengers. If he had visited the Prophet Muḥammad (peace be upon him), the latter should be taken as God's Messenger. He expressed his wish to serve the Prophet (peace be upon him). When Khadījah asked ʿAddās about Gabriel, he was astonished. For in a town reeling under idolatry none discussed Gabriel, God's angel who visited only the Messengers.[50] The above report is endorsed also by the report which states that Waraqah had drawn a parallelism between the angel visiting him and the Prophet Moses (peace be upon him).[51]

The popular Christian belief about the Prophet Jesus (peace be upon him) is that he is, God forbid, the son of God. However, genuine Christians regarded him no more than as the word of God and His spirit, as is borne out by the debate on this issue in Negus's court.

According to Imām Bukhārī's report, Umm Ḥabībah and Umm Salamah had seen a church with images during their stay in Abyssinia. When they recounted it to the Prophet (peace be upon him), he explained that when a pious Christian died, they erected the place of worship at his grave and engraved his image. Such would be reckoned as Allah's worst creatures on the Day of Reckoning.[52] The above clarifies the beginning of idolatry in Christianity, which culminated later in the worship of Mary and the Prophet Jesus (peace be upon him). It distorted their monotheistic doctrine and gave rise to the notion of sonship and divinity of the Prophet Jesus (peace be upon him).

Reference to some Christian teachings and rituals appears also in Salmān al-Fārsī's quest for truth. He was drawn to Christianity on observing them in prayer in a church. Gradually he was persuaded of the truth and superiority of this faith. About a practising Christian scholar of Syria he reports: 'I did not come across anyone more punctual in prayers, concerned about the Hereafter, indifferent to this world and devoted to worship than him.' He was critical of popular Christianity which was removed far away from the original faith. His mentors practised true Christianity.[53]

About the Christian mode of worship there appears an interesting report in the context of the Christian delegation of Najrān that had called on the Prophet (peace be upon him). After *ʿAṣr* prayer they performed their prayer at the Prophet's mosque, facing eastwards. As the Kaʿbah was declared the Muslims' *qiblah*, they faced southwards. The Prophet allowed Christians to pray facing their own *qiblah*.[54] A degenerated Christian scholar of Syria was notorious for usurping others' belongings, especially charity money. This points to the concept and practice of charity among Christians.

Notions about the Superiority of Christianity and Judaism: The Makkan Quraysh and their chiefs held the two major faiths – Christianity and Judaism in awe, and regarded these as superior to their own faith. They acknowledged their truth and exalted status. What accounted for it was the Quraysh's ignorance of and deprivation from the Scripture and divine faith. They were overwhelmed by the religious knowledge possessed by the Christians and Jews and the latter's conviction that these were the best faiths. Accordingly the Quraysh turned to them in all religious affairs and trusted their opinion. In view of the same impression many Arab seekers of truth had abandoned their ancestral faith and converted to Christianity or Judaism. This is borne out by the account of the three Ḥunafā'. One had even preferred Christianity to Islam. It emerges from the event related to ʿAddās that his Qurayshī masters, ʿUtbah and Shaybah regarded his faith superior to Islam, even when ʿAddās bore out the truth of the Prophet's message and kissed his hands and feet.[55]

Several Qur'ānic verses and reports of the day point to the Quraysh's belief in the superiority of Christianity and Judaism in Makkah.

The same point comes out in Salmān's quest for truth. He was originally a Magian of Iṣṭakhr and was impressed by Christian worship in a church. He regarded it as superior to his faith. According to another report, he turned into a Christian, as he was deeply moved by the conduct of a monk. He visited Syria in his quest for truth and gained insights into Christianity as he lived in the company of a Church father there. After his death he stayed with other Christian scholars in Syria, Ninevah, Nuṣaybīn and ʿAmūriyyah. At the latter's directive he came to Arabia to call on the Prophet Muḥammad (peace be upon him). Because of the treachery of his companions he was enslaved and arrived as a slave in Madīnah. After meeting the Prophet (peace be upon him) he embraced Islam.[56]

Judaism, Christianity and Islam as Perceived by the Quraysh:

After the Prophet's advent the religious scene of Makkah was changed altogether. It affected the social life greatly with far-reaching ramifications. Although the Makkans believed in the superiority of the People of the Book, their faith and their knowledge, it did not disturb their social life in the least. Their religious institutions and thought were not influenced by it. Judaism did not have any bearing on the Makkan social life. For there was not any sizeable Jewish presence there before or after the Prophet's advent. The few Jews there were absorbed in the wider community. This is evident from the affair of Adina, the Jewish neighbour of ʿAbd al-Muṭṭalib al-Hāshimī. This was an isolated incident without any implication for the local society.[57] Christians were more in number. However, most of them were slaves and did not influence the course of events. However, when Ḥunafā' accepted Christianity, it made some ripples which died down soon. For two Christians left Makkah and one turned to Islam. The Ḥanīf faith did make some sections of Makkah and many individuals weary of the conventional religion of the Quraysh, provoking them into looking for a sound faith.

It was in this social setting that the preaching of Islam commenced, encompassing almost every family and member of the Quraysh. According to Ibn Isḥāq, Islam had made its way into almost every Quraysh household. Not only isolated individuals, entire families or most of their members had embraced the new faith. What hurt the Quraysh and Makkan chiefs most was: i) Their youth had accepted Islam which hurt their interest. It constituted a sort of rebellion on the part of the youth against the elders, especially their supremacy and ii) All the Qurayshī families stood divided, with some as Muslims and others clinging to the ancestral faith. The latter hit them harder for it dented their family and social life.

Islam posed a serious threat to their faith. Such a danger was not faced by them from Christianity or Judaism. The major articles of Islamic faith – monotheism, afterlife and messengership – had changed their religious outlook which had its deep bearings on their society. These beliefs, together with other Islamic teachings sounded a death knell for idolatry and polytheism in Makkah. The Islamic code of conduct had pitted Muslims in real life as a formidable rival to the polytheistic Quraysh. The Quraysh chiefs realized it well that the success of Islam would deal a deadly blow to their political, religious and social order. They feared obliteration and it was a justified apprehension.[58]

The irony was that the Quraysh chiefs and Makkan opponents of the Prophet (peace be upon him) recognized that Islam is a genuine faith which spelled out a sound, correct way of life. They acknowledged the veracity of Islam and the Prophet Muḥammad (peace be upon him) yet they could not affirm it publicly or verbally. The language and style of the Qur'ān, its message and teachings and the pious conduct of its bearer, spread over forty years, compelled them to uphold the soundness of Islam yet they were prevented by their interests to do so. It spelled their death politically. As a result of this conflict they suffered from psychological problems. They therefore resorted to a variety of pretexts and tricks for opposing Islam which weakened their own faith further. They took to hurling baseless charges against the Qur'ān, the Messenger of Islam and the Islamic faith. They knew well the falseness of their allegations. They sought help from Jewish scholars for discrediting Islam and for leveling a host of charges. All this, however, brought into sharper relief the truth of Islam which convinced even them. The only resort open to them was to assassinate the Prophet (peace be upon him) for putting an end to Islam. This nefarious practice has been followed all along by the forces of falsehood. In contrast, true faith always seeks to win over the heart and mind of people, ensuring them the best in both the worlds. This conflict between truth and falsehood always gives rise to such responses. Falsehood tries to banish truth. The bearers of truth are forced to emigrate. In line with the same, Muslims had to leave Makkah and take refuge elsewhere.

CHAPTER 2

Evolution of the Muslim Minority in Makkah

By quirk of fate the true faith of Islam always had its beginning and progress in a polity dominated by non-Muslims. Muslims were always in minority in their town. It helped establish their identity in a multi-faith, pluralistic society. Their religious order was set up in opposition to the mainstream culture and civilization. Little wonder then that Islam faced stiff opposition. The old order could not put up with them, especially the reform introduced by Islam. This battle between truth and falsehood has been waged from the days of the Prophet Ādam to the Prophet Muḥammad (peace be upon him), the Final Messenger. This is the very belief of Islam and is at the heart of the cultural, community and religious history of Islam. It would not be out of place to assert that it has been a persistent tradition of world civilizations.

The battle between the old and the new orders led to many outcomes. In the phase preceding the Prophet Muḥammad's advent ancestral faith generally gained ascendancy while the true believers were exiled and martyred. The forces representing falsehood were, however, destroyed in line with Allah's practice. Divine penalty overtook them reducing them to naught. Earlier believers were sometimes rewarded with success or gained power in their land of emigration. At times the whole community was transformed.

The Prophet Muḥammad (peace be upon him), it must be recalled, was the final Messenger and Islam the universal, eternal faith for everyone. It was, therefore, inevitable that his message be preserved for ever. Accordingly it is destined that Islam had its beginning and evolution in the non-Muslim milieu of Makkah. The accomplishing phase took place in Madīnah as Islam was ascendant. Makkan Islam, nonetheless, served as the basis for Islam in Madīnah. The latter represents the extension and completion of the former. Moreover, Makkan Islam provides the Prophetic role model for the growth of Islam in a non-Muslim society, an example to be emulated by Muslim minorities in all lands until the Last Day.

These are two features of the universal message of Islam. Historical factors and laws of nature throw ample light on the rise and fall of all communities.

Several Qur'ānic verses as principles and the stories of Prophets as parables clarify these stages explicitly. While addressing Muslims the Qur'ān makes it plain that Islam is universal whereas the rise and fall of the Muslims is contingent upon the laws of nature, especially of causality. If Muslims fulfill necessary conditions for gaining ascendancy, pursue consistently the path of hard work, they are bound to attain success. If they fail to do so, they would be consigned to the abyss of fall and degeneration. This divine exhortation appears thus in the Qur'ān: 'If you turn back from the path, Allah would substitute you with another people, then they would not be like you.'[1] The same is pronounced as the unalterable way of Allah. It is made clear that Muslims would undergo rise and fall in proportion to their conduct. This divine promise came true in the very early days of the Makkan phase that Makkan Muslims would achieve heights of success. They were told unequivocally that in the event of their violation of divine commands the Prophet's teachings and laws of nature, they would be subject to loss and destruction. Many Qur'ānic verses of the Makkan period bring home the above point. These bear out the above truth.

The construction and evolution of the Muslim ummah in the Makkan phase and its consolidation and perfection in the Madīnan phase underscore the same divine law. Every community is subject to growth and decline. The Muslim community is subject to growth and decline. The Muslim community is not an exception to it. These verses thus reinforce the universality, timelessness and meaningfulness of the Qur'ānic message which the gifted souls cannot afford to ignore.

As it became apparent that Muslims would undergo both rise and fall, it was imperative that relevant laws for these two stages be in place. The same distinction pervades the Makkan and Madīnan *sūrahs* in terms of their rulings and teachings. Makkan commands and exhortations are the guidelines for Muslim minorities while Madīnan ones cater for the powerful Muslim community. The Qur'ān exhorts man to reflect and act insightfully. In line with this it emerges that the division between Makkan and Madīnan phases is premised on the same wisdom, emanating from laws of nature. For, it was not beyond Allah's power to bless Muslims with power in the Makkan phase itself. The Makkan Quraysh would have pledged subservience. However, Allah intended that the Muslim community should face both the situations. Accordingly, ascendancy was granted only in the Madīnan phase.

The distinct difference between the two phases was sharpened by divine revelation and hence it was perceived by the Prophet (peace be upon him). The leading Companions and their followers too, appreciated this important point. The Quraysh chiefs who were gifted with far-sightedness and a balanced approach to things did discern this philosophy of ascendancy and subservience and of majority and minority, to some extent. As guided by Allah, the Prophet (peace be upon him) devised his strategy in the Makkan phase while the Quraysh chiefs acted in their own ways. The Makkan model was formulated in the light of Makkan *sūrahs* and other divine commands. For thirteen years Muslims were trained how to live as a minority and how to construct their society for achieving progress and success. It enabled them to do well in the Madīnan phase and helped produce a blue print for Muslim minorities, providing them with a way of life and of constructing their society.

The Prophet's Career: Rationale behind Makkan and Madīnan Phases

Generally speaking, traditional biographers of the Prophet (peace be upon him), who abide by Oriental values, do not analyze vigorously the Makkan phase of the Prophet's career. They faithfully follow primary sources. They are so much swayed by Ibn Isḥāq's and Ibn Hishām's work, *Al-Sīrah al-Nabawīyah,* that they blindly follow in their footsteps. They betray sheer ignorance of the factors and phases of the evolution of the Prophet's career. So doing, they keep the readers in the dark. Generally their practice is to describe the thirteen long years of the Prophet's Makkan phase from 610 CE to 623 CE in terms of providing an account of the ills of the *Jāhiliyyah* period and relating the Prophet's ancestors and his assuming the office of messengership. They strictly follow the line adopted by the classical masters, Ibn Isḥāq and Ibn Hishām. Then they offer a traditional overview of the sending down of revelation, the gradual revelation of the Qur'ān, the divine command for making a call to Islam, early Muslims' acceptance of Islam, the preaching of Islam in both secret and public and other familiar events. Their treatment of the Islamic commands and Qur'ānic teachings does not advance understanding. By mentioning only the beliefs and some other religious commands they fail to present a complete picture of Islam. This is on account of the lack of a detailed analysis. As a result, they fall short of projecting how the Muslim community was constituted in the Makkan phase.

The truth of the matter is much more complex, varied and multi-layered. The Prophet had adopted a particular strategy for this phase of subjugation. He had devised it with reference to the Qur'ānic directives and other divine instructions. His main objective was to erect the Muslim community. It is clear from some Qur'ānic passages and *aḥādīth* that at times, the Muslim community comprised a single individual. For example, the Qur'ān brands the Prophet Abraham (peace be upon him) as a community unto himself. In a similar vein, the Prophet (peace be upon him) spoke of Zayd ibn Nufayl as a single community. A single votary of Allah thus constitutes unto himself a community. Another note-worthy point is that a single person has the potential to blossom into an entire community. Presently it is only in its potential form. However it can grow into a full-fledged community. This potential has existed since the days of the Prophet Adam (peace be upon him) and passed on to his progeny. It pervades man's primordial covenant and also the community embodied by the Prophet Abraham (peace be upon him). Being his successor and the seal of Messengers, the Prophet Muḥammad (peace be upon him) was a community unto himself.

Viewed against this background when the Prophet (peace be upon him) embraced Islam in preference to the Quraysh's ancestral faith, the Qur'ān branded him as the first of believers and Muslims. It is worth-reiterating that Muslims did not exist then. Yet in view of the vast potentials the Qur'ān conferred upon him the above honour. His acceptance of Islam established the principle that everyone is free to choose his faith. The Qur'ān, other Scriptures and traditions of all communities recognize this basic right.

Right to Choose Faith

It is borne out by the *jāhiliyyah* practices of the Makkan Quraysh and of later history that every member of Makkan society enjoyed the freedom to choose their faith. This explains why there were Christians, Jews, idolators, pagans, Ḥunafā' and followers of the Abrahamic faith in Makkah. No one ever challenged their right to profess the faith of their choice. When the Quraysh chiefs learnt about the Prophet's new faith, they accepted it as an instance of his choice. This is endorsed by several reports.

The Prophet (peace be upon him) professed the Abrahamic faith in its original form and this was accepted by his elders and Quraysh chiefs. When Abū Ṭālib ibn ʿAbd al-Muṭṭalib ibn Hāshim, the Prophet's patron and head of Banū Hāshim, saw the Prophet (peace be upon him) praying, he enquired about his faith. The latter clarified that it was the faith handed down by the Prophet Abraham (peace be upon him). The former did not deter him from doing so. Rather, he accepted it. He allowed his own young son, ʿAlī ibn Abī Ṭālib to accept the new faith.[2] This incident is reported at length by Ibn Isḥāq and Ibn Hishām. For example, in response to Abū Ṭālib's query about the new faith, the Prophet (peace be upon him) introduced it as the faith approved by Allah hence it is the faith of angels, messengers, and of the patriarch Prophet Abraham (peace be upon him) with which he was sent down for mankind. Abū Ṭālib not only let him and ʿAlī profess the faith of their choice, he pledged to lend them all help and support.[3] Regarding ʿAfīf al-Kindī's acceptance of Islam it is stated that al-ʿAbbās ibn ʿAbd al-Muṭṭalib al-Hāshimī had granted him this right. Al-ʿAbbās was the Prophet's uncle and a leading member of Banū Hāshim and Quraysh.

This point comes out more sharply in the context of ʿUmar ibn al-Khaṭṭāb's acceptance of Islam. When some Quraysh leaders took to beating ʿUmar for his crime of embracing Islam, Al-ʿĀṣ ibn Wā'il al-Sahmī, a prominent leader of Makkah and the Quraysh dissuaded them from it saying that they had no business as ʿUmar had exercised his right to choose a faith. He asked them to leave ʿUmar alone.[4] Ibn Isḥāq, Ibn Hishām, Ibn Saʿd and other biographers inform that the Prophet (peace be upon him) made a call to Islam both openly and secretly and people responded positively to it yet the Quraysh did not stop it. However, when the Prophet (peace be upon him) criticized their idols, they took to opposing him.[5]

Ibn Saʿd's additional report is that some young persons and members of the weaker sections accepted Islam. As a result, the number of Muslims increased. Yet the unbelieving Quraysh did not object.[6]

The above account is reinforced by reports about the acceptance of Islam by many persons. It is clear that the Quraysh never contested as to why they had embraced the new faith. This applies to both the young of the Quraysh elite and the poor Muslims. In accordance with Quraysh norms everyone was free to profess a faith of his choice. Muslims availed themselves of the same. There was no element of compulsion in these conversions. It was widely accepted that the excellent teachings of Islam, the miraculous features of the Qur'ān, the Prophet's unblemished conduct and ideal character had paved the way for Islam. In addition, the following two factors were at work: i) Islam was the natural way, as is asserted in the Qur'ān and *ḥadīth*. Man is attracted by faith which was the ancestral faith of the Makkans. Even the Quraysh chiefs could not dare deny it. This truth comes out in the Prophet's conversation with Abū Ṭālib al-Hāshimī. It stresses also the law of nature that Islam is the only faith acceptable to Allah. It has been the faith of earlier Messengers and of the angels enjoying proximity with Allah. This links Islam to earlier Messengers. The above truth is reiterated in the Qur'ān. Islam is the faith with Allah.[7] The Islamic concept of the unity of faith served as the clinching argument for the People of the Book. The Qur'ān introduces itself as the Scripture confirming and reinforcing the truth of the Torah and the Gospels.[8]

The universality of the Qur'ān goes hand in hand with the concepts of the unity of faith and the oneness of the Muslim *ummah*. Since all messengers presented the same faith and all Scriptures confirm one another and Islam is the only faith, all the believers naturally represent one single community. While speaking of earlier Messengers and their communities the Qur'ān describes them as a single community. The latest form of this community was to be organized in Makkah, consisting of Muslims. The articles of faith, earliest Islamic teachings of Makkah and the Prophet's statements held Makkan Muslims as a single entity. It was to be expanded at a later date on a vast scale. Both the Makkan and Madīnan *sūrahs* present this concept, which was imbibed well by Muslims. We will take up this point later.

Right to Preach

It has been the right of the members of all civilized societies to profess a faith of their choice and to preach it in a peaceful manner. This lesson was taught by nature at an early date to man and was followed by all earlier nations, groups and individuals. Freedom of faith is logically linked with the right to preach. What one likes is preached by him for others. This right is universally recognized. However, this right is subject to the condition that no compulsion, temptation or financial incentive be there in calling people to embrace a particular faith. A proper understanding is essential. These points are generally acceptable to everyone. There is the oft-quoted Qur'ānic verse: 'Let there be no compulsion in faith.'[9] Another explicit verse to the same effect is: 'Would you compel mankind against their will to believe?'[10] For preaching and warning Allah prescribed the ruling for the Prophet (peace be upon him) that it should only be for conveying the message and for communication and understanding. The same was perfectly accomplished by the Prophet (peace be upon him). Peaceful preaching was the golden principle of the mission of all the Messengers. Reference to the same occurs in the Prophet Noah's context: 'Shall we compel you to accept it when you are averse to it?'[11] Many Qur'ānic verses, Prophet's statements and incidents from Islamic history may be cited in support of the above proposition that the call to faith and preaching of Islam must be pursued only peacefully. Any compulsion is undesirable.

As the main preacher of Islam the Prophet's mode was always peaceful, natural, flexible and based on proper communication. To this was added the excellence of his conduct. The Qur'ānic model of spreading the good word was at the heart of his preaching: 'Invite all to the way of your Lord with wisdom and beautiful preaching.'[12] He stood out for his sincerity, his seeking good for everyone, his selfless devotion to Islam, his unfailing efforts in this cause and his readiness to sacrifice everything. Even Allah asked him not to exert so much in this cause. He did so out of overflowing love. Allah was, no doubt, intent upon the spread of His faith yet He did not want the Prophet (peace be upon him) to be hurt. For his safety ensured the success of Islam. With him around Islam could spread at its own pace. The Qur'ān pays tribute to the Prophet (peace be upon him) for having discharged his duty well. He preached and warned people. This he did out of his utmost dedication to Allah. *Sūrahs al-Kahf* and *al-Shuʿarā'* are both Makkan. These contain the following observations: 'You would only perchance fret yourself to following after them, in grief, if they do not believe in this message.'[13] 'It may be you fret your soul with grief that they do not become believers.'[14]

The Prophet's Model for the one Calling to Faith

In the Makkan phase the Prophet (peace be upon him) adopted the following three ways for preaching Islam:

1. He personally went to everyone for instructing them in Islam. In the same vein, he visited homes, meeting places, localities, gatherings, markets even fairs for reciting the truth of Islam. It is evident from early sources that he did not wait for others to call on him. Rather, he took the lead in visiting them and blessed them with the message which would bring them success in both the worlds.[15]

2. He made each Companion of his a missionary preacher. Many reports indicate that the Qurayshī Companions and others carried out the preaching in their circles. Thanks to Abū Bakr al-Ṣiddīq's efforts six important members of the Quraysh accepted Islam. These early Muslims served as sincere preachers and spread the mission of Islam in their own ways. Like the Prophet (peace be upon him), their approach was broad and multi-directional.[16]

3. Another mode related to preaching Islam outside Makkah and in foreign lands. The Prophet resorted to it in the Makkan phase. It was his practice from early days to train such Muslims who came from distant places for preaching Islam among their people on their return. This strategy bore rich fruits. For it helped introduce Islam in the entire Arabian Peninsula. Often did it succeed in conveying the message of Islam to foreign lands. Some instances in point are: Abū Dharr al-Ghifārī to Ghifār and Aslam tribes; Abū Mūsā al-Ashʿarī to Ashʿar tribe; Ṭufayl ibn ʿAmr al-Dawsī to Daws; Ashajj ʿAbd al-Qays to ʿAbd al-Qays tribe of Bahrain and many others in different parts.[17]

Two Modes of Da'wah

Two basic modes were used for preaching Islam in the Makkan phase. One was the secret mode of preaching and the other was public. These were not some temporary measures. Rather, these constituted an eternal practice. Both were interrelated in that one was to be followed by another. First, preaching was done privately and after its success it was carried out publicly. This order cannot be reversed. For there are many considerations behind this arrangement. In a non-Muslim society it is always imperative to preach in private. For it alone ensures success. This was the practice of earlier Messengers. The Prophet (peace be upon him) did so for three years, avoiding any public preaching. This secret exercise helped increase the number of Muslims. It avoided any unrest in the non-Muslim society. Nor did it incur any hostility which would have hampered the progress. After the success of this phase, public preaching was allowed. During the three years there was a sizeable number of Muslims. Reports make it plain that it was not a strictly surreptitious activity. The Quraysh chiefs as well as the general public knew about this call. However, they did not react publicly. They did not oppose the Prophet (peace be upon him) vehemently, for his call was in a low key. According to Ibn Isḥāq, many Makkan elites had accepted Islam owing to the Prophet's secret preaching. He provides a list of these converts and clarifies that at a later date men and women accepted Islam en masse. As a result, Islam gained currency in Makkah and was a common topic of discussion.[18]

It may be argued that a nucleus community should exist prior to making a call for preaching. Otherwise, non-believers might react so furiously that the nascent community of believers would perish altogether. This had happened prior to the emergence of the Muslim community. When the Prophet took to preaching Islam publicly, it evoked the ire of the Quraysh chiefs which shook the foundation of the Muslim community. In the first phase of preaching many Muslim groups had emerged in and around Makkah. It was no longer possible to obliterate them altogether. In number they were formidable and in terms of their resources and conviction too, they were too firm to be removed. Islam had spread in Arabia in the three year long phase of preaching privately.[19]

After this private phase, there was a switch over to making the call publicly. It led to the inevitable opposition. However, Muslims, by then, were able to withstand the hostility. As a result of public preaching, new dimensions were added. The message of Islam reached every part of the Arabian Peninsula. Rather, it moved into even foreign lands. This ten year long phase of public preaching in Makkah stands out as the golden period in terms of quantity and quality, efficacy and deep rooted results.

Settlement of New Muslims in a Safe Area

This consideration was central to the Prophet's strategy that whenever he realized that new Muslims would not be able to maintain their faith in their tribe or region, he would settle them in a safe area. They were settled mostly in Makkah or other areas. In so doing, he resorted to the traditional Arab practices of extending protection and amnesty or agreement. The weaker individuals or sections were placed in the custody of a Makkan family while those of strong descent were made allies of an Arab family. His objective was to place new Muslims in a safe ambience, away from hostility and such forces that attacked their faith. Further discussion on this issue follows in the chapter on the construction of the society.[20]

The Prophet (peace be upon him) followed all the prevailing norms and practices in preaching Islam. The following are some of the most important ones adopted in the Makkan phase:

a. Reciting the Qur'ān and instructing people who visited him.
b. Joining non-Muslim gatherings and reciting the Qur'ān and instructing them there.
c. Having discussions with the local chiefs with a view to conveying the message of Islam to them.

d. Arranging for meals for his kith and kin and community leaders for teaching them about Islam.
e. Winning people's good will by presenting them gifts and endearing himself to them.
f. Engaging in public welfare acts for bringing home the excellence of Islam.
g. Bringing them closer to Islam by acts of mutual cooperation and interaction and presenting Islam as the faith of peace and amity.
h. Professing and practising high moral standards in trade and business and social relations for persuading them of the truth of Islam and the moral superiority of Muslims.
i. Removing the objections against Islam and issuing rejoinders to the queries and charges about Islam.
j. Convincing non-Muslim chiefs about the goodness of Islam and persuading them of their own success on accepting Islam.[21]

Right to Practise Faith

The Prophet (peace be upon him) set a glowing example during his Makkan phase on how to live in a non-Muslim majority society while adhering to Islam and its sharʿīah and observing all Islamic commands related to its moral, religious and legal system. Muslims are entitled to profess their faith notwithstanding the opposition and hostility against them. By the same token, non-Muslims are free to follow their faith. 'For you your faith and for me my faith.'[22] That is the standing principle valid for all time and place. No civilized society can dare deny it.[23]

Performance of Prayer

After the Prophet's advent and revelation of the Qur'ān, the Prophet (peace be upon him) and all Muslims were obliged to offer prayer. *Wuḍū'* (ablution) was prescribed as a prerequisite for prayer. Gabriel instructed the Prophet (peace be upon him) in both of these, a point borne out by *ḥadīth* and *sīrah* studies.[24] Regarding the obligatory duty of prayer Ibn Isḥāq and Ibn Hishām clarify that Gabriel instructed the Prophet (peace be upon him) in prayer and *wuḍū'*. The latter then taught the same to Khadījah. Prior to his acceptance of Islam, ʿAlī had observed the Prophet (peace be upon him) praying inside the home and asked him about the same. As already noted, at the appointed hours of prayers the Prophet (peace be upon him) and his Companions would go to a valley in Makkah and pray there. We will revert to this point later.

As in the case of preaching, initially the Prophet (peace be upon him) prayed privately at home or at a secluded spot. As Muslims grew into a small group, they went to a Makkan valley and offered prayer there in congregation. The Companions had the standing instruction to pray privately.[25] Prior to the night journey only *Fajr* and *ʿAṣr* prayers were obligatory. Later on, five obligatory prayers were prescribed. In the Makkan period only two *rakʿahs* were prescribed for *ʿAṣr* prayer. The rationale was not to provoke undue hostility on the part of the opponents.[26]

Yet the Muslims had the right to worship and pray in their own way which they held very dear. For them it was a religious duty which served as the dividing line between faith and unbelief. This explains when ʿUqbah ibn Abī Muʿīṭ, an utterly hostile Quraysh member sought to prevent Muslims from praying in a valley, a Muslim youth Saʿd ibn Abī Waqqāṣ al-Zuhrī took him to task and made him concede his mistake in denying Muslims their basic right. ʿUqbah did try to mobilize the Quraysh chiefs for preventing them from offering prayers. He was, however, reprimanded by them. Thus the non-Muslim dominated society and its chiefs acknowledged this right of the Muslim minority.[27]

Praying Together

Another wise step taken by the Prophet (peace be upon him) was that at the time of praying together he offered *Ẓuhr* prayer in the Kaʿbah courtyard inside the Sacred Place of worship.[28]

The Quraysh also prayed at that hour and did not object to the Prophet's prayer. According to a report, Muslims initially offered only *Ẓuhr* and *ʿAṣr* prayers, the former together with the Quraysh and the latter at a secluded place lest the Quraysh might object. *Ẓuhr* prayer was one of the remnants of the Abrahamic faith and was performed with all its components by the Quraysh. It may thus be called as the joint prayer of the Makkans. It was a peculiar situation. Some other rituals of the Abrahamic faith were common to the Muslim minority and the Makkan Quraysh. Of these, *Ẓuhr* prayer was quite marked.

The Prophet (peace be upon him) offered *Ẓuhr* prayer in congregation. Another rite was the fast on 10th Muḥarram. The same may be said of Ḥajj rituals. Ḥajj was the annual worship of not only the Makkan Quraysh but all Arabs. Under the Prophet's guidance and leadership Muslims performed pilgrimage according to their capacity. In so doing, however, they observed the dictates of morality and nature and shunned the innovations committed by the Quraysh. They avoided going around the Kaʿbah in a naked state or not staying at ʿArafāt, and returning to Makkah without going there or entering their houses by the back door etc. They shunned these unethical practices as a matter of principle.[29] This establishes the principle that in a multi-faith society the Muslim minority may join festivals and rituals of other faith, provided these do not impair morals.[30]

Avoiding Polytheism and its Manifestations

On the important issue of social interaction and praying together the Prophet (peace be upon him) laid down the basic principle that Muslims must avoid polytheism and its manifestations. Included amid these are idolatry, making offerings to these, vows for them, and participating in any polytheistic ritual etc. He illustrated this through his practice. It was obligatory for Makkans, the Muslim minority and by extension for all Muslim minorities. They must keep away from polytheistic worship and its rituals. It is the religious duty of Muslims which the majority community cannot take away. It is antithetical to monotheism to make any adjustment with polytheism and bear with it.[31]

Building and Managing Place of Worship

1. *The first place of worship in upper Makkah*:
Soon after the revelation of the Qur'ān in the Makkan period, the Prophet (peace be upon him) was asked to offer prayers. Gabriel instructed him in *wuḍū'*, and purification in that these are prerequisites for prayer. He taught the Prophet (peace be upon him) how to offer prayer and gave him detailed instructions about two *rak'ah* and four *rak'ah* prayers, its postures and its beginning and end timings. He told also how to select a place for saying prayer. The first spot where the Prophet (peace be upon him) prayed after receiving Gabriel's extensive instructions was a corner of the valley in upper Makkah.[32]

2. *The Prophet's domestic Place of worship*:
It emerges from the *sīrah* that the Prophet (peace be upon him) had selected a spot inside his house for prayer. Soon after accepting Islam Khadījah started praying as the Prophet (peace be upon him) led prayers. A little later, 'Alī joined the Prophet's prayer. It was the beginning of congregational prayer and of the place of worship inside the house. Reports clearly indicate that the Prophet (peace be upon him) offered prayers inside his house. He directed Khadījah and 'Alī how to purify and do *wuḍū'*. It was again he who identified *qiblah*. Ibn Isḥāq reports that three Quraysh chiefs – Abū Sufyān ibn Ḥarb, Abū Jahl ibn Hishām al-Makhzūmī and al-Akhnas ibn Shurayq al-Thaqafī went out at night separately to listen to the Prophet's recitation of the Qur'ān while hiding themselves. They did so near the Prophet's domestic place of worship. For three nights they listened to him.[33] Ibn Isḥāq further reports that when the Prophet (peace be upon him) used to pray inside his house, mischievous neighbours poured rubbish on him. For avoiding this he put up a

stone and he prayed beneath it.[34] According to Balādhurī, Sa'īd ibn Zayd, son of Qurayshī Ḥanīf Zayd ibn Nufayl and brother-in-law of 'Umar ibn al-Khaṭṭāb, reports that Muslims used to pray either behind closed doors or in a far-off Makkan valley.

3. *The Prophet's place of worship in Minā*:
Regarding 'Afif al-Kindī's acceptance of Islam it is reported that the Prophet, (peace be upon him) Khadījah and 'Alī prayed in Minā and that he learnt about religious issues from Ibn 'Abbās.[35]

4. *Places of worship in Makkan valleys*:
In the early Makkan period the Prophet's other place of worship was in a Makkan valley. For Ibn Isḥāq reports: As the time of prayer approached, he would go to a valley. He was accompanied by 'Alī who joined him without letting his father Abū Ṭālib know about it. He hid it from other leading members of the community. Both prayed there and returned at dusk. They did so as long as Allah willed it.[36] In the above quoted report about Sa'īd ibn Zayd and other reports there is reference to places of worship in valleys.

The third person to join the prayer in congregation was Zayd ibn Ḥārithah, the Prophet's freed slave. According to Ibn Isḥāq he was next to 'Alī in accepting Islam and offering prayers.[37] Some reports indicate that the next persons to join were Abū Bakr and Bilāl being the fourth and fifth persons respectively who offered prayers led by the Prophet (peace be upon him) in Makkan valleys. Later on, other Muslims joined the congregational prayer in Makkan valleys at the appointed hours.[38]

5. *Nakhlah place of worship*:
As already noted in Ibn Isḥāq's report that Abū Ṭālib had expressed his astonishment when he saw his son 'Alī joining the Prophet (peace be upon him) in prayer. He asked about the prayer and the new faith. On coming to know the details he let his son pray and believe in Islam. However, he refused to accept Islam, saying that he would not abandon his ancestral faith at any cost. Al-Suhaylī makes two points about this report by Ibn Isḥāq and Ibn Hishām:

(i) It was at Nakhlah that ʿAlī had prayed along with the Prophet (peace be upon him) and (ii) the next point is related to a posture of prayer, as one raises his buttocks.[39] According to the editor and scholar, many places were known by the name of Nakhlah. One was Nakhlah Maḥmūd, in the vicinity of Makkah in Ḥijāz, which abounded in date-palm trees. Then there was Nakhlah Shāmiyyah located at Dhāt Araq. More importantly, it was the territory of Banū Saʿd ibn Bakr, the foster family of the Prophet. (peace be upon him) Nakhlah Yamāniyyah was a distant valley with a place of worship associated with the Prophet (peace be upon him).

6. *The Prophet's places of worship on Makkah and Ṭā'if highway*:
On his return from Ṭā'if the Prophet (peace be upon him) offered prayers at various spots which were known as the Prophet's places of worship.

7. *Abū Bakr al-Ṣiddīq's place of worship at home*:
Ibn Isḥāq reports that Abū Bakr had built a place of worship near his house in the locality of Banū Jumaḥ and prayed there. Being a tender-hearted person he cried when he recited the Qur'ān. It moved greatly children, slaves and women, drawing them towards Islam. The Quraysh chiefs complained to the Aḥābīsh leader Ibn al-Daghnah who had extended protection to Abū Bakr, that Abū Bakr hurt their family members. Ibn al-Daghnah asked Abū Bakr to shut the place of worship and do inside his house whatever he wished. The latter, however, declined to do so and returned his protection deal. This place of worship lasted for a long time.[40] The above report is cited by Imām al-Zuhrī on ʿĀ'ishah's authority with reference to ʿUrwah. Moreover, the reference to Abū Bakr's place of worship features also in Bukhārī's *Kitāb Manāqib al-Anṣār, Bāb Hijrat al-Nabīy wa Asḥābihī ilā al-Madīnah*.[41] This report too, is on ʿUrwah ibn Zubayr's authority.)

8. *Other Makkan places of worship located in houses*:
It is in order to speculate, irrespective of the availability of reports or otherwise, that many Muslims must have built places of worship,

like Abū Bakr, in the yard of their houses and offered prayers there. It is stated in the *ḥadīth* on the night journey that the Prophet (peace be upon him) had offered *ʿIshā'* near the house of Umm Hānī bint Abī Ṭālib al-Hāshimī. The latter too, had prayed.[42]

ʿAmmār's place of worship: Balādhurī has recounted some reports about the places of worship erected by Makkan Muslims in and around their houses, which confirm the above speculation. There are two reports about ʿAmmār ibn Yāsir al-Madhḥijī: (i) He was the first Makkan to set up his own place of worship and pray in it and (ii) His was the first to erect a place of worship in a house.[43]

Places of Worship outside Makkah

Wherever Muslims lived outside Makkah, they had their places of worship in houses. At some places, there was more than one place of worship in that the Muslims there could not be accommodated in a single place of worship.

1. *Place of worship of Ghifār and Aslam:*
According to reports, Abū Dharr al-Ghifārī led his people in prayer. There is a variant report, however, stating that Aymā' ibn Ruḥḍah led the prayers in that he was the tribal chief, though he had accepted Islam at a later date.[44] Although places of worship are not specifically mentioned in these reports, it is certain that there were places of worship of different groups within the tribe.

2. *ʿAbd al-*Qays *place of worship in Bahrain*:
The ʿAbd al-Qays tribe of Bahrain had built its places of worship. Of these one was the central place of worship of Jawashi built in the Makkan period. This was the second such place of worship, next to the Prophet's place of worship in which Friday prayer was offered.[45] The earliest Muslim of their tribe, Ashajj and his friends had accomplished this.[46]

3. *Place of worship in Madīnah during the Makkan phase:*
It is a historical fact that some places of worship were built in this period in Madīnah. About early Madīnan Muslims it is stated that under the leadership of Asʿad ibn Zurārah al-Khazrajī they prayed at a place owned by Ḥarrah of Banū Bayāḍah, known as Naqīʿ al-Khadamāt. Forty persons joined prayers there.[47] As their number grew places of worship were built by their families and tribes, generally in their courtyards in which prayers were offered on a regular basis.[48] Ibn Ḥajar clarifies that some places of worship predated the Qubā' place of worship. He cites Jābir's report to the effect that Muslims had built places of worship a few years before the Prophet's arrival and they used to offer congregational Prayers there.[49] According to Balādhurī, the number of these places of worship was nine which had gone up later.

Education and Training of Muslims

After the commencement of the Qur'ānic revelation in the Makkan period arrangements were made for educating and training new Muslims among the Quraysh and Makkans. The Prophet (peace be upon him) was the unlettered teacher. Although he did not have a teacher, he was the supreme teacher. This education system was based essentially on comprehending, memorizing and interpreting Qur'ānic verses and this continued throughout the Makkan period. The Qur'ānic passages revealed by then were scribed and preserved. Many Companions had the privilege of being the scribes of the Qur'ān. Instructions were issued about such religious duties as bodily purification, *wuḍū'*, prayer rituals and postures, morals and manners of spiritual development. There was an extensive syllabus for educating and training Makkan Muslims which was followed through the period.[50]

For imparting training to out stationed new Muslims a shorter syllabus was in place, lasting from a week to two months. They could not stay in Makkah for long and called on the Prophet (peace be upon him) for a limited period. They were trained soon after their acceptance of Islam. They were not allowed by the Prophet (peace be upon him) to settle down in Makkah. They were taught Qur'ānic *sūrahs*, basic teachings of Islam and other important religious duties which sufficed for their leading life as Muslims. The following Companions were sent back to their respective areas after receiving the above training – Abū Dharr al-Ghifārī, Zammām ibn Thaʿlabah al-Azdī, Ashajj ʿAbd al-Qaysī, Abū Mūsā al-Ashʿarī, Ṭufayl ibn ʿAmr al-Dawsī, ʿAmr ibn ʿAbasah, Ḍamād al-Azdī, Juʿl ibn Surāqah al-Ḍamrī and several others. Apart from the Prophet, (peace be upon him) many Companions were associated with this training programme. Among them were Abū Bakr, ʿUmar, ʿUthmān, Khabbāb ibn al-Arat al-Tamīmī, Muṣʿab ibn ʿUmayr al-ʿAbdarī and ʿAmr ibn Umm Maktūm al-ʿĀmirī. There were others too, engaged in it.[51]

Both the local and out stationed Muslims had the privilege to call on at their convenience the great teacher, the Prophet (peace be upon him) and visit the headquarters of their faith, Makkah, for learning about their faith, culture and morals. They maintained close contact with the Prophet (peace be upon him) through their emissaries, caravans and letters. The latter responded to their letters and queries.[52]

Organization of Centres: Makkan Centres

The Prophet (peace be upon him) set up several centres for the training of Makkan and out stationed new Muslims. His blessed house, the Kaʿbah courtyard, and parts of the sacred place of worship were some of these centres. There was the special centre, Dār al-Arqam. Companions' houses also served as training centres. The Prophet (peace be upon him) was an outstanding and constant source of guidance yet some centres were set up for imparting the training in an organized manner.[53]

The House of the Prophet's Family

Many women and men were trained in Islam at the Prophet's house. It helped them embrace Islam and learn about the Qur'ān, *sunnah* and articles of faith. The Prophet's first wife Khadījah bint Khuwaylid al-Asadiyyah, the Prophet's daughters, and all those associated with his household such as slaves and his relatives received the training there. Among others were Zayd ibn Ḥārithah and his wife Umm Ayman, ʿAlī ibn Abī Ṭālib and many freed slaves of the family. Some members of Banū Hāshim, for example, Jaʿfar and Asmā' bint ʿUmays learnt Islam there. Among the Prophet's friends Abū Bakr accepted Islam there and had his basic training.[54]

Companions' Houses

Abū Bakr's house: At a later date Abū Bakr's house turned into a training centre. For the Prophet (peace be upon him) visited it every day and consulted Abū Bakr. The latter's daughters and son had received their training in the same house. For example, the house of ʿUmar ibn al-Khaṭṭāb's sister Fāṭimah and his brother-in-law Saʿīd ibn Zayd was a training centre where Khabbāb ibn al-Arat taught the Qur'ān.[55] Some houses of Makkan new Muslims performed the same role. These were many in number. Interestingly, even some houses of sympathetic non-Muslims served the same purpose. One cannot deny in this context the significance of the houses of Abū Ṭālib and other relatives of the Prophet (peace be upon him). At Abū Ṭālib's house the Prophet (peace be upon him) had been brought up. It was his refuge. It may be regarded as the consultative assembly of Muslims in that the Prophet had discussion there with the Quraysh chiefs on Islam. The Prophet utilized this house for preaching Islam. A public call to Islam was made from a house when, at divine directive, the Prophet (peace be upon him) invited forty-five members of Banū ʿAbd Manāf and presented before them the message of Islam.[56]

The Courtyard of the Sacred Place of Worship

The Kaʿbah had a large courtyard. Since early days the Quraysh chiefs had their meetings there. The Prophet (peace be upon him) fully utilized this tradition and set apart a spot there for holding meetings on Islam. The Quraysh chiefs recognized this right of his, for he was a respectable, trustworthy person and the leader of a particular group. Reports indicate that he was seated there at different hours, instructing Muslims in the Qur'ān, *sunnah*, morals and manners and introduced Islam to non-Muslims. The Quraysh chiefs met him there and had discussions with him on Islam. Out stationed persons called on him there for making enquiries about Islam. He received foreign delegations there as well. It may be therefore legitimately called the Prophet's meeting place, no less in significance than the Quraysh's. It was recognized so by the Quraysh chiefs.[57]

Valleys, Mountains and Caves of Makkah

In the Makkan period the valley, mountain passes and caves of Makkah too, served as Islamic centres. We have already noted how these were utilized for offering prayers. These did play an important role. It was from the height of Mount Ṣafā that the Prophet (peace be upon him) made the first public call to all the tribes of the Quraysh and Makkah to accept Islam.[58] The sending down of divine revelation is obviously an illustrious aspect of the Prophet's career. Many *sūrahs* and verses were sent down at these valleys or caves. The Prophet (peace be upon him) met Gabriel and angels there. He was granted many divine commands at these spots. He performed many important social, religious and cultural duties there. It was at the valley of Abī Ṭālib that he had suffered persecution. For three years it served as the Islamic centre. He received some delegations there in private, for example, his pledge with Aws and Khazraj of Madīnah. These agreements changed the course of events.

Ibn Saʿd narrates the following significant report: On the day the Prophet (peace be upon him) addressed the Quraysh at Mount

Ṣafā, he did not return home until evening. This upset his loving uncle, Abū Ṭālib who went out along with some youth looking for him. On the way they met Zayd ibn Ḥārithah who informed them that the Prophet (peace be upon him) was engaged in conversation with his Companions at a house near Ṣafā.[59]

The Islamic Centre of Dār al-Arqam

The Islamic centre of Dār al-Arqam occupies great importance in the history of Islam and the Prophet's mission. Its account is related at length in primary sources. Recent biographers of the Prophet (peace be upon him) have accordingly highlighted its role, to the exclusion of other Islamic centres of Makkah. Undoubtedly Dār al-Arqam played its unique role in the history of Islam.

Some biographers are of the view that in the last days of the Prophet's private preaching when Muslims had grown in number, this centre was set up, probably after two years of the Prophet's advent i.e. in 612 CE. This centre had come up, however, in the early days of the Prophet's mission, for it was there that many early Muslims had embraced Islam, as is specified by Ibn Saʿd. Among them were ʿAmmār Ibn Yāsir al-Madhḥijī, Ṣuhayb ibn Sinān and Abū Dharr al-Ghifārī who had accepted Islam in that period. Abū Dharr al-Ghifārī is among the early Makkan Muslims, who was converted in the very early days of the Prophet's preaching. While dealing with conflicting reports about the date of his conversion, however, Ibn Ḥajar says that it happened two years after the Prophet (peace be upon him) assumed office.

This centre was selected for being the house of an influential and affluent Companion, al-Arqam ibn Abī al-Arqam al-Makhzūmī. It therefore came to be known as Dār al-Arqam. It was located near Ṣafā and Marwah, away from the main populace of Makkah. Situated at an isolated place it was a perfect site for the training, character building and education of Muslims, for one could reach there with some effort. The Prophet (peace be upon him) stayed there regularly and engaged in organizing Islamic activities. Abū

Dharr al-Ghifārī, Ḥamzah, ʿUmar and others had accepted Islam and were trained there.[60]

The progress of Islam and Dār al-Arqam was phenomenal. Early sources identify those who accepted Islam there and their dates. Such leading Quraysh chiefs as Ḥamzah ibn ʿAbd al-Muṭṭalib al-Hāshimī and ʿUmar ibn al-Khaṭṭāb had embraced Islam there. Among the out stationed ones the most prominent was Abū Dharr al-Ghifārī. Apart from being an Islamic centre, it was an educational institution, monastery, training ground, consultative assembly, place of worship and the Prophet's meeting place. It was truly an important Islamic centre during the Makkan period.[61]

1. *Rural centres outside Makkah*:
Out of his wisdom the Prophet (peace be upon him) directed out stationed new Muslims to return to their home towns and to engage in preaching Islam among their people there. Implicit in it was his directive for organizing Muslims and for forming the Muslim community. It is aptly observed by someone that the community exists wherever Muslims live, irrespective of their number and even in non-Muslim majority areas. We have already referred to the Islamic centres outside Makkah. It would be in order to outline their role in the propagation of Islam and the emergence of Muslim communities.

a. The tribes of Ghifār, Kinānah, Aslam and Khuzāʿah: These tribes were settled along the highway from Makkah to Madīnah. During the phase of the private preaching of Islam when Abū Dharr Al-Ghifārī learnt about the Prophet's mission, he deputed his elder brother Anīs Ghifārī to gather information. The latter's report on return did not satisfy him. Therefore, he himself went to Makkah and met the Prophet (peace be upon him) at Dār al-Arqam. He embraced Islam on listening to the Prophet. The latter, however, directed him to return to his tribe and preach Islam among them. Imām Bukhārī cites the Prophet (peace be upon him) thus: 'Go back to your people and warn them until my command reaches you.' Ibn Ḥajar explicates it on Abū Qutaybah's authority: 'Keep this matter secret and return to your people for instructing them. You should join us on learning about our ascendancy.'[62] However, before his return he declared before the Quraysh his acceptance of Islam. He was therefore, reprimanded. Al-ʿAbbās al-Hāshimī managed to protect him against the Quraysh's ire, pointing out that he belonged to the strategic route of trade with Syria. Any harm to him would deprive them of this trade route. After his return he vigorously preached Islam in his region. First, his elder brother, Anees and his mother accepted Islam, followed by others. By the time of the Prophet's emigration to Madīnah half of the tribes of Ghifār and Banū Aslam had been won over to Islam. During the Prophet's emigration journey the rest too, entered the fold of Islam. These two tribes stand out perhaps as the first organized Muslim community outside Makkah.

b. Banū Ḍamrah/Kinānah: Kinānah, an Arab tribe, was settled in Madīnah. Its members accepted Islam at an early date. The earliest among them was Juʿl ibn Surāqah al-Ḍamrī. It was by dint of his efforts that a branch of Muslim community sprang up there. Among other early Muslims of another branch of this tribe were ʿAbdullāh and ʿAbd al-Raḥmān al-Kinānī. They belong to Banū Bakr ibn ʿAbd Manāt. The following members of yet another branch of this tribe, Banū Wā'il – ʿUwayf ibn ʿAdbat, Sāriyah ibn Zanīm and Anīs ibn Zanīm had also embraced Islam in the Makkan period. Thus Islam had made its way into several branches of this tribe.

c. Banū Salīm: This tribe settled between Makkah and Madīnah was both large and powerful. They were settled in Ṣafā, Hizzah and other hamlets. ʿAmr ibn ʿAbasah was the first Muslim among them. He claimed to be the fourth of the earliest Muslims. On coming to know about the

Prophet's mission he visited Makkah and accepted Islam. He wanted to live in the Prophet's company. However, he was sent back with the directive to preach Islam in his home town and to join the Prophet (peace be upon him) after he launched his mission publicly. His tribesmen embraced Islam later. However, thanks to his efforts, a small Muslim community had come into existence there.[63]

d. Daws: This tribe of western and southern Arabia was introduced to Islam during the private preaching phase of the Makkan period. Muʿaqab ibn Abī Fāṭimah al-Dawsī, the earliest Muslim of the tribe, had returned to his tribe and carried on preaching among them. Many of his tribesmen accepted Islam, thanks to his efforts. Another prominent Muslim of this tribe was Ṭufayl ibn ʿAmr al-Dawsī who was a poet and tribal chief. His high status facilitated the spread of Islam in his area. In the Makkan period itself a small Muslim community had come up there. Of them, the most renowned one was Abū Hurayrah. The entire family of Ṭufayl ibn ʿAmr and other families accepted Islam. In 7/629 around 70-80 families of this tribe emigrated to Madīnah while many preferred to stay at home.[64]

Ḍamād al-Azdī too, was a prominent early Muslim of this tribe. However, he did not belong to the Daws. During the *Jāhiliyyah* period he was the Prophet's friend and business partner. He visited Makkah and accepted Islam after learning about the Prophet's mission. Not only did he pledge obedience to the Prophet (peace be upon him), he did so also on behalf of his people. As a result, another Muslim community surfaced there.[65]

e. al-Ashʿar tribe was a leading tribe of southern Yemen. Abū Mūsā al-Ashʿarī is its famous representative. In the beginning of the Makkan period he accepted Islam and returned to his tribe, devoting himself to the spread of Islam. Abū Bardā' and Abū Raḥm, the two brothers and at least, fifty members of his tribe embraced Islam as a result of his efforts. Thus in the extreme southern region a small Muslim community managed to come up and flourished even after the Prophet's emigration to Madīnah.[66]

f. Saʿd al-ʿUshayr: It figures among the tribes that were introduced to Islam. This particular tribe was of southern Yemen. Many of its members along with the leaders had embraced Islam.

g. ʿAbd al-Qays of Bahrain: They lived in eastern Arabia in the Persian border. Among its earliest Muslims were Ashajj ʿAbd al-Qays and his nephew, ʿAmr ibn ʿAbd al-Qays. The latter representing the former called on the Prophet (peace be upon him) in Makkah and accepted Islam. On his return he carried the invaluable present of *Sūrahs al-Falaq* and *al-Fātiḥah*. At his behest Ashajj too, became Muslim and took up the preaching of Islam in his area. After some time he went again to Makkah along with twelve or seventeen members of his tribe and gained knowledge of Islam during their stay in Makkah. On his return the preaching of Islam continued. By the time of the Prophet's migration to Madīnah, there were so many Muslims that they built a large place of worship at Jawthī, which was next only to the Prophet's place of worship in terms of having arrangements for Friday prayer. His efforts helped introduce Islam among other tribes of the region.[67]

It is an extensive topic which calls for detailed research. In sum, it may be concluded that many small Muslim communities had been formed among the Arab tribes settled outside Makkah. Later on, they grew into larger communities. An analytical study of these Islamic centres and groups is yet to be made. It is nonetheless on record that branches and sub-branches of the Muslim community flourished in almost every part of Arabia, with Makkah as the headquarters where the Prophet (peace be upon him) was stationed and they were in constant touch with him.

2. *Urban centres outside Makkah*:

Makkah was, no doubt, the main centre in view of the Prophet's presence. In the thirteen years of the Makkan period it was the headquarters. Moreover, the largest Muslim community flourished there. By the middle of the Makkan period, however, some other towns and centres surpassed Makkah in terms of the size of the Muslim population. Even if the Muslims in southern Arabia belonging to Ashʿar and Daws tribes and ʿAbd al-Qays tribe of Bahrain were less, the Muslims of Ghifār and Aslam tribes certainly outnumbered Makkan Muslims. Reports say that they were, at least, 1500-2000. For this was half the strength of these tribes that had embraced Islam. Yet Makkah enjoyed its central position.[68] In the last three years of the Makkan period i.e. between 620 and 623 CE Madīnah excelled Makkah in the number of Muslims and their organization. Islam spread there far and wide. Three years before the Prophet's migration, only six Khazrajī chiefs were Muslims there, in addition to a few others who had converted to Islam during pilgrimage or trade journeys as a result of their contact with the Prophet (peace be upon him). In 620 CE the Khazrajī chiefs took the preaching of Islam as their mission and many turned into Muslims. Twelve of them called on the Prophet (peace be upon him) in Makkah and in 620 CE contracted the first pledge of ʿAqabah at his hands. At their request the Prophet (peace be upon him) deputed to them Muṣʿab ibn ʿUmayr as the Qur'ān teacher who instructed them in Islam and *fiqh*. These efforts bore fruits as a large number of the members of Aws and Khazraj tribes embraced Islam. Their seventy-five representatives entered into another agreement with the Prophet (peace be upon him) which is known as the second pledge of ʿAqabah.

Till then Asʿad ibn Zurārah al-Khazrajī, the dynamic chief was in charge of the training and organization of local Muslims. He himself had taken up this responsibility. He led them in prayer for being their tribal chief. As the Prophet's representative Muṣʿab ibn ʿUmayr assumed the religious leadership of another group of Anṣār. Being the Prophet's emissary he occupied an exalted position. The second pledge of ʿAqabah led to the reorganization of Madīnan Muslims which had significant, far-reaching implications. It reconstructed their political and religious life and set up an Islamic centre.

Conventional biographers of the Prophet (peace be upon him) rest content with stating that the Prophet (peace be upon him) had appointed nine and three leaders of Khazraj and Aws respectively, with a chief overseeing them all. On the eve of the first pledge of ʿAqabah he had appointed, at the request of Madīnan Muslims, a leader of prayer, preacher and teacher as his representative. This does not indicate clearly the organization of the society. It was a very significant step politically and religiously and also in terms of the tribal traditions of the day.

Nine representatives for nine families of Khazraj were appointed. The same was done in the case of Aws by appointing three representatives. The Prophet (peace be upon him) had issued them directives before appointing them.[69]

Al-Suhaylī and Ibn Sayyid al-Nās interpret the appointment of twelve representatives as being identical with the appointment of twelve chiefs for the Prophet Moses's community, as referred to in verse 12 of *al-Māʾidah*. Imām Bukhārī has recorded *aḥādīth* only regarding the first pledge of ʿAqabah. However, Ibn Ḥajar has discussed reports by several *ḥadīth* scholars with a view to appreciating this appointment. In Imām Aḥmad ibn Ḥanbal's report about the second pledge there is a pointed reference to the conditions laid down by the Prophet (peace be upon him). Some other *aḥādīth* reinforce the above point.[70]

Although they were community chiefs, they were accountable to the Prophet (peace be upon him) for being his representatives. Both the Aws and Khazraj tribes had their own family and tribal organization. They also had an additional responsibility, for at their appointment the Prophet (peace be upon him) had told them: 'You are the custodians of your people as the disciples of Jesus, son of Mary were. I am a custodian over my community.'[71] Above them there was the chief, signifying the superstructure of this organization. More importantly, they were accountable to the head of the Islamic community, the Prophet Muḥammad (peace be upon him) stationed in Makkah. They abided by all his directives and commands. It was a major step towards organizing Madīnan society, for putting an end to the class system in the Muslim community and for merging different units into a single whole for creating the single ummah. Various dimensions of this important step, particularly its political and organizational significance have not been studied so far. A glimpse of the same may be seen in the same effective system which followed a century after in the ʿAbbāsid period. As a result, Abū Muslim al-Khurāsānī and his twelve representatives overthrew the Umayyads. The appointment of Muṣʿab as the teacher and religious head, in deference to the wish of the Madīnans, is equally significant, for he symbolized religious unity and religious leadership. As the Prophet's nominee, he was answerable to him. All these steps helped in the emergence of a strong Islamic political power, initially known as Anṣār, and later as the Muslim community itself. The emigrants from Makkah were joined by them in the bond of fraternity and this again resulted in shaping the greater Muslim community. In number Madīnan Muslims were the largest. They were superior to Makkan Muslims politically, strategically and financially. The Makkans merged well with them.

3. *Urban centres outside Arabia:*

Chronologically, prior to the emergence of the Madīnan community, another offshoot of the Muslim community came up during the Makkan period. In the fifth year of the Prophet's mission in 615-616 CE this community appeared on the scene, with variations in its size. However, during the entire career of the Prophet it flourished in Abyssinia. Even after the return of Muslim migrants in 7/629, Muslims of Abyssinian descent lived there. It is in order to mention them before the Madīnan community that it was the first foreign manifestation of the Muslim community which flourished in Abyssinia, outside the Arabian Peninsula. For twenty years from 615 to 629 CE it comprised refugees and emigrant Arabs who had taken shelter for defending their faith in a non-Muslim kingdom of a just Christian king. They were no more than 100-125 yet they were important socially, politically, religiously and culturally. They enjoyed a position of honour in a non-Muslim society and had their religious and cultural rights. Their lives, property and honour were safe. Socially too, they were held in esteem.

As a result of enjoying their religious rights, these Muslim migrants influenced non-Arabs and local Abyssinians. Some of them accepted Islam. Their patron and the Abyssinian king Negus Aṣḥamah was won over to Islam. Others naturally followed him. Although being slow, the trends of conversion to Islam continued there, as more and more Abyssinians entered the fold of Islam. They created a niche for themselves in the local society and maintained religious, social and cultural links with the Islamic headquarters Makkah, and the Prophet (peace be upon him). At a later date, they forged political and military contacts with the head of the Islamic state, pledging loyalty to him. This Abyssinian branch of the Muslim community had remarkable international dimension. For it flourished outside the confines of the Arabian Peninsula, in a non-Arab land. The universality of the Prophet's mission was reflected first there. Later on, it turned out to be an incontrovertible feature of the Muslim community. In the next chapter other aspects of this branch of the Muslim community in Abyssinia are examined.

CHAPTER 3

The Muslim Community of Abyssinia

After the emigration to Abyssinia, the construction of a Muslim community in a non-Muslim dominated country was the next inevitable phase. It was not something new. For in its own homeland, Makkah, the Muslim community had been a minority in the polity ruled by the Quraysh. At most, the stay of Muslims in Abyssinia may be regarded as the extension of the experience which the Makkan Muslim minority had. The only major difference was that some Muslims from now onwards lived in the midst of non-Muslims of a place other than Makkah. With all their social, cultural and religious distinctions they were placed in a non-Muslim society. It was something akin to the Muslim presence in the Quraysh society. There they did not enjoy peace on account of their practising a new faith. However, in Abyssinia they had relatively more peace. The Makkan society discriminated against them in social, political and cultural matters whereas in Abyssinia they enjoyed justice and tolerance. As a result, the persecuted Muslims of Makkah were allowed to emigrate towards the just non-Muslim Abyssinia. It laid down the Islamic principle that it is obligatory on Muslims to emigrate from an unjust country. The emigration could be to another town within the same country, as it happened with the emigration to Madīnah or to a foreign land such as Abyssinia. We will discuss historical, jurisprudential and other issues on this subject later.

In the non-Muslim Abyssinian society a section of the Makkan Muslim community led a peaceful life for around twenty years. Their social rank was similar to the one held by Makkan Muslims. However, they were not faced with a hostile and biased society. Initially, they too, had to face some opposition yet they were not persecuted. In other respects, they, nonetheless, resembled their Makkan counterparts, with some minor differences. However, a clear picture cannot be formed about them by focusing on the similarity with the Makkan experience. Let us study at some length the presence, evolution and performance of Muslims in Abyssinia.

The Relations Between Makkah and Abyssinia

Arabs had trade links with neighbouring countries. This relationship was established centuries before the Prophet's advent. Trade links led to cultural exchange between Arabs and Persians in the east, with Iraq and Syria and through these to the Roman Empire in the north; with Egypt and the Roman Empire in the north-west; with Abyssinia in the middle east and with Christian, Abyssinian and Persian kingdoms in the south. Makkah was, no doubt, the nerve centre of Arabia and the Quraysh enjoyed a prominent position. Not unsurprisingly they had relations with all these communities and countries.

Trade and Religious Links

In the spread of Christianity in Arabia, apart from the Roman Byzantine Empire the Abyssinian kingdom played a major role. According to a critic, if we go by the statements of Ibn Khaldūn and Orientalists, links between Arabia and Abyssinia had been established before the third century. Najrān was the headquarters of Christianity in Yemen. Before the fifth century Christianity had reached there. In 496 CE the entire Yemen was under the rule of a

Christian kingdom. This naturally led to the spread of this faith there. Abrahah, governor of Yemen, played a key role in preaching it. His plan to demolish the Kaʿbah was part of the same design. Quṣayy ibn Kilāb, the forefather of the Quraysh and founder of Makkah, was helped by the Roman Emperor in establishing his rule over Makkah. Romans and Abyssinians had provided the enterprising Quraysh youth with trade and transport facilities. ʿAbd Manāf's four sons – ʿAbd Shams, Hāshim, Nawfal and al-Muṭṭalib had developed special relations with neighbouring countries and secured trade license there. ʿAbd Shams had entered into such agreements with the Roman Emperor and King Ghassān; Nawfal with the Persian Emperor; al-Muṭṭalib with the Ḥimayrite king and Hashim with the Abyssinian king, Negus. According to Ibn Saʿd, the Roman Emperor had sent a letter of recommendation for Hāshim to Negus. Transport facilities had their bearings on the trade links between Arabia and Abyssinia since early days. Arab traders exported their leather, gum, incense and woollen clothes and imported grain from there.[1]

It emerges from Balādhurī's report that Hāshim had got trade license from the Roman Emperor and his elder brother, ʿAbd Shams from the Abyssinian king in that his trade was mainly in Abyssinia. These four illustrious sons of ʿAbd Manāf had laid the foundation of trade caravans, in winter to Yemen, Abyssinia and Iraq and in summer to Syria.[2] These trade links had forged their friendship with Abyssinia. On one occasion ʿAbd al-Muṭṭalib al-Hāshimī proposed that Negus of Abyssinia should act as the arbiter in a local dispute with Ḥarb ibn Umayyah. However, Negus declined to oblige him.[3]

Slave Trade

It is evident from several reports that Abyssinian slaves were brought to the Arabian Peninsula in general and to Makkah in particular. This trade was conducted in Abyssinia directly and at other places indirectly. As a result, there were a large number of Abyssinian slaves and their children in Makkah. Their children are referred to as 'Mawalladūn' in historical sources. Their association with the Prophet's life and Islamic history is deep and varied. Both the slaves and freed slaves of Abyssinia figure in it. Clues about their families are found in the history of Makkah of the *Jāhiliyyah* period.

Bilāl of Abyssinia and his Family

Among the Arabs of Abyssinian descent, the most prominent figure in the Prophet's Makkan period is of Bilāl. He belongs to the category of 'Mawalladūn' in that he was born in Makkah. His father, Rabāḥ was an Abyssinian. So was his mother, Ḥamāmah. According to reports, their ancestors had arrived in Makkah as slaves. They served an important Quraysh family. As stated by Ibn Isḥāq and Ibn Hishām, Bilāl and his family, namely his parents and brothers and sister were slaves to the Banū Jumah chief, Umayyah ibn Khalaf al-Jumaḥī. The Prophet (peace be upon him) referred to Bilāl as an Abyssinian, though his family had settled for long in Sarāt, a town near Ṭā'if.[4]

On the authority of Ibn Saʿd, Ibn Ḥajar states, that Bilāl came from upper Ṭā'if and his mother was Banū Jumah's slave. Ṭabarānī recounts the popular report that Bilāl was of Abyssinian descent.[5]

Umm Ayman

Nonetheless, the Abyssinian person with whom the Prophet (peace be upon him) came first into contact and for a long time was Umm Ayman. She was the slave to the Prophet's father, ʿAbdullāh. She had brought him up after his weaning. When he grew up, he freed her and got her married to Zayd ibn Ḥārithah. Usāmah was their son.[6] Barakah was her real name. She was of Abyssinian descent.[7] The Prophet (peace be upon him) had visited Madīnah along with his mother, Āminah, when he was only six years old. Umm Ayman accompanied them and after Āminah's death at al-Abwā', she brought back the Prophet (peace be upon him) to Makkah and looked after him. In Makkah she was married to ʿUbayd ibn ʿAmr al-Khazrajī who was on pilgrimage there. After marriage she went to Madīnah and gave birth to her son, Ayman and came to be known as Umm Ayman. After ʿUbayd's death, the Prophet got her married to Zayd ibn Ḥārithah. Usāmah was born to her as a result of this marriage. Ayman ibn ʿUbayd attained martyrdom in the battle of Ḥunayn. Zayd had a daughter too, Zaynab.[8]

Other Abyssinian Freed Slaves of the Prophet

Reference to some other slaves of Abyssinian descent occurs in the works on the Prophet's life. Of them, there was Anjashah, bearing the appellation, Abū Māriyyah. He was the Prophet's camel driver and sang songs to spur on the camels.[9] For Ibn Saʿd, Anjashah, like Bilāl, was the son of a slave of Sīrat. Rabāḥ,[10] with the partronym Abū Ayman, was the caller of the Prophet's meetings. He was a black person. After Yāsir's martyrdom at ʿUraynah he succeeded him and looked after the Prophet's camels.[11] According to Ibn Saʿd, Ṣāliḥ Shaqrān was an Abyssinian, whose original name was Ṣāliḥ ibn ʿAdiyy, who was initially ʿAbd al-Raḥmān ibn ʿAwf al-Zuhrī's slave. The Prophet (peace be upon him) bought him in view of his qualities. He emigrated to Madīnah and served as incharge of the booty and captives in the battles of Badr and Muraysiʿ.[12]

The Visit of Abyssinian Individuals and Groups

Many bits of evidence indicate the visit of Abyssinians to Makkah and its vicinity. Ibn Isḥāq's report on this count is very significant in that it is related to the Prophet's childhood. Ḥalīmah al-Saʿdiyyah, the Prophet's foster mother hastily returned the Prophet (peace be upon him) to Makkah in view of some extraordinary events. Of these, the most popular one is the opening up of his breast. Unable to comprehend this Ḥalīmah turned panicky. Another reason, as stated in Ibn Isḥāq's report, is that when Ḥalīmah was returning after the Prophet's weaning, a group of Anṣār spotted him and asked her about him, after inspecting him carefully. They told her:

'We would make it a point to take this child and keep him in our country, for he is destined to attain glory. We recognize him well.' Ḥalīmah secured his release and rushed to Makkah.[13]

The Business Centre of Abyssinia

Since early days trade links existed between Abyssinia and Makkah and Madīnah in particular and other Arab towns in general. A significant report about the emigration to Abyssinia is that some Muslim emigrants had reached the Shuʿayb port on foot, others on some mount. By chance they got two boats of traders which carried them to Abyssinia; charging them a fare of only half a dīnār. The Quraysh, who had some inkling about it, pursued them yet they could not detain anyone.[14] One of the factors for emigration to Abyssinia, according to Tabari, was that it had been a trade centre of the Quraysh. The latter had benefited much from it during peace period.[15]

Emigration to Abyssinia

Emigration has been a familiar practice in history. In the Prophet Muḥammad's mission emigration flowed from a divine directive. It played a major role in the life of the Prophet (peace be upon him) and of the Makkan Muslim community. On being faced with persecution and hardships Muslims have resorted to emigration in every age. During the Makkan period as persecution became intolerable, the Prophet (peace be upon him) allowed resourceful Muslims to emigrate. That Abyssinia was a land of truth and purity was the main consideration behind the Prophet's permission to do so. Another factor was that justice prevailed there. No injustice was apprehended. Moreover, despite the protection emanating from the tribal way of life in Makkah, Muslims could no longer survive in Makkah. Therefore, the practice of emigration was revived. It is significant that some members of the Makkan Muslim community were allowed to be the subjects of a just Christian ruler of a foreign country.[16] Abyssinia was part of the African continent, away from Arabia, under a non-Arab ruler.

Significantly enough, no Arab territory was used as the land of emigration. For all other towns like Makkah were under non-Muslim rule. They had the same protection system which was in force in Makkah. Yet religious differences denied any justice to Muslims. Any other Arab town would have been as hostile to Muslims as Makkah was. Although being not part of Arabia, Abyssinia was the nearest place to Makkah for return.[17] It was easier for Makkan Muslims to maintain ties with Makkah while being in Abyssinia. This important step served as an experiment for the Prophet's universal mission and for the global Muslim community. It conveyed the message loud and clear that the Muslim community is universal, open fully to non-Arabs.

Emigration to and Settlement in Abyssinia

According to classical biographers of the Prophet (peace be upon him) and standard sources, Muslims migrated to Abyssinia twice; the first being in 615 CE or the fifth year of the Prophet's mission when fourteen Muslims left Makkah for Abyssinia. After a year around eighty men, women and children migrated there, taking the figure of Muslims in Abyssinia to around one hundred.[18] Some scholars, however, insist that the emigration took place only once, and people went there at regular intervals.[19] As a result of this emigration spread over one and a half year, around one hundred Muslims settled there. Their number increased later.

All the classical and modern biographers of the Prophet (peace be upon him) have recorded the names of families and chiefs of the emigrants to Abyssinia. Notwithstanding variant reports, ten to fourteen persons were the first to emigrate. All the reports nonetheless unanimously state that ʿUthmān ibn ʿAffān and his wife Ruqayyah, the Prophet's daughter were among the earliest emigrants. ʿUthmān was the first to go there along with his wife, as is recorded in *ḥadīth*. According to Ibn Ḥajar, the Prophet (peace be upon him) received a delayed report about their reaching Abyssinia. Some women informed that ʿUthmān was seen, with his wife riding a donkey hence the Prophet's remark on it. The above report does not specify the place where ʿUthmān and his wife were spotted.

After a year in the second phase of emigration, Jaʿfar ibn Abī Ṭālib went there, as is reported by Ibn Ishaq. Dr. Hamidullah has recounted on Ṭabarī's authority this significant report that the Prophet (peace be upon him) had given Jaʿfar a letter for Negus, writing to him: 'I have sent my cousin Jaʿfar to you, along with some Muslims. When he calls on you, treat him well. Do not be unjust to him.' Although it is an introductory letter, it indicates the Prophet's familiarity with Negus, if not close relations. Other Muslims joined Jaʿfar, assembling and settling down in Abyssinia. Some went there along with their families and some without them. Sources list the emigrants belonging to the Quraysh families. There is some divergence of opinion on their names. Yet it is an extensive list.[20] Among them are eighty-three men. Their accompanying children or those born there are not mentioned. Mention is made of the poems on this migration and the Makkan poets.[21] Little information is on record how these emigrants were received there. The usual account is that they lived there in peace, praising Negus's protection and devoting themselves to worshipping Allah in that they enjoyed security there. Negus treated them well, providing them with facilities for their stay.[22] A detailed study of some reports sheds light on the migration of this Muslim minority to a non-Muslim country, its stay and settlement there, its social and economic life and the cultural and religious issues confronted by it.

There are extensive reports in the primary sources on the migration to Abyssinia. However, the writers on *sīrah* rest content with providing only a bare outline about the Quraysh delegation in Negus's court and their plea for deporting the Muslim emigrants to Makkah, Negus's discussion with Muslims and his dismissal of the Quraysh's demand and the eventual stay of Muslims there in peace and comfort.[23] Their accounts do not analyze the issues faced by the

Muslim minority of Abyssinia. An attempt is made below to delve into these issues.

According to Ibn Isḥāq and Ibn Hishām, the account of the Qurayshī delegation's discussion with Negus is based on the first-hand report narrated by Umm Salamah al-Makhzūmiyyah, herself an emigrant. It is significant for being an eye-witness account. The following points stand out in this report:

1. The conspiracy of the Quraysh chiefs: The Makkan enemies of Islam could not stomach the peaceful stay of the Muslims in Abyssinia and their profession of Islam there. Therefore, they hatched a conspiracy aimed at their return to Makkah. They resorted to deception in devising their steps:
   a. They decided to choose very intelligent and resourceful persons for the delegation to be sent to Abyssinia. Accordingly, ʿAbdullāh ibn Abī Rabīʿah al-Makhzūmī and ʿAmr ibn al-ʿĀṣ were selected, who were famous for their oratory, shrewdness and insightfulness as well as for their deceit. Some reports suggest that in addition to the above, another delegation comprising ʿAmr ibn al-ʿĀṣ al-Sahmī and ʿUmārah ibn Walīd al-Makhzūmī was also constituted. As the former failed in its mission, the latter was sent.
   b. Another device adopted by the enemies of Islam was to select the best gifts for Negus and his clergy chiefs. These gifts of leather were sent to every one of them in order to win them over in the move against Muslim emigrants. It was a blatant instance of bribery in diplomacy and politics.
   c. What was more sinister was their advice to the delegation members not to let the Muslim emigrants approach Negus. They must ensure their expulsion before Negus gets in touch with them. It would have forced the king to abide by his own order, even if he changed his mind later. This move was to be executed in connivance with Negus's clergymen.

d. The delegation faithfully observed these directives. First, they personally called on each clergyman and presented gifts to them. They made a forceful plea, stating that some ignorant youth of their country had fled to Abyssinia. They were guilty of having abandoned their ancestral faith. Nor had they accepted the faith of Abyssinia. They professed a new faith, unknown to both them and the Abyssinians. Therefore, they would like to request the king to order their return to Makkah. These clergymen should persuade the king to return the refugees to the delegation and not to get in touch with them. For they knew these refugees well and their crime. Each of the clergymen promised to help the delegation. Meeting them individually was part of the conspiracy lest in a meeting someone might not agree.

e. The next day the Qurayshī delegation made a forceful presentation. It was endorsed by Negus's clergy, as was planned. However, Negus decided to give a hearing to the Muslims' stance. The delegation apprehended and resented it. They dismissed it as a pointless exercise. Again, the clergy supported their contention. This infuriated Negus who ordered: 'We would never return them to you. For they have taken refuge with us. They have preferred us to others. I would send for them and enquire about your charges against them. If they are guilty as you contend, I would hand them over to you, returning them to their country. However, if this is not the case, I would help and protect them as long as they stay here. I would fulfill my obligations towards them.'

It was an effective political and diplomatic move on the part of the Quraysh. Bribery with a view to winning supporters among the ruling class, persuading them individually, deterring them from listening to the other party of victims and prevailing upon the ruler to secure the judgement in one's favour have always been part of diplomatic activity. However, Negus's just policy frustrated their plan.

Another nefarious conspiracy devised by the Quraysh delegation, which is not specified in Ibn Isḥāq's and Ibn Hishām's above-quoted report, is mentioned in some accounts and verified by other sources. The Quraysh delegation to Abyssinia comprised three members and the third member was ʿUmārah ibn al-Walīd al-Makhzūmī. For al-Suhaylī, it was the second delegation consisting of ʿAmr ibn al-ʿĀṣ al-Sahmī and ʿUmārah ibn al-Walīd al-Makhzūmī whereas the first delegation had ʿAmr ibn al-ʿĀṣ and ʿAbdullāh ibn Abi Rabīʿah as its members. The following points emerge from the report:

ʿAmr ibn al-ʿĀṣ Sahmi had gone there along with his wife. She tried to have illicit relations with ʿUmārah, which was naturally resented by ʿAmr ibn al-ʿĀṣ. ʿAmr was thrown by them into the sea and as he raised alarm, those on board rescued him. ʿAmr turned into ʿUmārah's foe, though he maintained silence then.

2. In Abyssinia ʿAmr suggested to ʿUmārah to seduce Negus's wife for achieving the objective of their delegation, for Negus would not turn down a case recommended by his queen, who was his favourite as well.

   ʿUmārah fell into this trap and became friendly with the queen. She was also attracted towards him. At that juncture ʿAmr, acting as Negus's well-wisher, divulged the secret to Negus and produced some bit of proof.

3. In view of the diplomatic immunity, Negus did not behead ʿUmārah. However, he directed magicians to cast a spell on him. Under its spell, ʿUmārah filed to the desert and lived amid beasts. It was during Caliph ʿUmar's caliphate that he died in the same state.

4. Although the above report reveals the misconduct of the two leading Qurayshi persons, it points to the conspiracy pervading their way of life. Had they succeeded in influencing the queen, it would have been an altogether different story. Moreover, one learns that abusing female sexual favours has been part of diplomacy in the past, as it is now. The above report is nonetheless generally branded as a fabricated one.[24]

The Muslim Stance in Negus's Court

The King Negus summoned Muslim emigrants to his court. They consulted among one another on the stance to be adopted in his court. They decided that irrespective of the consequences, they would make a faithful presentation of Islamic teachings, based on their knowledge and the training received from the Prophet (peace be upon him). According to recurrent reports, Jaʿfar ibn Abī Ṭālib made the presentation before Negus and pleaded the case for Islam effectively and eloquently. He brought home the message of Islam and its attendant transformation. It articulated fully the message of Islam as it was in the Makkan period and its impact. It is worth-quoting:

1. 'O King! We were a people steeped in *Jāhiliyyah*, given to idolatry, eating dead bodies, committing indecent acts, severing our blood ties, usurping the rights due to neighbours and the strong among us exploited the weak ones.
2. While we were lost in it, Allah sent down to us a Messenger from among ourselves. We know well his family background and his truthfulness, honesty and piety. He called us to the way of Allah, urging us to believe in His Oneness, worship him and abandon idolatry in which our ancestors indulged.
3. He directed us to speak truth, render our trusts, maintain ties of kinship, fulfill the obligations towards our neighbours, shun all that is unlawful and avoid bloodshed.
4. He dissuaded us from committing indecency, telling lies, devouring orphans' belongings and slandering chaste women.
5. He commanded us to worship the Only True God and not to associate anyone with Him. He asked us also to pray, fast and pay *zakāh*.'

   According to Umm Salamah, a witness to the incident, Jaʿfar recounted all these features of Islam before Negus and made the following concluding remarks.

6. 'We therefore testified to his message and believed in him. We followed him in all that God had revealed to him. We prayed only to the One True God and did not hold anyone equal to

Him. We refrained from all that he declared as unlawful for us. We regard it as lawful all that he has allowed us.

7. After we professed faith in him, our people took to persecuting us. They tried to make us revert to our ancestral faith and idolatry, driving away from worshipping Allah and regarding the unlawful as lawful.
8. When they inflicted much injustice on us and made life difficult for us, preventing us from practising our faith, we came to your country, preferring you to others. We liked to have your protection in the hope that we would not be treated unjustly under your rule, O king.'

   Umm Salamah reports that the king asked them whether they had a portion of divine message revealed to them. At the king's command Jaʿfar recited the opening verses of *Sūrah Maryam*.
9. Umm Salamah adds that on listening to the Qur'ānic passage, tears welled up in Negus's eyes and his beard was soaked with tears. His clergymen also cried. Their Scriptures were soaked as they listened to the Qur'ān.
10. Then Negus exclaimed: 'Undoubtedly this message and the one carried by Prophet Jesus (peace be upon him) have emanated from the same source of light.' Addressing the Quraysh delegation, he asked them to go away: 'By God! I would not hand them over to you. Never would they be deported from our country.'

Umm Salamah relates that when the two Quraysh representatives left court, ʿAmr ibn al-ʿĀṣ al-Sahmī said: 'Tomorrow I would produce against them a point which would strike at their roots.' ʿAbdullāh ibn Abī Rabīʿah al-Makhzūmī, the more pious of the two, however, said: 'We would not do so. For we have ties of kinship with them, though they have opposed us.' ʿAmr ibn al-ʿĀs, nonetheless, persisted in saying: 'I would make it a point to tell Negus that they regard Jesus, son of Mary as a mere mortal.' Accordingly they told him the next day: 'O King! They say something outrageous about Jesus, son of Mary. Summon them and find out their stance about him.' Negus again sent for the Muslims. When the Muslims came to know about it, they were worried regarding it as something disastrous. After a lengthy discussion they decided to state faithfully their belief, no matter what it might result in. In response to Negus's query, Jaʿfar said emphatically: 'Our belief about Prophet Jesus (peace be upon him) is what our Messenger told us. Jesus is the servant of Allah; His Messenger has His spirit; His word which Allah had sent down to the devout and chaste Mary.' While striking his head on the ground, Negus picked up a straw and exclaimed: 'By God! Jesus was no more than this piece of straw.' On hearing this his clergymen protested with their gestures. However, he ignored them and assured Muslims of his protection: Those hurting them would be penalized. He asserted this thrice: 'Even if I am given a mountain of gold, I would not like that any hurt should touch you.' He asked his ministers to return the gifts given by the Quraysh delegation, saying that these were not needed: 'By God! God did not take anything from me when He restored this country to me. How can I accept bribery? People obeyed me and I would follow them.' Both the Qurayshī delegations returned from his court in utter failure and despair. For even their gifts had been returned. The Muslims continued to live in comfort and peace in that excellent refuge.[25]

Some Events and issues related to the Muslims' stay in Abyssinia

Umm Salamah has recounted some incidents related to the stay of Muslims in Abyssinia during the Makkan period. These have a direct bearing on the issue of the Muslim presence in a land of unbelief. Al-Suhaylī and other scholars and jurisprudents have deduced many points with the help of analogy about the rights and duties of Muslims in a non-Muslim or multi-faith country.

It is on record that after Negus's proclamation of help and support an Abyssinian rose in revolt against him. Umm Salamah reports: 'We do not recall anything more worrying than this. For we apprehended that if that rebel prevailed over Negus and assumed power, he would not look after us as well as Negus had done.' Negus proceeded to quell this rebellion. The battlefield was beyond the river Nile. For long Muslims awaited the outcome of this battle. They felt disturbed as no news came. After mutual consultation they deputed al-Zubayr ibn al-ʿAwwām al-Asdī to cross the river and reach the battlefield. In the meantime they prayed to Allah for Negus's victory over his enemy and for his continued rule over the kingdom. After some time Zubayr rushed back to them, giving them the good news of Negus's victory. Umm Salamah informs that the Muslims were overjoyed. Negus returned victorious. Allah granted him stability and glory and strengthened the Muslim presence in Abyssinia. Muslims enjoyed his patronage until they returned to the Prophet (peace be upon him) in Makkah.[26]

The events related by Umm Salamah about the Muslim emigrants in Abyssinia are related to the first two years of their stay. The Muslims had reached there in 615 CE and as reported by Ibn Hishām, they returned to Makkah on several dates. By 617 CE all of them had returned. Some of them had returned earlier on hearing a false report. The false report reaching them was that the Makkans had accepted Islam. It was a distorted version of the Gharānīq incident. The truth of the matter is that the Prophet (peace be upon him) fell in prostration at the conclusion of reciting verses of *Sūrah al-Najm*. The Quraysh chiefs present there joined him in prostration. This led to the rumour that the Makkans had embraced Islam. When the Muslim emigrants to Abyssinia reached Jeddah port, they learnt the actual report, so many of them returned to Abyssinia. Thirty-three men and women, however, made their way into Makkah. Among them were Umm Salamah and her husband, Abū Salamah. These emigrants sought the protection of some Quraysh chiefs and stayed in Makkah until their emigration to Madīnah. Some, however, did not find such protection and were forced into leading a miserable life in prison until their moving to Madīnah. They went to Madīnah before and some after the battle of Badr. Some emigrated after the battle of Uḥud and some even at a much later date. Some passed away during their imprisonment.

Ibn Hishām, al-Suhaylī and others have provided lists of those who returned to Makkah, giving their brief account. One thus gets a clear picture as to who among them enjoyed protection, who was put behind bars and who died. Their securing protection is an important event. For, as their own family or tribe refused to extend them protection and expelled them some families granted refuge to these helpless Muslims and defended them.[27]

Some stray points about the religious and cultural life of these migrants to Abyssinia feature in the works on *sīrah* and history. However, little is known about their twenty years long social, political and economic life. It is not stated how they lived and had links with the majority community of Christians. Classical sources are silent on these issues. It, however, emerges from some clues as to what kind of life they led. Their social life may be reconstructed. This may be verified in the light of primary sources.

Social Insecurity and Persecution

It is explicitly stated in the sources on *sīrah* and the accounts of witnesses that King Negus had helped and supported the Muslim migrants minority. He assured them of professing their faith in his kingdom and tried to protect them against any persecution, torture and injustice. Ibn Hishām's version significantly states that Negus had enforced the law for protecting the rights of the Muslim minority that any Abyssinian or Christian citizen found guilty of hurting Muslims would have to pay the penalty of four dirham. As Muslims thought the penalty amount was too low, he doubled its amount. The above version is based on the reports shared by Ibn Hishām, al-Suhaylī, Ibn ʿAsākir and Ṭabarī. It is also mentioned that Negus took this step on learning from Muslim emigrants that some people harassed them. In other words, the non-Muslim society did not favourably tolerate the Muslim minority. They opposed Muslims. This had its beginning in the offensive remarks passed against them and led to even tormenting them. Yet the state took immediate remedial steps and provided legal redressal to the Muslim minority.[28]

Notwithstanding all the legal protection, Muslims did face some inconvenience. It is reported by Asmā' bint ʿUmays: 'We were within the range of strangers and on the enemy land. We were harmed. We spent our life in fear. We were persecuted on account of serving the cause of Allah and His Messenger.'[29] Perhaps the mischievous persons in the Abyssinian society were encouraged by state officials. For it is clear from reports that save Negus and his close ministers, all state officials and clergymen were hostile to Muslims. They had put up with the Muslim presence only under pressure from Negus's command. They might have instigated the mischief makers to harm the Muslims.

State Support for the Abyssinian Emigrants

There are some variant reports about Jaʿfar's speech at Negus's court and his other speech on the Islamic stance on Prophet Jesus (peace be upon him). Umm Salamah's report is much more authentic, as cited above. Another report is on the authority of ʿAbdullāh ibn Masʿūd al-Hadhalī, yet another from Abū Mūsā al-Ashʿarī. There is another report by Jaʿfar ibn Abī Ṭālib as narrated by his son, ʿAbdullāh ibn Jaʿfar. There are two important additions in these reports, which are recorded by the biographers of the Prophet (peace be upon him) and *ḥadīth* scholars. Among them are Ibn Ḥajar, Ibn Isḥāq, Wāqidī, Mūsā ibn ʿUqbah, Ṭabarī and Bukhārī.

It is indicated in ʿAbdullāh ibn Masʿūd's report that the next day, when Muslims stated their belief about Prophet Jesus's status, the Quraysh delegation reached court earlier. For instigating the king, his clergymen and courtiers they told them that Muslims would not prostrate on entering court. The Quraysh delegation had made it a point to offer this act of prostration. When Muslims reached there, they did not, of course, prostrate before the king. On being asked to explain their conduct, they clarified that they do not prostrate before anyone other than Allah. The king appreciated their response, asserting that it has been the way of true believers. Christians had introduced prostration for paying respect to kings in contravention of the teachings of their faith. It is further stated in the report that the king promised peaceful stay for Muslims and directed also that food and clothes be provided to them.[30] Ibn Kathīr verifies the chain of narrators of both the reports. Muslims were faced with the problem of meeting their basic needs. Food and clothes were provided to them as an urgent relief measure only for the time being. Muslims would have found it beneath their dignity to accept this on a regular basis. Furthermore, no state or society can provide such support to a minority permanently. Nor can it help the minority in the long term.

Trade Activities of Muslim Emigrants to Abyssinia

Keeping in mind the economic life of the Quraysh chiefs and youths it is easier to follow that Muslim emigrants, notwithstanding their acceptance of state help initially, soon picked up trade and business. For they came from a trading community and knew well how to earn money. The same accounts, at a later stage, for the Muhājirīn taking up their own business after enjoying initially the hospitality extended by the Anṣār of Madīnah. For these Muslims of Quraysh descent were not used to any help from others. They recognized that no one could afford sponsoring them for long. Islamic teachings too, had taught them not to depend on others for their living expenses. It was in addition to their economic background, their psyche and their social compulsions.[31]

Reports do not contain any details about trade activities of the emigrants to Abyssinia. Some clues contained in these, however, reinforce our viewpoint about their economic pursuits. According to Ṭabarī, the Quraysh used to have trade links with Abyssinians and had a roaring business there. This fact appears in several reports of the day. It is on record that Hāshim or ʿAbd Shams, a member of Banū ʿAbd Manāf, had secured a special letter from the king of Abyssinia for carrying out trade. In a similar fashion, other members of Banū ʿAbd Manāf had got special permits from the rulers of Rome, Persia and Egypt.[32] Ṭabarī relates that Muslim emigrants did not face much difficulty in view of their earlier trade links. They were engaged soon in trade. Again, they had no difficulty in attaining a social ranking there.[33]

Umm Salamah informs that Abyssinia was the main market for Makkan tanned leather and its goods. Abyssinians liked its quality much. Arab traders made it a point to import it there, for they got a good bargain. These goods were in great demand there. For the same reason the Quraysh chiefs had sent gifts of leather goods for the king and his clergymen.[34]

Other reports too, bear out the importance of leather goods in Abyssinia. On the eve of the battle of Badr the Quraysh and Makkan soldiers had brought there in a large quantity leather mats for selling these at a high price. Arabs carried out trade even during battles as it was indispensable for their survival.

Their Social Conditions

Some points about their social life may be gleaned from the reports of the day. These are related below for providing glimpses of the social life.

Newly-born Muslims in Abyssinia

Many Muslims had emigrated with their wives. Children were born to some of them. Among them were:

- ʿAbdullāh, the eldest son of ʿUthmān ibn ʿAffān and Ruqayyah, the Prophet's daughter. He was born in Abyssinia, returned to Makkah along with his parents and then went to Madīnah. According to some reports, he was born two years before the emigration to Madīnah and died in 4/626 at the age of only six years.[35] Amah bint Khālid, daughter of Khālid ibn Saʿīd was born in Abyssinia. She was brought up there and was adept in the local language. The Prophet (peace be upon him) had spoken to her in the same language in order to make her feel at home. Her brother Saʿīd ibn Khālid too, was born there.[36]

- ʿAbdullāh ibn al-Muṭṭalib was born to Muṭṭalib ibn Aẓhar and Ramlah bint Abī ʿAwf al-Sahmī.[37]
- Four children were born to Ḥārith ibn al-Taymī and Rā'itah bint al-Ḥārith al-Taymī – one son Mūsā ibn al-Ḥārith and three daughters, ʿĀ'ishah, Zaynab and Fāṭimah.[38]
- A daughter Zaynab bint Abī Salamah was born to Abū Salamah ibn al-Asad al-Mukhzūmī and Umm Salamah bint Abī Umayyah.[39] Al-Suhaylī states that her name was Barrah which was changed to Zaynab by the Prophet (peace be upon him). She was lovingly called as Zaynab, as it stated in *ḥadīth*.[40] The Prophet had given her the nick name of Zaynab, after his marriage to Umm Salamah. As he retired to privacy on the wedding night, Zaynab being a small girl, separated from her mother, took to crying. It was then that the Prophet lovingly called her as Zaynab and used the same name of her later.[41]
- ʿAbdullāh ibn Jaʿfar al-Hāshimī was born to Jaʿfar ibn Abī Ṭālib al-Hāshimī and Asmā' bint ʿUmays. Muḥammad too, was born there.[42]
- Umm Ḥabībah bint Abī Sufyān and her husband ʿUbaydullāh who later converted to Christianity, had a daughter born in Makkah and another one in Abyssinia.[43] Ḥabībah's brother ʿAbdullāh had probably died in Abyssinia.[44]
- Muḥammad Ibn Abī Hudhayfah, son of Abū Hudhayfah ibn ʿUtbah was born in Abyssinia.[45]
- According to Ibn Isḥāq and Ibn Hishām, five boys and five girls were born in Abyssinia.[46] It is not, however, an exact figure. The actual number was higher.

The Muslims who Died in Abyssinia

Some Muslim emigrants died in Abyssinia. Of them, reports specify the following ones:

- ʿAmr ibn Umayyah al-Asdī al Qurashī died in Abyssinia as a Muslim. However, Ibn Isḥāq makes no mention of him.[47]

- Sakrān ibn ʿAmr al-ʿĀmirī al-Qurashī, the former husband of Sawdah bint Zamʿah, died in Abyssinia, as is stated by Mūsā ibn ʿUqbah and Abū Maʿshar. Balādhurī cites this report, with the remark that the report about his death in Makkah is more authentic.[48]
- Khālid ibn Ḥizām al-Asdī Qurayshi, who migrated to Abyssinia in the second batch died on the way to Abyssinia.[49]
- ʿUbaydullāh al-Asdī too died in Abyssinia, though he had turned into a Christian.
- Muṭṭalib ibn ʿAbd ʿAwf al-Zuhrī and his younger brother Ṭālib al-Zuhrī also died in Abyssinia. They were the brothers of Aẓhar ibn ʿAbd ʿAwf, an emigrant to Abyssinia.[50]
- ʿAmr ibn Saʿīd's wife, Fāṭimah bint Ṣafwān al-Kināniyyah died in Abyssinia.[51]
- Jahm ibn Qays al-ʿAbdarī's wife, Umm Ḥarmalah bint al-Aswad died there.[52]
- Rā'iṭah bint al-Ḥārith al-Taymiyyah, wife of Ḥārith ibn Khālid al-Taymī died in Abyssinia. A report, however, states that she had died on the way to Abyssinia. Her son, Mūsā and two daughters, Zaynab and ʿĀ'ishah died there on account of drinking polluted water.[53]

Among other emigrants who died there were the following:

- ʿUrwah ibn ʿAbd al-ʿUzzā and his nephew, ʿAdiyy ibn Naḍlah ibn ʿAbd al-ʿUzzā.[54] Balādhurī speaks of him and ʿUrwah ibn Abī Uthāthah, which signifies that Abū Uthāthah was his father's patronym.[55]
- ʿAmr ibn Umayyah ibn al-Ḥārith, Ḥāṭib ibn al-Ḥārith and his brother, Ḥaṭṭāb ibn Ḥārith and ʿAbdullāh ibn al-Ḥārith Qays al-Sahmī.[56] Some others also died there.

The Return of Abyssinian Emigrants

Ibn Isḥāq and Ibn Hishām and some others have compiled a list of the migrants who returned by 7/629. These emigrants returned to Madīnah in three phases: (1) Some returned to Madīnah after the Prophet's emigration there (2) Some came to Madīnah before Jaʿfar's return (3) Some returned along with Jaʿfar.

To the first category belong the following: Yazīd ibn Muʿāwiyah al-Asdī Qurashī, Firās ibn al-Naḍr al-ʿAbdarī; al Ḥārith ibn al-Ḥārith al-Sahmī;[57] Qays ibn Ḥudhayfah.[58] Among those who returned a little before the battle of Badr were: ʿAbdullāh al-Asdī and ʿAmr ibn Ḥārith al-ʿĀmirī al-Qurashī.[59] Al-Nuʿmān ibn ʿAdiyy also returned there.[60]

The following returned to Madīnah a little before Jaʿfar's return: ʿAmr ibn Saʿīd and his wife;[61] ʿAmr ibn ʿUthmān al-Taymī; Hāshim ibn Hudhayfah al-Makhzūmī; Shuraḥbīl ibn Ḥasanah al-Kindī; Saʿīd ibn Qays ʿUthmān ibn ʿAbd Ghanam al-ʿĀmirī al-Qurashī; Hubār ibn Sufyān ibn ʿAbd al-Asad and his brother ʿUbaydullāh ibn Sufyān.[62]

The Prophet had written to the King Negus for the return of Jaʿfar and the rest of the emigrants. Accordingly, Negus sent all of them by two boats to Madīnah. Ibn Isḥāq's list includes sixteen men and eight women. In addition, there were children. The total number was twenty-four.[63] Thirty-four emigrants returned on various dates. All of them were men. The sources do not specify women and children.

Change of Faith

All the emigrants adhered fast to Islam. One or two of them were, however, carried away by the local non-Muslim ambience and converted to the faith of the majority community. The only instance on record is of ʿUbaydullāh al-Asdī who, as reports unanimously state, had converted to Christianity and died in the same state. His wife Umm Ḥabībah bint Abū Sufyān secured separation from him, consequent upon the change of his faith. ʿUbaydullāh criticized

Muslims for their blind following and claimed to have seen the reality.[64] It is noteworthy regarding him that he had earlier turned into a Christian, abandoning his ancestral faith. Then he embraced Islam and converted again to Christianity after reaching Abyssinia.

Negus's Acceptance of Islam

All the sources on *sīrah, ḥadīth* and history maintain that Negus had embraced Islam. This is reported only in passing by Ibn Isḥāq and Ibn Hishām and their followers. Other sources, however, relate it at length. Ibn Kathīr has cited such reports. Abū Nuʿaym states that after Jaʿfar's speech Negus had publicly declared: 'I testify that Muḥammad is the Messenger of Allah and he is the same person whose advent had been foretold by Prophet Jesus. Had I not been a king, entrusted with so many obligations, I would have called on the Prophet (peace be upon him) and kissed his feet.[65] It would be in order to quote the Qur'ānic verse, containing Prophet Jesus's prophecy about Prophet Muḥammad's advent: 'And remember, Jesus, the son of Mary, said: "O children of Israel! I am the Messenger of Allah sent to you, confirming the Torah which came before me, and giving glad tidings of a Messenger, to come after me, whose name shall be Aḥmad." But when he came to them with clear signs, they said: This is evident magic.'[66]

Ibn Kathīr records another report on the authority of Ibn ʿAsākir's *Tārīkh Dimashq* about Negus's acceptance of Islam. Although this report is of a later date, it reinforces the event of Negus's entry into the fold of Islam. This report goes back up to Jaʿfar ibn Abī Ṭālib and is narrated by his son, ʿAbdullāh ibn Jaʿfar al-Hāshimī: 'When the Prophet emigrated to Madīnah and gained ascendancy there we informed Negus of it and told him about our return, seeking his leave which he granted. He arranged for us boats and provisions and told us: "Tell our leader about my good treatment of you. I send with you my representative. I testify that there is no god besides Allah and that Muḥammad is His Messenger. Please request the Prophet to pray for my forgiveness."' It appears in the above report when Negus's representative called on the Prophet (peace be upon him) in order to convey the above message and Jaʿfar confirmed his acceptance of Islam, the Prophet did *wudu* and prayed thrice for Negus's forgiveness. His plea was reaffirmed by the Muslims present there. Although Ibn ʿAsākir brands the above report as 'Ḥasan Gharīb', Abū Nuʿaymm al-Iṣfahānī's version removes the doubt.[67]

Ziyād Bakrī's report, recounted by Ibn Isḥāq, contains the additional note that some Abyssinians had risen in revolt, charging Negus with retracting the ancestral faith. Before quelling that rebellion Negus had put a note on his chest in which he declared his profession of Islam.[68]

Another weighty evidence of Negus's acceptance of Islam is afforded by the Prophet offering funeral prayer for him *in absentia*, as recorded by Bukhārī and Muslim in their *ḥadīth* collection.[69] On Negus's death in 9/631 the Prophet (peace be upon him) offered his funeral prayer in congregation and prayed for his forgiveness. Reports say that a certain halo could be seen at his grave owing to his help and support for the Muslims. *Ḥadīth* scholars have cited such reports for deducing some points. Negus had to face rebellion on account of his abandoning the ancestral faith. However, he managed to overcome it. While going to the battle against the rebels he had directed Muslim emigrants to look for some other refuge in the event of his defeat. He promised them the same protection, if he prevailed over the rebels. Muslims prayed fervently to Allah for his victory. They were worried over the reports about the rebellion.[70]

Spread of Islam in Abyssinia

Negus's acceptance of Islam was not an isolated instance. Reports indicate that when Abyssinian Christians learnt about the Prophet's advent, their delegation comprising twenty persons went to Makkah in order to call on him and find out about the new faith. They met him at the Kaʿbah in the sacred mosque and had discussions with him. Under the influence of his teachings and on listening to the Qur'ān they embraced Islam. It appears from the internal evidence of these reports that this had happened after the Muslims' emigration to Abyssinia. Or it could be at an earlier date. This point is discussed in another section.[71]

Much is not on record about the spread of Islam in Abyssinia. Yet let us take up an important report on the issue, though of a later date. It is related to 7/629 of the Madīnan period when some Abyssinian Christians came to Madīnah along with Muslim emigrants. This delegation comprised seventy persons. According to a study, all of them were Muslims. They had accepted Islam even before reaching Madīnah. Others, however, maintain that they converted to Islam after calling on the Prophet (peace be upon him) in Madīnah. If we go by the former version it appears that owing to the efforts of Muslim emigrants, local Abyssinians kept on embracing Islam. If the latter report is true, it is evident that Abyssinians were converted to Islam after calling on the Prophet (peace be upon him). Some scholars resolve the issue, holding the view that they had turned into Muslims in Abyssinia and declared the same when they visited the Prophet (peace be upon him) in Madīnah. It was done for pledging their oath of allegiance to the Prophet in person. This view is more plausible and fits in with relevant reports.

In the literature on the Prophet's Companions, there is little material on the spread of Islam in Abyssinia. Some names do appear and their number is also mentioned. On that basis an account of those who embraced Islam in Abyssinia may be compiled. The following points in this context deserve mention:

1. *Al-Iṣābah* specifies that forty persons accepted Islam, though their names are not stated.
2. It is recorded in *Usd al-Ghābah* that as Muslims attained victory in the battle of Badr, those who had accepted Islam is Abyssinia expressed their wish to Negus that they would like to call on the Prophet (peace be upon him). With his permission they visited Madīnah and also took part in the battle of Uḥud.[72] He has compiled the list of the Companions of Abyssinian descent.

Of them the following deserve mention:

a. Abrahah, an Abyssinian Christian who was Negus's courtier. As Islam spread in Abyssinia with the arrival of Muslim emigrants, Negus himself and many Christian clergymen accepted Islam. Abrahah was one of them. He was part of the Abyssinia delegation that visited Madīnah along with Jaʿfar. He had the privilege of calling on the Prophet (peace be upon him).[73]
b. Idrīs was another Abyssinian who visited along with Jaʿfar as a member of the delegation. Along with Abrahah he accepted Islam.[74]
c. Ashraf was an associate of Abrahah and Idrees and also a member of the Abyssinian delegation. Nadvī reckons him as a member of clergy.)
d. Buḥayrah, one of the earliest Abyssinian Muslims and an associate of Abrahah, Idrīs and Ashraf.
e. Tamīm, a member of the Abyssinian delegation.
f. Tammām, another member of the Abyssinian delegation.
g. Duryad.
h. ʿAlqamah Dhū jinn.
i. Dhū Makhmar, Negus's nephew and his emissary to the Prophet (peace be upon him).
j. Dhū Munāṣib.
k. Dhū Mahdam.
l. ʿĀmir.
m. Nāfiʿ.

The Link between the Headquarters and the Muslim Minority in Abyssinia

It is generally held that after their emigration Makkan Muslims did not have any link with the Islamic headquarters in Makkah or Madīnah. For circumstances did not allow any interaction. It is nonetheless a false impression, based on a superficial reading of relevant reports. The truth is that the Muslim minority had maintained links during the Makkan period and these were strengthened with the establishment of an Islamic state in Madīnah. This truth is indeed impressive and worth-reiterating.

In the Makkan period

Few reports throw light on the link between Makkan Muslims and the Muslim emigrants in Abyssinia. Yet such reports are not non-existent altogether. May accounts assert that the two had strong links. Of these, the following are note worthy.

1. According to the popular version, the emigration to Abyssinia took place in two stages. The first one is in the fifth year of the Prophet's mission i.e. 615 CE and the second one, a year later. The latter batch of emigrants naturally carried the latest account of the Prophet (peace be upon him) and Muslims in Makkah.
2. On getting the report that Makkans had accepted Islam en masse, these Muslim emigrants returned home and arrived in Jeddah. However, they returned to Abyssinia on realizing that the report was not true. They too, took the latest reports to Abyssinia.
3. Those emigrants who secured a safe place in Makkah appraised fellow Muslims in Makkah of the situation of the Muslim minority in Abyssinia. The Prophet (peace be upon him) too, gathered information from them.
4. Through a special messenger the Prophet (peace be upon him) had sent gifts from Makkah to ʿUthmān and Ruqayyah in Abyssinia. On his return that emissary related the account of Muslims in Abyssinia. One might speculate that other couriers would have also gone to Abyssinia.
5. Abū Ṭālib al-Hāshimī had composed couplets, urging Negus to extend help and support to Muslims. Without being delivered to Negus, these would not have served any useful purpose. Ibn Isḥāq informs that these were duly sent to Negus. The courier related also the situation of the Prophet (peace be upon him) and Muslims in Makkah to the emigrants there.

6. Abū Ṭālib maintained ties of kinship with his Muslim son Jaʿfar ibn Abī Ṭālib and his daughter-in-law, Asmā' bint ʿUmays and supported them financially. Through his messengers Muslim emigrants must have learnt their situation. By the same token, on their return to Makkah, they must have informed Makkan Muslims about these emigrants.
7. It is evident from the example of both the Prophet (peace be upon him) and Abū Ṭālib that the Makkan relatives of these emigrants maintained their ties with them and communicated with them through traders, travellers and couriers. It naturally included the exchange of the latest news.

In the Madīnan period

1. Some emigrants to Abyssinia returned to Makkah on coming to know about the Prophet's departure for Madīnah and then emigrated to Madīnah.[75] This reinforces the point that these emigrants kept in touch with the headquarters and informed the King Negus of the latest developments.
2. Some emigrants went directly to Madīnah, travelling by boats from the Abyssinian coast.[76] Without their strong link with Madīnah, it could not be possible. These emigrants kept in touch in both Makkan and Madinan periods with fellow Muslims, as is borne out by their travel to Madīnah.
3. King Negus used to ask after the welfare of the Prophet and Muslims in Makkah and these emigrants furnished him with all the reports. Al-Suhaylī recounts a significant report on this count. One day Negus assembled all the Muslims and informed them that Allah had blessed His exalted Messenger with victory as he took on the enemy at the battleground of Badr. Allah inflicted a comprehensive defeat upon the enemy and defended His faith. On this auspicious occasion Negus dressed himself in the manner of Prophet Jesus. It is instructed in the Gospels that a servant of God should act modestly on being granted some divine blessing. The victory at Badr was no doubt, a mighty favour hence, he thanked God profusely.[77]

4. As already noted a delegation of Abyssinians comprising seventy persons had called on the Prophet (peace be upon him) and pledged obedience to him.
5. The Prophet sent ʿAmr ibn Umayyah al-Ḍamrī twice as his emissary to Negus's court.
6. It was during the period of the second delegation that the Prophet (peace be upon him) married Umm Ḥabībah bint Abī Sufyān. She was then in Abyssinia and her marriage was solemnized by Negus.
7. On different dates these emigrants returned to Madīnah. The last batch returned along with Jaʿfar in 7/629.

Influence of Abyssinian Culture

It is a truism that an interaction between two cultures or peoples of different socio-religious affiliations results in exchange and influence on each other's language, way of life, dress, food, customs and other cultural manifestations. They borrow from each other even in social life. Ibn Khaldūn reckons Islamic culture as universal. During their stay in Abyssinia these Muslim emigrants adopted many items of Abyssinian culture and influenced, in an equal measure, Abyssinians. This is quite natural and part of divine providence. Many bits of evidence on this count may be cited from the Qur'ān and *ḥadīth*. Islamic civilization abounds in instances of cultural borrowing and influencing others.

Interaction between Arabic and Abyssinian Languages

In view of the old trade links between Abyssinia and Arabia, especially Makkah, it is on record that they had learnt each other's language or at least, gained its working knowledge. Words of Abyssinian origin made their way into Arabic as a result of this cultural interaction. This point is affirmed by the sources on both *sīrah* and *ḥadīth*. Amah bint Khālid, daughter of Khālid ibn Saʿīd was born in Abyssinia and had gained mastery over the local language, as she had lived there for about fifteen years. On her return to Madīnah in 7/629 the Prophet (peace be upon him) gave her the present of a well-decorated cloth sheet. At that time she was clad in a yellow shirt. The Prophet employed some Abyssinian expressions, complimenting the beauty of her dress. His use is reflective of the import of certain Abyssinian words into Arabia. That she received this gift from the Prophet (peace be upon him) in her childhood is not plausible. For he addressed her as 'Umm Khālid', indicating as it does her married status.[78]

King Negus had addressed Jaʿfar ibn Abī Ṭālib al-Hāshimī and other Muslim emigrants in Arabic and the latter had also employed Arabic, for the relevant reports do not point to the presence of any Abyssinian interpreter. Negus and his clergymen comprehended well the contents of the Qur'ānic *sūrah*, *Maryam*. At that time too, no interpreter was pressed into service. Arabic was thus the second language of Abyssinia. The locals could express themselves well in it. This had become possible owing to their centuries-long relations with Arabia. Both the Abyssinians and Arabs had learnt each other's language for the same considerations.

Ibn Hishām and al-Suhaylī recount a report which should be of great interest for those interested in linguistic studies. While granting refuge to the emigrants Negus used the word 'shiyūm' which means 'safe and secure'. Its variant recitation is 'siyūm' which is an Abyssinian expression. Likewise, while prescribing the penalty for those abusing Muslim emigrants the expression 'Dhabrah' signified that the Abyssinians were not after money which would impel them to harass Muslims. 'Dabrī' is used of a gold coin.[79]

The Qur'ān does contain words of non-Arabic language. Amid these are Abyssinian expressions, for example, *Jibt, Ṭaghūt, Ṭūbā, Sakar, Sijjil, Mishkāt, Minsa'ah* etc. Some other words are also termed as Abyssinian in origin. A detailed account appears in Imām Suyūṭī's and Ibn Durayd's works.[80] Dr. V. Abdur Raheem is of the view that Arabs borrowed few words from Abyssinian language, as also from Hebrew and Indian languages. He, nonetheless, provides a list of loan words from Abyssinian into Arabic. These are: *al-Ḥawārī*, *al-Munāfiq, al-Fāṭir, al-Minbar, al-Miḥrāb, al-Muṣḥaf, al-Burhān, al-Mishkāt and al-Najāshī.*[81] Al-Suhaylī has provided a telling report about Negus Aṣḥamah's learning of Arabic at a young age. An Arab trader had bought him as a slave and brought him to Arabia. He was a member of Banū Ḍamrah, settled in Badr. There was a good pasture there and Aṣḥamah used to graze his master's goats there. As a result of his long stay there he learnt Arabic. This explains his ready comprehension of *Sūrah Maryam* when it was recited before him.[82]

Emigration to Abyssinia as a Theme in Arabic Poetry

It goes without saying that languages and literature are influenced by their milieu and socio-cultural traditions. Arabic poetry is no exception to it. It was part of the Arab tradition to record in their poetry every event, scene and geo-historical happening. They treated it as a theme in their works. The emigration to Abyssinia was indeed a major event for the Quraysh, both its elites and ordinary members and also for the Muslim emigrants and their kith and kin and friends in Makkah. Little wonder then that this theme appears in some passages of Arabic poetry. Ibn Isḥāq makes it a point to quote illustrative passages from Arabic poetry about every event. This trait of his has been, however, subject to some criticism. All of his quotations are not spurious. Many of these are authentic and repeated by Ibn Hishām.

Some emigrants to Abyssinia composed poems on this theme. Ibn Hishām has cited three passages from ʿAbdullāh ibn Qays al-Sahmī . He was called 'al-Mabraq' in view of his poems on the theme of emigration. His work may be regarded as the earliest attempt at emigration poetry in Arabic. Another renowned poet was ʿUthmān ibn Maẓʿūn al-Jahmī who satirized his cousin Umayyah ibn Khalaf al-Jahmī for his persecuting him. Umayyah was a leading Quraysh chief who was hostile to Islam. Ibn Hishām has quoted only the above two poets. Abū Ṭālib al-Hāshimī also composed poetry on this theme in which he suggests to Negus to help Muslims.[83]

Some social issues too, surface in the emigration poetry of Arabia:

1. The helpless Makkan Muslims are told that the emigrants have found refuge.
2. The point brought home is that Allah's power is boundless and that He delivers one from disgrace.
3. Therefore one should not put up with a life of humiliation and dishonour.
4. Muslims have followed the Prophet (peace be upon him) whereas others have disregarded his commands.
5. Allah is invoked to penalize the unbelievers and to deliver the believers from their persecution.
6. Fellow Makkans are told that the believers hold their faith dearer than their ties of kinship. They are, however, keen on fulfilling their obligations of kinship.
7. The unbelievers have disregarded totally the ties of kinship.
8. Muslims make it a point to treat well the weak and widows.
9. The Quraysh are guilty of disobeying Allah, as was the case with the people of ʿĀd, Madyan and al-Ḥijr.
10. They have tremendous respect for Prophet Muḥammad (peace be upon him) and express the same even when they are in Abyssinia, away from Makkah.
11. Umayyah ibn Khalaf is condemned for driving out Muslims, prompted by his hostility towards Muslims.
12. Muslims have been expelled from the peaceful Makkah and dumped into a place which has little interest for them.
13. The Quraysh took to fighting against noble people and destroyed those who could rescue them.
14. Soon the Quraysh would be overwhelmed by sorrow and suffering. The weak would be avenged.
15. Negus is requested to help and defend Jaʿfar, ʿAmr and other members of the community.
16. For Allah has granted abundance to Negus and blessed him with bounties.
17. Negus is such a noble and generous person who benefits not only his kith and kin, but also his foes.[84]

CHAPTER 4

Formation of the Muslim *Ummah* in the Makkan Period

Social System

Social organization is the most difficult part in the formation of a community. Many social, emotional and psychological problems and issues are involved in the separation of a minority from the majority community. The social disintegration and chaos within a minority poses a serious problem. Although being part of a larger society, a minority may not be integrated with it. It has its own set of priorities. Under intense psychological pressure a minority tends to be vulnerable. If a minority is not organized, it might be lost into oblivion. It creates more problems in the society, worsening the situation. For the despairing members of the minority cannot adjust themselves with the larger society, which results in chaos. Destined to obliteration, they sow the seeds of discontent in the broader community.

As the Muslim community was evolved as a result of the spread of Islam, it caused ripples in the Makkan society. The tribal order was hurt hard and old family ties crumbled. Centuries-old notions of unity and solidarity received a set back. The entire social edifice shook. Earlier they were united by the bonds of tribal affiliations and community life, especially in opposition to other Arab tribes. The old order developed cracks and it turned into a tragedy, engulfing every Quraysh member. The Makkan chiefs lamented over the collapse of their family, tribal and social order. They blamed the Prophet (peace be upon him) and his faith for it.

According to Ibn Isḥāq the first Quraysh delegation lodged this complaint with Abū Ṭālib: 'Your nephew reviled our gods and condemned our faith. He regards the wise among us as fools and our ancestors in error.'[1] The second delegation made an almost identical complaint to Abū Ṭālib.[2] Their main grudge was that, apart from opposing their faith, the Prophet (peace be upon him) created a rift among them, as it appears in the complaint of the third delegation as well.[3]

It was hard for Abū Ṭālib to withdraw his help and support for the Prophet (peace be upon him). Nor could he bear with the divisions in his own community. He had to make his choice and after much reflection he decided to continue his help and support for his nephew. As a result, his own extended family of Banū ʿAbd Manāf was divided into two. Banū Hāshim and Banū Muṭṭalib supported Abū Ṭālib while the two other families – Banū Umayyah and Banū Nawfal endorsed the Qurayshī position. This saddened Abū Ṭālib and created many problems. Of these, social disorder was the most disturbing one.[4] The Quraysh chiefs convened a meeting for resolving how to carry out propaganda against the Prophet's mission. They decided to dub him as a magician who causes separation between father and son, brother and brother, husband and wife and family members.[5] While visiting the Prophet, (peace be upon him) ʿUtbah ibn Rabīʿah, the renowned Quraysh chief protested against his message which had caused disunity among his community.[6] In their public meetings the Quraysh ire was directed against the division resulting from the popularity of Islam.[7]

ʿUmar, a perceptive and mighty figure among the Quraysh, felt the same before his acceptance of Islam. He dismissed the Prophet (peace be upon him) as a Sabean who had destroyed the unity among the Quraysh rank and file.[8] ʿUmar was not alone in entertaining this thought. All the Makkan chiefs and unbelieving Quraysh felt the same, as is recorded in several reports.

The Makkan chiefs were not altogether mistaken in forming this impression. It was a ground reality. Rather, it was inevitable, which no one could avoid or reform. This social disorder was imperative for the birth of a new community. It was part of the historical process necessary for the emergence of a dynamic community. Destruction was a prerequisite for the reconstruction. The Muslim *ummah* was to rise on the debris of the Quraysh society. The Prophet (peace be upon him) was set to demolish centuries-old decadent Arab society, reeling under injustice and inequality. His task was to build a just, pious society which was to be full of mercy for everyone and based on love for the entire mankind.

It was quite a task for the Prophet (peace be upon him) to construct a new society, a new community and a new *ummah*. It involved numerous hurdles and problems. He did not have enough resources to achieve it. As Islam appeared on the scene and grew in popularity amid Makkan families, some of them accepted Islam. The social problem it caused was that while some members of a family turned into Muslims, other members, constituting an overwhelming majority, clung to the old faith. Most of these Muslims were youth. They were the future hope of the Quraysh families and were dependent upon their elders financially. It was a totally unacceptable situation for heads of families. They took it as a revolt on the part of the young. They thought that the abandoning of the ancestral faith by their sons and daughters would spell the division of their families. Naturally, they could not reconcile to it at any cost. Even such Quraysh families that had converted to Islam were subject to internal social pressure, for they stood aloof from the mainstream Quraysh. This was bound to put an end to their unity and tribal solidarity.

Makkan Fraternity

The Prophet (peace be upon him) was faced with the problem of how to join together people belonging to a variety of families and different backgrounds. They were to be bound in a new fraternity, away from their unbelieving families. The new Muslims had to be protected against the social disorder and gaps. A unified Muslim *ummah* was the need of the hour.

Analysis of Reports

He resolved this vexing problem by establishing religious fraternity. It helped reconstruct their social life. Reports indicate that as the Muslim population became sizeable, he made members of the Quraysh as brethren in faith. Muḥammad ibn Ḥabīb al-Baghdādī (d. 245/860) is the first to discuss the Makkan fraternity, distinct from the one in Madīnah. He maintains: 'The Prophet introduced religious fraternity before his emigration to Madīnah. This fraternity was premised on mutual sympathy and truth. It was achieved in Makkah. He established this brotherhood between him and ʿAlī ibn Abī Ṭālib. The same practice was followed regarding Abū Bakr and ʿUmar, Ḥamzah and Zayd ibn Ḥārithah, ʿUthmān ibn ʿAffān and ʿAbd al-Raḥmān ibn ʿAwf al-Zuhrī, al-Zubayr ibn al-ʿAwwām al-Asdī and ʿAbdullāh ibn Masʿūd al-Hudhalī, ʿUbaydah ibn al-Ḥārith al-Hāshimī and Bilāl ibn Rabāḥ, Muṣʿab ibn ʿUmayr al-ʿAbdarī and Saʿd ibn Abī Waqqāṣ al-Zuhrī, Abū ʿUbaydah ibn al-Jarrāḥ al-Fihrī and Sālim, the freed slave of Ḥudhayfah, Saʿīd ibn Zayd and Ṭalḥah ibn ʿUbaydullāh al-Jahmī. Al-Baghdādī specifies that all this was part of the Makkan fraternity.

Another major historian who has recorded the same point is al-Ḥāfiẓ ibn ʿAbd al-Barr (Yūsuf ibn ʿUmar ibn Abd al-Barr al-Nimrī 368 AH-463 AH). Even before his emigration to Madīnah the Prophet (peace be upon him) had established fraternity among Makkan Muslims. Ibn ʿAbd al-Barr's list is identical with that of al-Baghdādī. However, he does not specify any such tie between the Prophet (peace be upon him) and ʿAlī ibn Abī Ṭālib. He mentions it, however, in the context of Madīnan fraternity, substantiating it with several reports.

The outstanding Andalusian biographer Imām ibn Sayyid al-Nās (Muḥammad ibn ʿAbdullāh ibn Yaḥyā 671 AH – 734 AH) has discussed both the Makkan and Madīnan fraternity. His account is as follows: For the first time in Makkah the Prophet (peace be upon him) forged fraternity among Muslims of Makkah based on the principles of truth and sympathy. His list resembles that of al-Baghdādī. He mentions such a tie between the Prophet (peace be upon him) and ʿAlī ibn Abī Ṭālib towards the end of the list while it is the starting point in al-Baghdādī's list.

The outstanding *ḥadīth* scholar and commentator on Bukhārī, Ḥāfiẓ Ibn Ḥajar al-ʿAsqalānī (Abū'l-Faḍl Shihāb al-Dīn Aḥmad ibn ʿAlī al-Miṣrī 773-852/1372-1447) has recorded more reports about the Makkan fraternity. He reiterates Ibn ʿAbd al-Barr's assertion that the fraternity was enacted twice, first in Makkah and later in Madīnah. On Ibn ʿAbbās's authority he relates that the Prophet (peace be upon him) had made Zubayr and ʿAbdullāh ibn Masʿūd as brethren in faith though both of them are Makkan Muslims. This report is cited by Imām Ḥākim and Ibn ʿAbd al-Barr and it has a sound chain of narrators. Ḥāfiẓ Ḍiyā' al-Dīn al-Maqdisī too, has narrated this report in his *Mukhtārah* on the authority of Ṭabarānī's *al-Muʿjam al-Kabīr*. Al-ʿAsqalānī bears out the authenticity of the report and reinforces it with Ḥākim's version about Makkan fraternity. In Ibn Taymiyah's view Ḥākim's reports are less authentic than al-Maqdisī's in *Mukhtārah*. Ḥākim recounts also ʿAbdullāh ibn ʿUmar's report that the Prophet (peace be upon him) had arranged for the brotherhood between Abū Bakr and ʿUmar and others as well. On ʿAlī's query he had declared himself as his brother in faith.

Imām al-Qasṭalānī, (Aḥmad ibn Muḥammad 851-923/1448-1517) another commentator on Bukhārī, also speaks of the fraternity in both Makkah and Madīnah and provides a list of the names found also in Ibn Sayyid al-Nās's version. He brings out also the advantages of this move.

Ḥusayn ibn Muḥammad ibn Ḥasan Diyār Bakrī (d.c. 966/1559) has discussed at some length the Makkan fraternity on the authority of Ibn Ḥajar, Ḥākim and ibn ʿAbd al-Barr. However, a more detailed account is provided by ʿAlī ibn Burhān al-Dīn al-Ḥalabī (975-1044/1567-1634). With reference to Zayd Ibn Abī Awfā he cites Ḥāfiẓ Ibn al-Jawzī (Abū'l-Faraj ʿAbd al-Raḥmān ibn ʿAlī ibn Muḥammad al-Qurashī al-Bakrī 510-597/1116-1200). The popular view is that the fraternity was enacted twice, for the first time among Makkan Muslims before the emigration and the next time between Muhājirīn and Anṣār after the emigration. Imām al-Ḥalbī states the number of persons who entered this bond and records further details of this bonding in Madīnah.

ʿAllāmah al-Zurqānī (ʿAbd al-Bāqī ibn Yūsuf al-Miṣrī 1020-1099/1611-1688) commences his account with quoting Ibn ʿAbd al-Barr to the effect that it had happened twice; the first time among Makkan Muslims and has provided the names. Al-Zurqānī has brought home the following points about the relationship with Ali and the Makkan fraternity.

According to Imām Ḥākim, Ṭalḥah and Zubayr had been made brothers in faith. Another report, however, says that it was between Zubayr and Masʿūd. Furthermore, after this was enacted, only ʿAlī was left. At his plea the Prophet (peace be upon him) took him as his brother in faith, a point confirmed by many *Aḥādīth*. Al-Zurqānī clarifies further that Ḥākim and Ibn ʿAbd al-Barr have quoted Ibn ʿAbbās to the effect that the Prophet (peace be upon him) had made Zubayr and Ibn Masʿūd brethren in faith, though both of them were Makkan Muslims. His version is akin to that of Ibn Ḥajar. It is followed by details of Madīnan fraternity, which throws ample light on the rationale behind this step.

Two persons of two different families were bound by a set of rights and obligations. This bond was similar to the one obtained between real brothers in the Makkan Arab society. They had legal, social, economic, moral and religious obligations towards each other. At one's death the other one inherited him in full. This was a life-giving measure for Muslims. It was indeed a message of mercy for them. However, it was vehemently rejected by the unbelieving Arabs. For it put an end to the remote chance of the return of their lost children to their fold. More importantly, it was a blow to their political prestige, social power and national unity. It amounted to the emergence of a rival order in their midst, which could be fatal for them. In contrast, for the Muslims of Makkah it brought a new life, comforting and strengthening them and blessing them with unity and solidarity in future. They, of course, needed all that badly.

Allowance for the Social Class

The principles underlying the Prophet's management of the Makkan fraternity underscores his insights into the social nuances. In establishing this relationship between the members of two different Qurayshī families he took into account their social background, family status, economic parity, social ranking, political position, individual talents and other factors. He saw to it that both of them were peers in every respect, ruling out any distance and gap between them. It would ensure perfect compatibility among them. Accordingly, the fraternity yielded the desired results.

On analyzing this fraternity, it emerges that the most significant pairing was between Abū Bakr and ʿUmar. ʿUthmān and ʿAbd al-Raḥmān ibn ʿAwf, Zubayr ibn al-ʿAwwām and ʿAbdullāh ibn Masʿūd, Ḥamzah and Zayd ibn Ḥārithah, ʿUbaydah ibn Ḥārith and Bilāl ibn Rabāḥ, Muṣʿab ibn ʿUmayr al-ʿAbdarī and Saʿd ibn Abī Waqqāṣ, Abū ʿUbaydah al-Fihrī and Sālim, Saʿīd ibn Zayd and Ṭalḥah ibn ʿUbaydullāh al-Taymī were made brethren in faith. The Prophet (peace be upon him) took ʿAlī ibn Abī Ṭālib as his brother in faith. This particular instance is nonetheless subject to discussion. Reports, however, bear out the same. It is a popular tradition.[9]

Makkan Brotherhood: A Permanent Structuring

This arrangement of fraternity was not a temporary phenomenon. Nor was it confined only to the above mentioned pairs. It was a permanent feature of the Islamic social system, binding all Makkan Muslims together. It infused a new energy among them. For as the Makkans embraced Islam, they joined this new brotherhood. This contributed to uniting Makkan Muslims as a single *ummah*. It stood in a sharp contrast to the non-Muslim Quraysh society. Historians and scholars have paid little attention to the emergence of Muslim society in Makkah. Nor has the Makkan fraternity been analyzed. However, this misperception should be laid to rest that the Muslim *ummah* had not developed during the Makkan period and that it was evolved only in Madīnah. Rather, the Madīnan fraternity and society developed along the lines which were established in Makkah itself. The different social units were united together in Makkah. This phenomenon was akin to all other aspects of Islam which had their beginning in Makkah. Madīnan Islam, no doubt, stands out as the developed and advanced form of Makkan Islam. By the same token, Madīnan community represented the perfect and larger version of the Makkan community.

The above point is adduced by reports related to *sīrah*. It is clearly mentioned in primary sources that the love and fraternity promoted by the Prophet's above-mentioned measure lasted until the last breath of the persons concerned. Rather, it grew in time. The perfect relationship between Abū Bakr and ʿUmar, between ʿUthmān and ʿAbd al-Raḥmān and all other pairs provides ample evidence for them. The same spirit later promoted the fraternity between Muhājirīn and Anṣār in Madīnah. The Makkan fraternity was a source of great strength for the Muslim minority during Makkan period. It helped the community withstand all the obstacles and brought glory to it. Such brotherhood alone can ensure the power and grandeur of a Muslim minority.

The Makkan Muslim Community's Capacity for Work

In the Makkan period, apart from constructing the Muslim community, one of the major tasks of the Prophet was to motivate it socially and enhance its mobility and productivity. As the Messenger of Allah and head of the community the Prophet did not rest content with forming only the community. For constructing something is easy, provided it is aided by favourable circumstances. Many reformers and community leaders have been successful in forging social unity. However, generally speaking, such efforts do not have a long life. The groups such formed are subject to tension, friction, conflict and dissension, often resulting in their disintegration. For such groups are formed, in the first place, on narrow considerations, not on any eternal principles. The Muslim community constructed by the Prophet (peace be upon him) in the Makkan period, which later grew into the broader Muslim *ummah* in Madīnah, was based on eternal and natural principles. Allah brands it as His special mercy which helped Muslims develop such mutual love and concern. The renowned Orientalist, Philip K. Hitti credits the Prophet (peace be upon him) with this unique achievement of uniting the unruly, uncouth, ignorant people of degenerate society into a highly serious, sincere and disciplined community.

It was quite a task to construct the Muslim community in the hostile, multi-faith Makkan polity that was dominated by non-Muslims. It was more difficult to ensure and maintain its collectivity, unity, solidarity, mutual relations and efficiency. That was the main challenge. The formation of the Muslim community in Madīnah was relatively easier. For the majority of Muslims were settled in Madīnah and the hostile forces lacked strength and offensive. The latter might have been more resourceful in their wealth and socio-political power and military strength. However, the numerical advantage of Muslims in Madīnah contributed to their emergence as a strong community. This was lacking in the Makkan period as the enemy was superior in every respect.

Collective Life

In the first thirteen years of Islamic history the Makkan Muslim community displayed utmost love, self-abnegation, unity and solidarity. It helped in its emergence as a united force. They had the privilege of enjoying the Prophet's leadership, which has remained unrivalled in history. They were fired by their conviction which made them a cemented force. The fraternity measure bound them in an orderly group. The hostility on the part of the unjust social order of the day made them all the more active. The call for struggle infused a new spirit into them. They had meagre material and financial resources, though not altogether devoid of these. More importantly, they resolved to make an optimum use of all they had, especially their spiritual, moral and religious strength. They grew into a social force with a distinct identity, as opposed to the non-Muslim majority community in their midst. This firm resolve, dynamic leadership and fervour turned them into a force to be reckoned with. They were not plagued by dissension or hypocrisy. Some instances of hypocrites in their midst are found in the Madīnan period but none in the Makkan phase. Both in its internal and external affairs the Makkan Muslim community displayed complete unity and acted in unison. They would reach a decision after mutual consultation. They would abide by the Prophet's directives at any expense and performed selflessly all that he commanded. It no doubt, presented a model of obedience to be emulated. Proper leadership, sincerity of purpose and good intention are unifying factors for a community. In the Makkan period the Prophet (peace be upon him) was the unquestioning leader. There were no tribal chiefs or family heads in this period. In contrast, in the Madīnan period, notwithstanding the Prophet's towering presence, there were tribal chiefs of Aws and Khazraj with their own loyal followers. The above was an important factor in the emergence of the community. It helped in the Madīnan period as well. However, there were initial problems and obstacles. The Makkan Muslim community was formed under the single leadership of the Prophet (peace be upon him) and attained its noble objectives.

Rallying Together the Weaker Sections

The above account of the pairs of brethren in faith should not give the wrong impression that the scope of the fraternity was confined to the Quraysh elites. It is evident from the examples of Bilāl and Zayd ibn Ḥārithah that the Prophet (peace be upon him) paired the Quraysh nobles with the slaves and freed slaves who had accepted

Islam. It was a historic instance of social equality as introduced by Islam. In the *Jāhiliyyah* Arab society non-Quraysh were taken as allies yet they held an inferior rank socially. Only some allies annexed an equal status by dint of their wealth and numerical strength. The Prophet's measure granted an equal status to allies and freed slaves.

More significantly, the Prophet (peace be upon him) liberated helpless Muslims from their unjust, unbelieving masters and set them free, according them the status of equal members of the Muslim community. It is generally held that some affluent Muslims had freed slaves. It was no doubt a noble gesture on their part. However, on a close study it emerges that it was the Prophet's strategy that they should be bought for securing their release from the clutches of their oppressive masters and for freeing them from exploitation. It was he who had exhorted rich Muslims to do so.

Muslim Women

Reports do not discuss the role of Muslim women in the emergence of the Muslim community and in the fraternity arrangements. This should not leave the odd impression that women had no role in the society or that they were not granted any place in the community. Women and children were under the care of male heads of families. Notwithstanding their individual position and service to the community they were counted as part of the family. They are not therefore mentioned separately. However, they were part of the fraternity and Muslim community. Being an indispensable part of the family unit, women were naturally included in the pairing. They behaved in accord with Islamic teachings as part of this fraternity.

Economic Life of the Makkan Muslim Ummah

The collectivity of the Makkan Muslim community is reflected at its sharpest in its dynamic economic life. Muslims were united in opposition to the Quraysh society. As the latter resorted to injustice and the Arab and tribal norms of unity, solidarity and protection failed to defend the helpless Muslims, the Prophet (peace be upon him) resorted to employing the principle of ransom and purchase. All the rich members of the community acted on his directive. The Prophet's first wife, mother of believers donated all she had in this cause, as the Prophet (peace be upon him) acknowledged. Abū Bakr secured the release of a large number of Muslims. It helped protect the weak Muslims against oppression. In the Makkan period Abū Bakr had more than forty thousand dirham in cash, besides his property and trade goods. He spent all this in the cause of Islam. At the time of emigration to Madīnah he was left with only five thousand dirham, and that too was meant for the Muslim community.[10] ʿUmar ibn al-Khaṭṭāb, ʿAbd al-Raḥmān ibn ʿAwf and many other affluent Makkan Muslims generously spent their wealth on buying and freeing slaves. ʿAbdullāh al-Naḥḥām sponsored several poor Makkan Muslims. Even the unbelieving Quraysh were so much impressed by his philanthropy that they did not let him emigrate to Madīnah, fearing that the orphans and poor persons supported by him would have no one to help them. He actively pursued the Islamic directive for charity and helping the poor.

For years the donations by the generous Muslims solved the financial problems of the community in Makkah. They met both individual and collective needs. The Prophet (peace be upon him) urged Muslims to donate and spend in Allah's cause. Accordingly, they spent even more than they could afford. They donated in both cash and kind for meeting their basic necessities of life. The funds so generated catered for the needs of Muslim emigrants to Abyssinia, of the Muslims subject to social boycott, expenses incurred on entertaining delegations and helping the poor Makkan Muslims.

Economy is the core of the economic life of a society. It assumes greater importance in the context of a minority. Wealth is like the blood supply that sustains the entire community. If people are not financially sound or dependent upon others, their life tends to be more difficult. A minority should not only support itself, it should learn how to survive in adverse circumstance and attain self-sufficiency and independence. The Prophet (peace be upon him) and Makkan Muslims of both Qurayshī descent or otherwise were essentially traders and knew well the significance of wealth in economic, social and community life.

The head and members of the Makkan Muslim community resolved to stand on their feet and to improve their economic life. Traders drew up a plan for their trade activities and acted on it systematically.

The Prophet's Trade

Since his young age the Prophet (peace be upon him) was engaged in trading on partnership basis. He used to take the goods of Makkan businessmen to Syria and Yemen and got his share in the profit. After his marriage to the wealthy widow Khadījah it was his source of income. The husband and wife had their joint business venture.[11] After assuming the office of Messengership he devoted himself fully to the cause of Islam. He did not have any time to carry on trade. Therefore, he sent his goods through leading Quraysh traders and non-Quraysh brokers to market. This improved his financial position. In the words of the Qur'ān, he became independent. Balādhurī cites a report to the effect that he had sent his goods through Abū Sufyān to Syria and reaped rich dividends. It was not an isolated instance. Rather, it was part of his trading activity. The above report is recorded by others as well.

Ibn Kathīr has narrated a report about a famous poet of the *Jāhiliyyah* period, ʿUthmān ibn Abī al-Ṣalt on the authority of Ṭabarānī and Ayman which is sound. In summary, the report reads as follows: Abū Sufyān went on a business trip to Syria along with his friend, Umayyah ibn Abī al-Ṣalt and returned to Makkah after two months. He then went to Yemen for the same purpose and returned after five months. People called on him in order to find out about their investments. The Prophet (peace be upon him) too, visited him while his wife Hind was playing with her children. He greeted Abū Sufyān and felicitated him on his safe return. He discussed with him his travel and stay there yet asked him no question about his share.

When he returned, Abū Sufyān told Hind: 'I marvel at this man. I do like him. Every Qurayshī who had given me his goods enquired about it. However, he did not ask me any questions.' A little later Abū Sufyān went to the Kaʿbah and met the Prophet (peace be upon him) there. He told the latter about his profit and asked him to take it from him. He refused to take the commission which he usually charged. The Prophet, (peace be upon him) however, declined this offer. He then told him to send someone who would carry his goods. He agreed on taking the standard commission.[11] Ibn Kathīr clarifies that Bayhāqī has recorded the same report in his *Kitāb al-Dalā'il* on Ismāʿīl ibn Ṭurayḥ's authority. He, however, prefers Ṭabarānī's report for being more extensive.[12] In a similar vein is Balādhurī's other report, which though brief is very significant. By coincidence it is also related to Abū Sufyān. At that time when the Prophet (peace be upon him) was also engaged in preaching Islam privately, Abū Sufyān returned from his trade journey to Syria. He had carried there the goods of the Prophet (peace be upon him) as of other persons. When he learnt about it, he said that Abū Sufyān would act honestly in this matter.[13]

It is clear from the reports by Ṭabarānī, Bayhaqī, Balādhurī and Ibn Kathīr that the Prophet (peace be upon him) continued to trade even after holding his Prophetic office. That it went on after his marriage to Khadījah is on record. However, the nature of his work changed. Initially the Prophet (peace be upon him) carried the goods of others to Syria or other markets. After marriage he only took his own goods and those of his wife. It was now a venture of equal partnership. This lasted for fifteen years i.e. from 595 to 610 CE. After his assuming the Prophetic office, the nature of his job changed again. He was fully busy with his mission, hence, he could not go to market. He entered into partnership with some Quraysh businessmen. It was another form of sharing profit. His link with Abū Sufyān in this trade activity brings home the following points: First, he entered into business partnership with such a leading Makkan trader and Quraysh chief as Abū Sufyān. Moreover, it points to his excellent social relations with him. Abū

Sufyān was involved in trade with both Syria and Yemen. The Makkan Quraysh businessmen journeyed to Syria and Yemen in winter and summer respectively. This point is borne out also by the Qur'ān. This trade was on alternate basis. After trade journey to Syria in summer they went to Yemen in winter. It was thus a trading cycle. Abū Sufyān carried the goods of Makkan traders and earned his profit. He earned commission in addition to his profit. Even after learning about the Prophet's mission Abū Sufyān did not abandon his trade or social links with him. Rather, out of love for him he refused to take his commission. Only at the Prophet's insistence he accepted commission. The Prophet (peace be upon him) had trust in Abū Sufyān's integrity as a trader and his business acumen. He did not rely only on Abū Sufyān for his trading. For no businessmen could rely on only one person. It is worth-noting that like Abū Sufyān he had trade links with other Quraysh and Arab tribal traders. Among his other trade partners the following feature prominently: ʿAbdullāh ibn Abī al-Ḥamsā' al-Taymi, al-Sā'ib ibn Abī al-Sā'ib al-Sayfī Makhzūmī and Qays ibn al-Sā'ib Makhzūmī. Both in the *Jāhiliyyah* period and the in the days of his Prophetic office they were his trade partners.[14]

Makkan Muslims' Trade

A detailed account of Makkan Muslims engaged in trade is found during the Madīnan period. Among them were the youth of both Quraysh and non-Quraysh families such as Abū Bakr al-Ṣiddīq, ʿUmar ibn al-Khaṭṭāb, ʿUthmān ibn ʿAffān, ʿAbd al-Raḥmān ibn ʿAwf, Ṭalḥah ibn ʿUbaydullāh, al-Zubayr ibn al-ʿAwwām, Abū ʿUbaydah ibn al-Jarrāḥ al-Fihrī, Saʿd ibn Abī Waqqāṣ, Saʿīd ibn Zayd, Khālid ibn Saʿīd al-Asdī, Yazīd ibn Zamʿah (ʿAbd al-ʿUzzā), Muṭṭalib ibn Azhar, Ṭulayb ibn Azhar al-Zuhrī, al-Miqdād ibn ʿAmr al-Kindī, Shuraḥbīl ibn Ḥasanah al-Kindī, Zayd ibn al-Khaṭṭāb al-ʿAdawī, ʿĀmir ibn Rabīʿah ʿAnzī al-ʿAdawī, Nuʿaym ibn ʿAbdullāh al-Naḥḥām al-ʿAdawī, ʿUthmān ibn Maẓʿūn Jumaḥī, and his elder brothers and other relatives, ʿAbdullāh ibn Ḥudhāfah and his brother Khunays al-Sahmī, Hishām ibn al-ʿĀṣ ibn Wā'il al-Sahmī, al-Arqam ibn Abī al-Arqam Makhzūmī, ʿAyyāsh ibn Abī Rabīʿah al-Makhzūmī, al-Walīd ibn al-Walīd ibn al-Mughīrah al-Makhzūmī and his several brothers and relatives, Abū Ṣabrah ibn Abī Ruḥm al-ʿĀmirī and his brothers and relatives, ʿAbdullāh ibn Jaḥsh of Banū Ghanam ibn Dawdān and ʿUbaydullāh ibn Jaḥsh and his relatives, who were the budding traders of Makkah. Of them, the following had established their credentials: ʿUthmān al-Umawī and ʿAbd al-Raḥmān al-Zuhrī. They were engaged in both local and international trade. They travelled up to Yemen and Syria and had, apart from cash and goods, agricultural property in and around Makkah, especially Ṭā'if. Unlike non-Muslim businessmen they were not very rich. However, they had started building their financial status. They were not dependent upon non-Muslim traders for the promotion of their trade or their income. The trade activities of Makkan Muslims have not been studied so far. A detailed study may be conducted on it. A pointer to the financial status of the Makkan Muslim community is afforded by the cash amount available with leading Muslims at the time of their emigration to Madīnah. According to his own statement, ʿUmar ibn al-Khaṭṭāb al-ʿAdawī was the richest among the Qurayshī emigrants. His cash must have been more then the four thousand dirham owned by Abū Bakr.[15]

Conventional *sīrah* writers focus on the miserable lot of Makkan Muslims and their religious life. As a result, they have not touched on their trade and their role and place in Makkan economy. Some reports of the day, however, indicate that they had strengthened their business activity even during such difficult times. Makkan Quraysh chiefs and other traders took trade caravans at least twice a year to Syria and Yemen. Several caravans left for these countries. It was a regular business activity. Moreover, they visited round the year different markets in Arabia. All these points are adduced by history. Makkan Muslim businesses joined these caravans both in groups and individually. Some reports to this effect exist and are dated around the period close to the emigration to Madīnah.

1. On his return from a Muslim trade caravan from Syria, al-Zubayr ibn al-ʿAwwām al-Asdī met the Prophet (peace be upon him) and presented him the gift of a dress. Significantly enough, the caravan comprised only Muslim traders.[16]
2. At the same time Ṭalḥah ibn ʿUbaydullāh al-Taymī travelled to Syria for business and met the emigrants on his return.
3. In the trade journey of Ṭalḥah ibn ʿUbaydullāh al-Taymī to Syria, the investment was also of Abū Bakr. According to another report, it consisted of garments. Ṭalḥah handed over the profit to Abū Bakr.[17]
4. On his emigration when Abū Bakr reached Madīnah along with the Prophet, (peace be upon him) he was readily recognized by Madīnans, for he used to pass through Madīnah on his trade journeys. In contrast, Madīnans had not seen the Prophet (peace be upon him) for long.[18]
5. The most important trade caravan was led by ʿUthmān ibn Ṭalḥah in that he left for Syria for business soon after or during the emigration to Madīnah.[19]

Handicrafts

As clarified by works on *sīrah* and Imām Muḥammad ibn Ḥasan al-Shaybānī, there were four main sources of income for Muslims: trade, agriculture, handicrafts industry and labour. Makkan Muslims had little opportunity for agriculture in that the land was arid and irrigation facilities were non-existent. However, they were engaged in it at Ṭā'ifian Nakhlah. Yet it played no important role in their prosperity or economic independence. They had avenues for handicrafts and labour. Muslim artisans had improved their condition in Makkah and some of them, according to the Quraysh chiefs, had accumulated wealth. Of them, there was Khabbāb ibn al-Arat Tamīm who manufactured arms and was also a goldsmith. He had raised the huge amount of four thousand dinar (around fifty thousand dirham) which he had paid as the price for his emigration to Madīnah to the Quraysh chiefs. Ṣuhayb ibn Sinān al-Rūmī was also a rich artisan who too, had given his wealth to the Makkan chiefs in return for their permitting him to emigrate to Madīnah.[20]

Labour Force

It was common for the Makkan Muslims to work as labourers, apart from their engagement in trade, handicrafts and industry. Obviously, labour workers could not gain prosperity. However, they met their basic needs, sufficient for sustaining them. They would sleep hungry or draw upon the help rendered by their Muslim brethren. Labour was the main preoccupation of Makkan Muslims.

ʿAbdullāh ibn Masʿūd al-Hudhalī grazed goats on wages. The same was the occupation of his brother, ʿUtbah ibn Masʿūd while his mother worked as a domestic help. This family had close ties with the Prophet's family.[21] ʿAmmār ibn Yāsir Madhḥijī, his father Yāsir and his mother Sumayyah worked as labourers. ʿAlī ibn Abī Ṭālib and his elder brother Jaʿfar also grazed goats and did labour work.

As to the weaker sections of Muslims, some of them were slaves, others the freed ones. Muslim slaves to both the Quraysh chiefs and leading Muslims served their masters. Some of their chores were: assisting in trade, drawing water, grazing cattle, handicraft and providing domestic help. They were supported by their masters. Prior to his freedom Zayd ibn Ḥārithah did these jobs at the Prophet's house. So was done by other slaves.[22] ʿĀmir ibn Fuhayrah was a slave to Abū Bakr and grazed his cattle. As Zayd and ʿĀmir were freed and they earned bread for their families. They, nonetheless, continued working as labourers. Some other freed slaves of Banū Umayyah and Banū Hāshim flourished under the patronage of their former masters and earned lots of money.[23]

Social Relations with the Majority Community

Islam believes in full cooperation and tolerance in a non-Muslim society for the Muslim minority in all legitimate social, economic, political and cultural matters. More importantly, it recommends full interaction and instructs Muslims to do so. It obliges them to treat well the non-Muslims as a religious duty. Reports related to the *sīrah* make it plain that after holding the Prophetic office the Prophet (peace be upon him) maintained social relations with his non-Muslim kith and kin and other Makkans. He continued cooperating with them on all national, community and cultural issues. He treated them well in order to press home the point that Islam stands for excellent behaviour and spells mercy for Muslims and non-Muslims alike. Some important points of this issue are discussed below in order to highlight the Islamic stance in a pluralistic society.

The Prophet's Meal Parties

After the divine command for preaching Islam publicly the Prophet (peace be upon him) arranged for a meal party for his close relatives belonging to Banū ʿAbd Manāf. He did so twice, for the first party did not yield any result. Even the second one was not very fruitful. Nonetheless, it illustrates the Prophet's practice that meal gathering may be useful for spreading the message of Islam and for improving social relations, especially for the non-Muslim majority. Some reports specify that before drawing up the list of invitees the Prophet (peace be upon him) had consulted his affectionate maternal aunts. Women were not invited, for they were bound by the views of their male relatives. Around fourty-five male members of Banū ʿAbd Manāf were invited. The party had a good impact. Ali was incharge of organizing it. Some *ḥadīth* scholars have contested parts of relevant reports. However, no one has objected to the meal party itself.[24] The Prophet threw this party not only once. It was reflective of Arab social tradition and the Prophet's and Companions' regular practice. *Aḥādīth* relate many such parties, of which some happened in the Makkan period. The Prophet (peace be upon him) lived in the midst of his non-Muslim relatives and friends. Logically, it is unlikely that he did not invite them. With the preaching of Islam it became a strong social tradition. Rather, it became all the more necessary. Abū Bakr had invited ʿUthmān ibn ʿAffān, al-Zubayr ibn al-ʿAwwām, Ṭalḥah ibn ʿUbaydullāh, ʿAbd al-Raḥmān, ibn ʿAwf and Saʿd ibn Abī Waqqāṣ before their acceptance of Islam. Ibn Isḥāq's report points to the gathering, in which a meal must have been served.[25]

The Prophet's Presence in the Gatherings of the Majority Community

The Quraysh chiefs and other Makkans generally treated Makkan Muslims well, except in religious matters. This point comes out in their invitation to the Prophet (peace be upon him) and Muslims to their meals. Such invitations were heartily accepted by the Prophet and Companions. For this could serve as the platform for conveying to them the message of Islam. A Makkan chief Ubayy ibn Khalaf al-Jumaḥī prepared a meal and invited the Prophet (peace be upon him) and his Companions to share it. Reports indicate that in fulfillment of his role as the Prophet he insisted that he would join Ubayy only if he recited the creedal statement of Islam: 'There is no god besides Allah'. When he did so, the Prophet (peace be upon him) accompanied him. On the way Ubayy met ʿUqbah ibn Abī Muʿīṭ al-Umawī, his friend who asked him whether he had recited it. To this Ubayy replied in the affirmative, saying that he had done so in order to make the Prophet accept his invitation, even though Islam was not his belief.[26] This party did not end well, for Ubayy misbehaved at the instigation of his friend, ʿUqbah. Yet, it brings home two points: (i) The non-Muslim Makkan chiefs and other Quraysh leaders invited Muslims to meal parties, as it was part of their social tradition. They did so instinctively. (ii) Muslims accepted such invitations especially of their dear Quraysh brethren.

The Prophet (peace be upon him) and the Companions lived in the midst of non-Muslims. It is wrong to assume that there was total segregation between Muslims and non-Muslims. For no social group can exist, being cut off completely from the mainstream. This is the law of nature as well that the majority community cannot disregard altogether a minority.

During the three years of misery when the Muslims were confined to a valley, they were helped by their non-Quraysh non-Muslims. It is reported that Ḥakīm ibn Ḥizām al-Asdī, nephew of the Prophet's wife Khadījah bint Khuwaylid, occasionally provided them with wheat. If the opponents tried to obstruct him, he fought with them. Once when Abū Jahl sought to stop him, he was abused by Ḥakīm. Another Quraysh chief Abū al-Bukhtarī even hit Abū Jahl. They could not uphold that a relative be obstructed from helping his kith and kin in distress.[27] After citing Ibn Isḥāq's above report Ibn Kathīr adds that during the three years long social boycott Muslims were helped by such kind Quraysh members who recognized the ties of kinship.[28]

Social Relations Among Muslims and Polytheists

On the basis of some reports about the social life it would be wrong to infer that all the Makkan Muslims had been subject to the boycott, as is erroneously projected by writers on the *sīrah*. The boycott involved only Banū Hāshim and Banū Muṭṭalib. For they had refused to hand over the Prophet (peace be upon him) to the Quraysh chiefs. Apart from the Muslims of these two families, their non-Muslim members had also been subject to the boycott. Other Muslims were spared. Nor were they victimized in any other way. As they had been living under the pact with the Quraysh in Makkah, they carried out their normal social relations with Makkans. The Prophet (peace be upon him) never resorted to boycotting non-Muslims. He maintained normal social relations even with his enemies, sharing their sorrow and happiness and had trade links with them. He would pay them courtesy visits. Accordingly, Muslims followed this practice of the Prophet and had excellent social relations with their non-Muslim neighbours, relatives and residents of the town. They even had matrimonial ties with them until the Qur'ān prohibited it.

Trade and Matrimonial Links between the Two

There are frequent references to the Prophet's trade links with non-Muslims. The following points are recapitulated below. Among his trade partners the Prophet (peace be upon him) had excellent relations with Ḥakīm ibn Ḥizām al-Asdī and his family. Although Ḥakīm was then a non-Muslim, he had cordial relations with him. Among the Companions ʿAbd al-Raḥmān ibn ʿAwf had non-Muslim partners. His close friend and partner was Umayyah ibn Khalaf al-Jahmī, a leading Makkan figure opposed to Islam. Yet he was close to ʿAbd al-Raḥmān and this lasted even up to the Madīnan period.

Muḥammad ibn Ḥabīb al-Baghdādī and other writers on the *sīrah* have covered extensively the Quraysh trade partners. Al-Baghdādī speaks of fifty-eight such partners. Al-ʿAbbās ibn al-Muṭṭalib al-Hāshimī, and Abū Sufyān were good partners. Other reports specify that these two chiefs of ʿAbd Manāf remained close friends, partners and associates until their death. Wars did not dent their ties. Nor did religious differences estrange them. Notwithstanding being a Hāshimī, al-ʿAbbās was regarded as a friend and supporter of Umayyah.[29]

Al-Walīd, son of the Quraysh chief ʿUtbah ibn Rabīʿah was another Umawī friend and trade partner of al-ʿAbbās al-Hāshimī. Their cordial relations continued during both *Jāhiliyyah* and Islamic periods until al-Walīd was killed in the Battle of Badr.[30] ʿUthmān al-Umawī and Rabīʿah ibn Ḥārith ibn ʿAbd al-Muṭṭalib al-Hāshimī had been friends and trade partners in both the Jāhiliyyah and Islamic periods and this bond continued until ʿUthmān's caliphate.

In the Makkan period an outstanding instance of the matrimonial tie between Muslims and polytheistic Quraysh is of the marriage between the Prophet's eldest daughter, Zaynab and Abū'l-ʿĀṣ ibn Rabīʿ al-Abshamī. According to popular reports, this tie had been fixed by Khadījah in the *Jāhiliyyah* period. For Abū'l-ʿĀṣ was her dear nephew. It is, however, likely that the marriage was solemnized during the Islamic period. At least, it is beyond any shadow of doubt that this tie lasted during the Islamic period and was to the Prophet's liking. The Prophet (peace be upon him) had tremendous love for their children, ʿAlī and Umāmah.[31]

An interesting and significant report is that initially ʿĀ'ishah was to be married to Jubayr, son of a Makkan chief Muṭʿim ibn ʿAdiyy. It was Muṭʿim who had extended protection to the Prophet (peace be upon him) after Abū Ṭālib's death. When the Prophet's proposal reached Abū Bakr, he was slightly upset because of the initial plan. He first talked to Muṭʿim and his family. They, however, refused to accept a Muslim girl as their daughter-in-law lest she might preach the same in their family. This incident again points to the matrimonial ties between the two communities.[32]

Political Alliances

At the time of the Prophet's advent, the Quraysh tribe held twelve positions and these where the hereditary offices of the twelve most important families of Quraysh. They had these for ages. For example, Ḥijābah, Sidānah and Liwā' were in the custody of Banū ʿAbd al-Dār, namely ʿUthmān ibn Ṭalḥah and ʿĀmir ibn Hāshim. Dār al-Nadwah and Rifādah were with Ḥakīm ibn Ḥizām of Banū Asad. Al-ʿAbbās ibn ʿAbd al-Muṭṭalib of Banū Hāshim looked after Siqāyah and Mushāwarah by Yazīd ibn Rabīʿah al-Aswad of Banū Asad. Abū Bakr ʿAbdullāh ibn Abī Quḥāfah of Banū Taym enjoyed the offices of Diyyah and Maghārim while Sifārah and Munāfarah by ʿUmar ibn al-Khaṭṭāb of Banū ʿAdiyy. Qiyādah was the hereditary office of Abū Sufyān ibn Ḥarb of Banū Umayyah. The twin positions were held by Khālid ibn al-Walīd of Banū Mukhzūm. Azlam and Aysar was the hereditary office of Banū Jumaḥ, held by Safwān ibn Umayyah while Amwāl was looked after by Ḥārith ibn Qays of Banu Sulaym.

Some of them had embraced Islam. For example, Abū Bakr al-Ṣiddīq al-Taymī was the earliest Muslim. At a later date ʿUmar ibn al-Khaṭṭab accepted Islam. Al-Abbās ibn ʿAbd al-Muṭṭalib al-Hāshimī is taken as an early Muslim while ʿUthmān ibn Ṭalḥah al-ʿAbdarī and Khālid ibn al-Walīd al-Makhzūmī entered the fold of

Islam in 7/729. Almost half of these Quraysh chiefs had abandoned their ancestral faith and accepted Islam. Yet they did not relinquish their office. In other words, Makkan chiefs did not depose them. Even as Muslims they carried on, looking after the affirms of their tribes and cooperated with Makkan chiefs until their emigration to Madīnah. It may be therefore said that Makkan polity was ruled by a coalition of Muslim and non-Muslim office bearers. It was a mixed government of both majority and minority communities. It provides a role model for the participation of a Muslim minority in bodies dominated by non-Muslims. The evidence is provided by the Prophet's endorsement of the continuance in office of ʿUthmān ibn Ṭalḥah al-ʿAbdarī for Ḥijābah and of Al-ʿAbbās ibn ʿAbd al-Muṭṭalib al-Hāshimī for Siqāyah, as reported in *ḥadīth* and *sīrah* works.[33]

Ibn Ḥajar adds the following significant points. When ʿUthmān ibn Ṭalḥah al-ʿAbdarī went home to collect the key to the Kaʿbah, his mother Sulāfah bint Saʿīd refused to part with it, saying that once the Prophet (peace be upon him) took it, they would never get it back. However, he did bring the key and the Kaʿbah was opened. When the Prophet (peace be upon him) came out, he paused near the well. At that point ʿAlī exclaimed that his family was granted the Prophethood, Siqāyah and Ḥijābah and that no one else was more deserving of these. The Prophet, (peace be upon him) however, disliked it and handed over the Kaʿbah key to ʿUthmān ibn Ṭalḥah al-ʿAbdarī, as it had been in his custody for long. Ibn Abī Shaybah and Ibn Isḥāq report the same. Ibn Jurayj states that ʿAlī had requested the Prophet (peace be upon him) that both Ḥijābah and Siqāyah be given to them. At that juncture the following Qur'ānic verse was sent down: 'Allah commands you to render back your trust to those to whom they are due.'[34] He let ʿUthmān ibn Ṭalḥah retain the key, as it was in the custody of his family for long.

For details of the office of Siqāyah held by al-ʿAbbās ibn ʿAbd al-Muṭṭalib al-Hāshimī since the days of *Jāhiliyyah*.[35] Ibn Ḥajar makes an important observation that al-ʿAbbās had inherited the office of Siqāyah from his father ʿAbd al-Muṭṭalib ibn Hāshim and was held by him until the advent of Islam. The Prophet (peace be upon him) let him hold the office.

Ibn Jurayj's report, as cited by Ibn Ḥajar, reads as follows: al-ʿAbbās had requested the Prophet (peace be upon him) that both Siqāyah and Ḥijābah be granted to him. The latter, however, found the request as unreasonable and let every custodian retain his office.[36]

Many bits of evidence indicate that the Quraysh families of Banū ʿAbd al-Dār and Banū Hāshim held the offices of Ḥijābah and Siqāyah. They retained their hereditary positions. The same may be said about other office bearers. The information about the following office bearers is regrettably defective: Abū Bakr, ʿUmar and Khālid ibn al-Walīd al-Makhzūmī. However, their being in office is supported by *aḥādīth* and historical accounts. This underscores the point that in political as well as socio-cultural and economic matters the Prophet (peace be upon him) adopted the policy of cooperation. The Quraysh too, pursued the same in their own interest. The Quraysh were known for their forbearance. The Prophet (peace be upon him) always pursued the path of cooperation and interaction.

The issue needs further discussion which cannot be continued in this work for the constraints of space. However, the above account proves our point that in the Makkan period Muslims had friendly and cordial relations with their non-Muslim relatives. This is the right Islamic approach and the Prophet's role model which we must emulate.

CHAPTER 5

The Defence System and the Right to Defend

Generally, writers on the *sīrah* make this sweeping statement that Muslims did not have the permission in the Makkan period to wage jihād. For them it includes fighting, killing and every defensive mechanism. It leaves the odd impression that Muslims were asked to surrender to the unjust order of the day and the Prophet (peace be upon him) and the Companions acted on this directive. Total surrender, rather subservience is the brain child of such persons who believe in non-dynamic Islam. The above view about surrender is belied by the reports of the day; *aḥādīth* and history. The Prophet (peace be upon him) did not and could not act so, for such conduct is contrary to the temper of Islam.

No doubt Makkan Muslims were not commanded to take up arms in jihād. Yet they had every right to defend their faith, life, property, honour and social, and collective life. They were obliged to defend their lives and their faith. It is the natural right of a community and its religious duty as well. Otherwise, fanatics belonging to the majority community would devour minorities. Nor would they ever allow a minority to follow its faith or construct its social order or improve its condition. Fanatics have behaved in the above fashion throughout history. It is evident from *sīrah* literature that Makkan Muslims had the right to protect their life and honour and to promote their faith and identity. The tribal security system came to their rescue, as is illustrated later in this work. Under the same code Makkan Muslims enjoyed the right to defend their life, property, honour and faith. No evidence in the *sīrah* literature or historical works points to the contrary that Muslims had no such right in the Quraysh society.

Tribal Code of Security and Support

As in every society, the Makkan society followed a code of social security and support based on tribal norms. Every tribe was bound to defend the life, honour, property and faith of its every member. Tribal solidarity alone ensured life and safety in adverse circumstance. Accordingly, individuals remained all along loyal to their tribes, for it gave them safety and security. Like other Arabs, Makkan Muslims were faithful to their families and tribes. Notwithstanding their acceptance of Islam, their tribesmen were bound to help and defend their members. They could not violate their code even if they wished so. For it was a disgraceful act. They would have been condemned by all Arab tribes. They would have been branded as cowardly, brazen and spineless people, unable to defend their own people. Tribal norms dictated that one should give up his life defending even his enemy, once he had granted protection to him.

The Prophet (peace be upon him) and all Quraysh families enjoyed this tribal support and defence. It was widely recognized that no outsider could harm them. They could be oppressed by their own tribesmen. When the enemies of Muslims, the Quraysh, decided to teach them a lesson, they realized that any harm inflicted by outsiders would engender civil war. They themselves should take action against Muslims. Makkan Muslims were, therefore, harassed and unjustly treated by their own family members and relatives. They did not let others inflict any harm on them.[1]

Family chiefs extended help and support to their members and all Muslims drew upon it. The Prophet (peace be upon him) enjoyed the protection of the Banū Hāshim chief, Abū Ṭālib and also of other leaders of Banū ʿAbd Manāf. Only Abū Lahab had the audacity to flout the centuries-old code. He was accordingly reviled by his own tribe.[2]

The Prophet (peace be upon him) and all Makkan Muslims benefited from the tribal code of solidarity and protection. For it defended their life, property and honour and also their faith and way of life. It helped protect and expand Islamic society. Whenever a tribe or family was found too weak to defend them, they sought the protection of some other chief or family. For example, Abū Bakr had accepted the custody of the Aḥābīsh chief, Ibn al-Daghnah.[3] ʿUmar also got, on a temporary basis, protection from al-ʿĀṣ al-Sahmī.[4] Many other Makkan Companions had secured similar help and support from Arab families with a strong sense of honour.[5]

As the slaves lost their protection on gaining freedom, Muslim families, who had secured their freedom by buying them, offered them protection. This applied to their whole family. For example, Abū Bakr extended protection to Bilāl, many other freed slaves and their families. He could offer little help yet it was a great relief for many oppressed Muslims and they managed to enjoy relatively more peaceful and secure existence.[6]

Those cowardly families that refused to protect their members were granted safety by other families. When Abū Ṭālib died and his protection was no longer available, another family chief of Banū ʿAbd Manāf, Muṭʿim ibn ʿAdiyy extended him protection which he had until his emigration to Madīnah.[7] When the emigrants to Abyssinia returned to Makkah on hearing a false report and their families refused to extend them any help and support, other Qurashyī chiefs and families provided them with protection. Such an arrangement made them like members of the same family and they were entitled to equal rights. Balādhurī has compiled a list of the Quraysh chiefs who had offered projection to the emigrants to Abyssinia.[8]

The Principle of Individual Amnesty

The peace agreement between the Makkan Quraysh and the Muslim *ummah* is illustrated by the individual contracts. Since the Prophet (peace be upon him) approved it, it may be regarded as the Islamic law of collective cooperation. It was in accord with old tribal code of conduct hence it covered defence and social security. Without this, there could not be any guarantee of social life and tribal system. Reports speak of another agreement in the same vein which was contracted by two individuals. Again, as it carried the Prophet's approval, it may be included in the above category.

Agreement for the Protection of Interests

Bukhārī quotes a report to the effect that ʿAbd al-Raḥmān ibn ʿAwf had entered into an agreement with a Makkan chief, Umayyah ibn Khalaf for protecting mutual interests. ʿAbd al-Raḥmān is on record saying: 'I had an agreement with Umayyah ibn Khalaf that he would defend my family and property in Makkah and I would reciprocate the same in Madīnah. We had put this to writing.'[9] While defining the term '*Ṣāghiyah*' Ibn Ḥajar explains that it stands for family, property and defending life. Basically, the above was an agreement of mutual interests. It is clear from Bukhārī's account that a Muslim, of the land of war or of Islam, may enter into an agreement of '*Wakālah*' with even those who are at war. ʿAbd al-Raḥmān had made Umayyah his custodian in Makkah and the latter held the same position in Madīnah. As pointed out by Ibn Ḥajar, the Prophet (peace be upon him) knew well about this agreement. Rather, he endorsed it. It appears that these two close friends had entered into the agreement before the emigration to Madīnah. Other reports underscore their close ties. In line with the same agreement ʿAbd al-Raḥmān tried to offer security to Umayyah and his son, ʿAlī in the battle of Badr and the latter expressed his consent to pay ransom money. However, both of them were killed by some Muslims.[10]

Right to Defend

The Companions' defensive measures: Once In the early days of the Makkan period while Saʿd ibn Abī Waqqāṣ was offering prayer along with the Companions in one of the Makkan valleys, a group of polytheists passed by and resenting the Muslims' act they reproached and even beat some Muslims. In retaliation Saʿd hit a polytheist with a camel bone and the victim started bleeding profusely. This was the first instance of spilling blood in the cause of Islam. This report features in early sources. Balādhurī adds that Saʿd ibn Abī Waqqāṣ, Saʿīd ibn Zayd al-ʿAdawī, Khabbāb ibn al-Arat al-Tamīmī, ʿAmmār ibn Yāsir Madhḥijī and ʿAbdullāh ibn Masʿūd al-Hudhalī were engaged in prayer in Abī Dubb valley. Abū Sufyān, al-Akhnas ibn Shurayq, and other polytheists hit the Muslims. When the Muslims retaliated and a polytheist was hurt, it unnerved them. Muslims drove away the polytheists from the valley.[11]

Bukhārī informs that as ʿUqbah ibn Muʿīṭ al-Umawī tried to strangle the Prophet (peace be upon him) to death, while the latter was performing prayer, Abū Bakr pushed him away from the Prophet (peace be upon him).[12]

Another important report is that once the Prophet (peace be upon him) and Abū Bakr were going round the Kaʿbah, holding each other's hand. ʿUqbah ibn Muʿīṭ al-Umawī, Abū Jahl Makhzūmi and Umayyah ibn Khalaf abused them whenever they passed by them in each round. In the fourth round Abū Jahl tried to obstruct the Prophet (peace be upon him). At this ʿUthmān pushed him while Abū Bakr and the Prophet pushed Umayyah ibn Khalaf and ʿUqbah respectively.[13]

The incident related to ʿAbdullāh ibn Masʿud al-Hudhalī is in the same vein. He recited verses of *Sūrah al-Raḥmān* before the Quraysh chiefs in their gatherings and was beaten by them. He, however, continued doing so.[14] Prior to his accepting Islam, Ḥamzah ibn ʿAbd al-Muṭṭalib al-Hāshimī had wounded Abū Jahl ibn Hishām al-Makhzūmī in the head for his misconduct towards his nephew, Prophet Muḥammad (peace be upon him). Soon after this incident he accepted Islam. Abū Jahl conceded his aggression and avoided taking revenge. In other words, he acknowledged the right to defend.[15] Writers on the *sīrah* state that Ḥamzah's acceptance of Islam played a crucial role in the defence of Islam and the Prophet (peace be upon him). The hostile Quraysh were too terrified to resort to any mischief, for they realized that the Prophet (peace be upon him) derived strength from Ḥamzah.

According to Ibn Saʿd, in his childhood al-Zubayr ibn al-ʿAwwām al-Asdī had a fight with someone and thrashed him so hard that he had to be carried away. The report does not specify the cause of this fight.[16] Even if this incident had happened during the *Jāhiliyyah* period, Saʿd ibn Abī Waqqāṣ displayed similar bravery after he turned into a Muslim. Among the emigrants to Abyssinia who had returned to Makkah was ʿUthmān ibn Maẓʿūn al-Jumaḥī. Since he was no longer under the protection of al-Walīd ibn al-Mughīrah al-Makhzūmī, someone hit him hard. Unable to put up with it, Saʿd hit the unbeliever on the face, smashing his nose, avenging the injustice done to his Muslim brother.[17]

On ʿUmar ibn al-Khaṭṭāb's acceptance of Islam, his Makkan compatriot and early Muslim, ʿAbdullāh ibn Masʿūd al-Hudhalī's comment is as follows: It was the day of victory. Reports invariably speak of ʿUmar as a man full of power and glory who could not be overcome.[18] The entry of ʿUmar and Ḥamzah into the fold of Islam strengthened Muslims so much that they ultimately overpowered the Quraysh.[19]

Ibn Kathīr provides further details how ʿUmar first declared his acceptance of Islam in the gatherings of unbelievers and beat Quraysh chiefs and then informed the Prophet (peace be upon him) of his embracing Islam. The Prophet (peace be upon him) left Dār al-Arqam, with ʿUmar and Ḥamzah in front of him. Together they went round the Kaʿbah and offered *Ẓuhr* prayer. Then they returned to Dār al-Arqam along with ʿUmar. After this, ʿUmar left for home alone.[20]

Another telling report on this count by Ibn Kathīr is that after his acceptance of Islam, ʿUmar went round the Kaʿbah. The Quraysh members just watched him as they had come to know about his conversion. ʿUmar went to the unbelievers' gathering, proclaiming his belief in Islam. When Abū Jahl asked him about his faith, he recited the creedal statement of Islam, affirming his new faith. The Quraysh surrounded him. ʿUmar got hold of ʿUtbah and took to beating him, forcing his fingers into ʿUtbah's eyes which made him yell in agony. This terrified the unbelieving Quraysh. Then ʿUmar released ʿUtbah. He made life difficult for the Quraysh. In all public meetings he declared his conversion to Islam. He reached the Prophet (peace be upon him) in a state that he was dominant over the enemies of Islam.[21] Ibn Masʿūd relates that Muslims could not offer prayers near the Kaʿbah until ʿUmar embraced Islam. He took on the Quraysh and prayed near the Kaʿbah. Other Muslims joined him.[22]

In 616 CE ʿUmar accepted Islam at the Prophet's hands at Dār al-Arqam. It pleased the Prophet (peace be upon him) so much that he exclaimed '*Allāhu Akbar*' (Allah is Great). The Prophet's family came to know about this event. Companions came out of their houses. They were much encouraged by the entry of Ḥamzah and ʿUmar into the fold of Islam. They recognized that both of them would protect the Prophet (peace be upon him) and help the Muslims take revenge against their enemies.[23]

ʿUmar's acceptance of Islam and his declaration of the same before the Quraysh chiefs underscore the Muslims' right to defend themselves and their efforts for jihād. ʿUmar directed a local messenger Jamīl ibn Muʿammar al-Jumaḥī to convey this news to the Quraysh, who propagated it. He announced the same to the Quraysh chief. ʿUmar himself went to their meetings and proclaimed it. This enraged the Quraysh so much that they took to beating him. ʿUmar took them head-on. It lasted until evening. When he paused, he told the Quraysh: 'You may do whatever you want. By Allah, if our number increases to 300, we would either leave Makkah or you would have to vacate it for us.' Meanwhile, al-ʿĀṣ ibn Wā'il al-Sahmī passed by. He asked about the matter and made the following important observation: 'Leave him alone.

He has preferred something for himself. What do you ask of him? Do you think Banū ʿAdiyy ibn Kaʿb would leave their member at your mercy? Leave him alone.' At this people moved away from ʿUmar.[24] It must be said to ʿUmar's credit that the next morning he went to the staunchest enemy of Islam, Abū Jahl al-Makhzūmī to inform him about his new faith. Although Abū Jahl was his real maternal uncle, he cursed ʿUmar for his accepting Islam.[25]

The Prophet's Defensive Measures

During the period of his persecution at the hands of the Quraysh the Prophet (peace be upon him) displayed exemplary perseverance. Yet it did not betray any note of surrender, defeatism or forfeiting the right to self-defence. The Qur'ān issued a series of severe warnings to the Quraysh against their reproaching, reviling and persecuting Muslims. They were warned against the terrible punishment in the Hereafter and against penalty in this world as well. This was done at a time when the Prophet (peace be upon him) did not have any semblance of power or authority. The Qur'ānic warnings during the Makkan period may be analyzed in an independent article.[26] The Prophet's utterances during this period bring into light the Muslim defence system clearly.

According to Ibn Isḥāq, some Quraysh chiefs were assembled somewhere in the period of public preaching of Islam. They were infuriated over the Prophet's call. Suddenly the Prophet (peace be upon him) entered the holy mosque, touched the black stone and walked in front of the Quraysh chiefs while going round the Kaʿbah. Some of them passed comments which were resented by the Prophet (peace be upon him). Yet he continued going round the Kaʿbah. When he passed by them again, someone reproached him. He again felt unhappy yet overlooked it. When it happened for the third time, he paused and addressed them in a strong voice: 'O the great Quraysh chiefs! By Him Who exercises control over my life, I have brought to you killing and slaughtering.' Narrators inform that upon hearing this, those present fell into silence. They sat mute and spell-bound. On gaining poise, the rudest Qurayshī spoke to him very gently for winning his heart: 'O Abū'l-Qāsim! Please go away. By God, you are not a fool.' Then he left the mosque. The next day the Quraysh chiefs gathered at the same spot and discussed that incident. At the same time the Prophet (peace be upon him) entered. All of them surrounded him, asking him whether he had given that threat the other day. He replied in the affirmative. They started dragging him. However, Abū Bakr came to his rescue and the Quraysh dispersed.[27]

The Prophet's uncle, Abū Lahab's enmity towards the Prophet (peace be upon him) is well known. The Qur'ān has condemned him for the same in *Sūrah al-Lahab*. For tormenting the Prophet (peace be upon him) he made his sons divorce the two daughters of the Prophet. He directed ʿUtbah to harm him. When he came to the Prophet (peace be upon him), the latter was engaged in reciting verses from *Sūrah al-Najm*. He reviled the Lord. At this the Prophet cursed him, and warned him that Allah would set one of His beasts on him. When ʿUtbah was in Syria, a tiger devoured him while he was asleep.[28] Another notorious Quraysh chief was Abū Zamʿah Aswad ibn Muṭṭalib al-Asdī. He and his associates taunted the Prophet (peace be upon him), Islam and Muslims and hurt them in every conceivable way. As the last resort, the Prophet (peace be upon him) cursed him, praying to Allah that he be rendered as a blind person and that his children should leave him in the lurch in his miserable condition. Allah accepted his supplication. One day he went outside Makkah in order to receive someone. While he was seated under the shadow of a tree, Allah deprived him of his eyesight.[29] His children dumped him. This incident was full of lessons for the Makkans.

Many scholars of *ḥadīth* and *tafsīr* report that the Prophet (peace be upon him) was offering prayer at the Kaʿbah when the notorious enemy of Islam, though a close relative of the Prophet, ʿUqbah ibn Muʿīṭ al-Umawī drew close to the Prophet (peace be upon him) and tried to strangle him. Abū Bakr reached there and pushed him away from the Prophet, saying: 'Do you kill him who says that my

Lord is Allah and who has brought to you clear signs from your Lord.'[30]

The Prophet's Warning

The Prophet being immensely merciful did not curse anyone. However, provoked by religious fervour he occasionally cursed the culprits, especially those of the Quraysh. A curse pronounced by him is reported in several works on *ḥadith* and *sīrah* in view of its many implications. This is a highly popular report, cited by Ibn Kathīr on the authority of many sources. He discusses it at length, as is evident from the account below. ʿAbdullāh ibn Masʿūd al-Hudhalī narrates: 'Only once I saw the Prophet cursing the Quraysh in general. While he was offering prayer, a group of Quraysh chiefs was seated beside him. There lay the entrails of a camel. The Quraysh chiefs urged the people there to place it on the Prophet's back. ʿUqbah ibn Abī Muʿīṭ did so. The Prophet was overburdened with its weight as he was in the posture of prostration. Fāṭimah came there and removed it. After finishing his prayer, the Prophet cursed them: "O Allah! Punish this group of the Quraysh. O Allah! Inflict punishment on ʿUtbah ibn Rabīʿah, Shaybah ibn Rabīʿah, Abū Jahl ibn Hishām, ʿUqbah ibn Abī Muʿīṭ, Ubayy ibn Khalaf (or according to a variant report, Umayyah ibn Khalaf)."' According to the narrator, all of the above persons were slain in the battle of Badr. Their bodies lay in a well. Ubayy ibn Khalaf being a bulky person was cut into pieces.

Apart from specifying the sources, Ibn Kathīr clarifies some points, especially the reaction of the Quraysh to this outrageous deed. Initially they laughed heartily over what they had done. When Fāṭimah came, she criticized them. When the Prophet (peace be upon him) finished his prayer, he raised his hands and cursed them. On noting this, the Quraysh chiefs stopped laughing. They were terrified of his curse. He had specifically cursed seven persons present there. (Some reports mention six and others only five names.) Other variant names are of Walīd ibn ʿUtbah and ʿUmārah ibn al-Walīd, as specified in Bukhārī's report.[31] Ibn Kathīr clarifies that Bukhārī has related this report under several chapters and in each instance with a new chain of narrators and a variant text. The text appears in its both shorter and longer versions.[32] According to Ibn Ḥajar, this is a more extensive report. This and other reports indicate that the Prophet (peace be upon him) pronounced the curse thrice upon the Quraysh. It hurt them badly for they knew that a supplication made in Makkah is accepted.

The Prophecy about the Ascendancy of Islam

The Prophet had conviction in the universal feature of his mission and that Islam and the Muslim *ummah* would ultimately gain ascendancy. His belief was based on the divine revelation received by him. Many Makkan *sūrahs* point to this promise made to him. These verses both exhort and warn the Quraysh: Muslims were clearly told that if they consistently follow faith, they would be victorious.

Verse 44 of *Sūrah al-Anbiyā'* reads as follows 'Do they not see that We gradually reduce the land (in their control) from its outlying borders? Is it then they who will win?' Shāh ʿAbd al-Qādir interprets it in terms of the gradual spread of Islam. He borrows this idea from his illustrious father, Shāh Walīullāh Dihlavī who brings out the point how Islam was gaining from strength to strength even in Makkah. Another relevant verse: 'Already Our word has been passed before this to Our servants sent by that they would certainly be assisted and that Our forces, they surely must conquer.'[33] Ibn Isḥāq's account of the Prophet's advent opens with reference to Allah's promise about his eventual ascendancy. He refers to the covenant with messengers mentioned in verse 181 of *Sūrah Āl ʿImrān*. Actually this belief is rooted in the Qur'ānic account of the primordial covenant which explicitly states that the Messengers of Allah are destined to victory. Many other verses of a similar tenor may be adduced. However, it is an altogether independent topic which may be studied in its own right.

It is logical to assume why the ascendancy of Islam and the Muslim *ummah* was promised. As Islam projects itself as a universal faith for all people of all times which would last until the end of the world, it is inevitable that it would be dominant somewhere and at some time. The religious scholars of the day, conversant with the history of Allah's Messengers, recognized this, for example, Waraqah ibn Nawfal al-Asdī who testified to the Prophet's veracity and promised to help the cause of Islam. It was not wishful thinking on his part. Aided by his foresight he discerned the future events. In *ḥadīth* it is recognized as a believer's quality. Some reports state that Waraqah had foretold that soon the Prophet (peace be upon him) would be directed to wage jihād.[34] In another account he is found foretelling that the Prophet (peace be upon him) would face fighting and killing.[35]

The Prophet (peace be upon him) had a strong belief in his success and the ascendancy of Islam from the very beginning and throughout the Makkan period. He believed so even when he had no supporter. He expressed the same belief in the dark days of severe persecution in Makkah and even when he faced adverse and hostile conditions both in and around Makkah, he knew that victory was imminent.

In the early days Muslims were only a handful. Yet the Prophet (peace be upon him) firmly believed that his mission would be successful and Islam would be a global force. In the early days of the Prophet's career Afif al-Kindī saw the Prophet (peace be upon him) offering prayer along with ʿAlī and Khadījah in a Makkan valley and enquired the Prophet's uncle, al-ʿAbbās ibn Abd al-Muṭṭalib about the new faith. To this al-ʿAbbās replied: 'He is Muḥammad ibn ʿAbdullāh. He thinks that Allah has sent him down with this faith. He claims that he would soon have control over the treasures of Roman and Persian empires.'[36]

When the Makkans unleashed persecution against the weak Makkan Muslims, some Companions were naturally disturbed and requested the Prophet (peace be upon him) to supplicate to Allah for defending them and for cursing the polytheists. They were keen on divine help and support. The Prophet (peace be upon him) urged them to practise perseverance and consistency, clarifying that the believers in earlier times were persecuted more harshly yet it did not deter them. They should not lose patience. He comforted and consoled them that Allah would help in accomplishing this mission, making Islam ascendant and propagating it in every part of the world. Islam would be so firmly placed in all the countries that a rider would travel from San'ā' to Ḥaḍramawt, without fearing anyone except Allah. They should not be impatient.[37]

The Quraysh chiefs and other enemies of Islam were dismayed at the success of the Prophet's mission and resorted to every possible move for frustrating him and for depriving him of the tribal protection he enjoyed. As part of this objective, the Quraysh chiefs had a series of meetings with the Banū Hāshim chief and the Prophet's guardian, Abū Ṭālib al-Hāshimī. Amid the issues discussed were the Islamic teachings, the Prophet's efforts and the Quraysh proposals for peace. However, the Prophet (peace be upon him) firmly reiterated that Islam would be dominant soon in the whole of Arabia, rather the entire world. Ibn Isḥāq has recounted the deliberations of the meeting of the third Quraysh delegation with Abū Ṭālib. After Ḥamzah's acceptance of Islam they called on Abū Ṭālib, who sent for the Prophet (peace be upon him). After listening to the Quraysh and Abū Ṭālib, the Prophet said: 'O Uncle! I present before you a message, by the acceptance of which you would be the rulers of the entire Arabia and the whole of non-Arabia would pledge obedience to you.'[38] Different wordings of the above statement by the Prophet (peace be upon him) appear in various reports. Common to all of these is the Prophet's assertion that Islam would soon gain ascendancy in the world.[39]

The Prophet (peace be upon him) met Abū Ṭālib when the latter was on his death bed. As on earlier occasions, the Prophet (peace be upon him) invited him in particular and the Quraysh chiefs present there to the message of Islam: 'I tell them to recite only one formula. On pronouncing it Arabs would be subservient to them and the same would fetch them *jizyah* from non-Arabs.'[40]

The Prophet (peace be upon him) contacted Arab tribes, asking them to embrace Islam and for seeking their help and support. For this end he visited Arab tribes in Ḥajj season. Bayharah ibn Firās, chief of Banū ʿĀmir ibn Ṣaʿṣaʿah said after meeting the Prophet: 'By God, If I sponsor this Qurayshī youth, I would devour the entire Arabia.' However, the Prophet (peace be upon him) declined his conditional offer of help. His condition was that he should inherit the rulership after the Prophet (peace be upon him). The latter refused to accept any such condition. He was not prepared to make anyone as his partner in rulership.[41]

When the Quraysh chiefs resolved at Dār al-Nadwah to assassinate the Prophet (peace be upon him), they were assembled for this evil act on the night the Prophet was to emigrate to Madīnah. At that time Abū Jahl said: 'Muḥammad says that if you follow him, you would assume the rulership of Arabia and the rest of the world. When you would be raised after your death, you would have gardens like those of Jordan. If you do not listen to him, he would cause killing and slaughtering among you and Hellfire would be prepared for you when you rise after death. You would be consigned to Hellfire.'[42] The narrator adds that the Prophet (peace be upon him) came out at that juncture. He had a bowl of dust in his hand and he said: 'Yes, I do say so. You would be in this condition.' Allah sealed their sight in that they could not see him. This report too, is indicative of the Prophet's warning to the Quraysh chiefs and of his enemies' affirmation of the same.[43]

Belief in the Veracity of the Prophet's Warnings

Even the Quraysh chiefs and other enemies of Islam did believe in the Prophet's honesty and truthfulness. They recognized also the truth of faith preached by him. For these reasons and in view of the Qur'ānic pronouncements they were afraid of his warnings. With their worldly knowledge and insights and of the implications of Islam they recognized that the Prophet (peace be upon him) is bound to be ascendant.[44] They were cognizant of the fact that the Prophet (peace be upon him) could not be suppressed and that he would be one day dominant over not just Arabia but the entire world. They wanted to leave him to his own in order to thwart his ultimate success. The following pieces of evidence support the above proposition.

1. With the consent of the Quraysh chief a leading Quraysh figure, ʿUtbah ibn Rabīʿah al-Asbshamī had a talk with the Prophet (peace be upon him) in order to resolve the contentious issue of Islam. He made three offers: (i) That the Prophet should give up preaching Islam. In response the Prophet (peace be upon him) recited verses 1-5 of *Sūrah Fuṣṣilat.* ʿUtbah reported back to the Quraysh that they should better follow the Prophet (peace be upon him). For he is blessed with great tidings.[45]
2. Once Abū Jahl tried to crush the Prophet's head with a stone. At that time Gabriel appeared before him in the form of an ostrich which terrified Abū Jahl and he returned. On listening to this account, a Quraysh leader al-Naḍr ibn al-Ḥārith al-ʿAbdarī advised the Quraysh to withdraw their charges of magic, sooth saying, poetry and madness against the Prophet (peace be upon him). He testified to the Prophet's pious character and asked the Quraysh to revise their stance. For great tidings were being conveyed to them.[46]
3. After finding out the signs of a genuine Messenger of God from Jewish rabbis the Quraysh chiefs posed before the Prophet (peace be upon him) questions about the people of the cave, Dhū'l-Qarnayn and the spirit. They were provided with a satisfactory reply about all these three in *Sūrah al-Kahf.* It brought home the veracity of the Prophet's message. However, their pride and jealousy prevented them from accepting Islam. They rather decided not to listen to the Qur'ān at all. For any debate with the Prophet (peace be upon him) would result only in his victory.[47]
4. After the revelation of *Sūrah al-Muddaththir* the Prophet remarked: 'I am an open warner.' An Arabic idiom it signifies the one who warns clearly and strives to do so. He warned the Quraysh against the terrible consequences of their rejection of the call to Islam.[48]

It is borne out by works on *tafsīr, ḥadīth*, *sīrah* and history that in 614-615 CE the Prophet (peace be upon him) and Muslims found life extremely difficult in Makkah. They were in such plight that around 100 helpless and victimized Muslims had to leave their homes and take refuge in a foreign land. *Sūrah al-Rūm* was sent down at that juncture. Its opening verses predict the following two major events:

a. The Roman's defeat against the Persian in only a blip. They would soon regain strength and overwhelm their enemy.
b. Muslims too are weak and subjugated presently. However, Allah would soon help them gain ascendancy.

We cannot discuss the whole historical context of the above two incidents. The Roman's defeat at the hands of the Persians had turned the event into a battle between Christians and Magians. The Makkan Quraysh were naturally inclined favourably towards the Persians for both of them were idolators. In contrast, Muslims sided with Christians in that both of them believed in divine revelation, Messengership and divine faith. The Makkan Quraysh threatened Muslims with obliteration like the Persians had devastated the Romans. In the given circumstance the victory of Muslims was unthinkable. However, the Prophet (peace be upon him) delivered the good news about the ultimate victory of the Romans. He also said that the Muslims' ascendancy was imminent.[49]

Rejoinder to the Quraysh Propaganda

The Quraysh chiefs and enemies of Islam carried out a propaganda war against Islam, the Prophet and the Muslim community. This move against the Muslim minority has always been adopted by anti-Islam elements. It is evident from the Qur'ān, *aḥādīth* and *sīrah* reports that in every age the Messengers and reformers have been opposed by mischievous sections of their own society. The Prophet (peace be upon him) had to face the malicious propaganda campaign in Makkah. Yet he responded vigorously to it. Rather,

Allah strongly refuted it in the Qur'ān. Muslims too, responded in both prose and poetry. The Arabs were proud of their poetic accomplishments. Both the Qur'ān and the Prophet (peace be upon him) were successful in countering this propaganda.

The Three-pronged Makkan Propaganda

(i) To denounce the Qur'ān and discredit it as the word of God, which would make people suspicious about its divine origin (ii) To oppose the Prophet and to deny his Messengership. To mock his humanness and to cast aspersions on him (iii) To launch a hostile campaign against the Muslim community and to dismiss it as the faith of the weaker, backward sections of the society.

There was not even an iota of truth in this propaganda campaign. However, the enemies of Islam knew it well that telling lies constantly would give them credence. However, they disregarded the obvious point that a lie cannot be taken as truth forever. Falsehood does not have any legs to stand on, irrespective of the fervour with which it is uttered. The Prophet (peace be upon him) and other preachers of faith recognized this point. Apart from presenting the message of truth they kept on refuting the false propaganda against Islam. They did so cogently and persuaded people of the truth. As a result, Islam spread far and wide. They expose the untruth of the propaganda.

a. Propaganda against the divine origin of the Qur'ān

That the Qur'ān is of divine origin is stressed repeatedly in the Qur'ān. Were one to cite the verses to this effect, it would fill this volume. Let us draw attention to only the main points. The Qur'ān first quotes the historical evidence that the Qur'ān represents the continuation of the divine revelation, sent down to Prophet Ādam, the first Messenger of Allah. Moreover, the Qur'ān confirms all earlier Scriptures. Thus the Qur'ān is the continuing link between earlier and final versions of divine message. A believer in the Qur'ān testifies to the truth of all the earlier Scriptures. This proves beyond any shadow of doubt that the Qur'ān is not the product of the human mind.[50]

The Quraysh chiefs and their ideologues realized that the Qur'ān is not the work of some human being. This explains why they listened to its recitation secretly and marvelled at it. They recognized its divine credentials. They were awe-struck on listening to it and forgot for the time being their silly charges against it. Faced with the miraculous beauty of the Qur'ān they found it hard to criticize it. For truth overtook them and its marvels left them spell-bound. Yet they resorted to the following false charges against the Qur'ān:

1. The Prophet (peace be upon him) is its author. The Qur'ān, however, refutes it stoutly and insists that it is divine in origin. The Qur'ān threw open a challenge to them that they should produce some verses like unto it, if they regard it as a work by some human being. The Quraysh claimed to be the most eloquent among Arabs and had mastery over Arabic language and literature. They were asked whether any of the marvels of the Qur'ān was to be found in any of their literary masterpieces. That the Qur'ān is in chaste Arabic is also brought home.[51]

2. The Qur'ān adduces two weighty arguments on this count. First, the Prophet (peace be upon him) had stayed in their midst for long. He was conversant with the literary style of the day. However, the Qur'ānic style is altogether different. In his day to day life when he engages in conversation, it has nothing in common with the Qur'ānic idiom. This in itself is a strong argument for the divine origin of the Qur'ān. Moreover, if it is the work of a human being, they should produce something similar to it. The Qur'ān proclaims that all men and jinns together cannot produce anything similar to the Qur'ān, what to say of composing the Qur'ān itself.

3. The Quraysh and other enemies of Islam claimed that the Qur'ān is composed by a Christian born and brought up in Makkah. The Qur'ān, however, points to his non-Arab credentials. Given this, he could not produce the Qur'ān which is in chaste Arabic. This was commonplace in everyone's knowledge.[52] The objections

against the Qur'ān had no substance. These were not supported by logic. For example, it was asked as to why the whole of the Qur'ān was not sent down at one time or why it was not sent to some leading Quraysh or why in Arabic, not some other language or why it contained tales of the ancient people. They dismissed the Qur'ān as a book full of parables and myths.[53]

b. Propaganda against the Prophet's character

Another major allegation of the Quraysh and other enemies of Islam was against the Prophet's claim to Messengership. For them, he was not a genuine Prophet. The same was done in relation to earlier Prophets. Even today the same false charge is pressed. The Qur'ān refutes the above charge and argues that he is a genuine Messenger. It specifies further that his message is directed at the entire humanity and for all time until the Last Day. He stands out as the final Messenger and Prophet and mercy unto all the worlds. His advent is foretold by earlier Messengers. Prior to assuming office he led a pious, unblemished life. His excellent conduct itself proves that he is a true Messenger. Earlier Scriptures testify to his appearance, a point known well to the religious scholars. Above all, the Qur'ān, the word of Allah testifies that he is a Messenger and Prophet.[54] Those indulging in propaganda could not counter any of these arguments or bits of evidence. They took to hurling other baseless charges. For example, they dubbed him as a poet and the Qur'ān containing only his ramblings. Then they accused him of a being a mad person, given to gibberish. They charged him with practising magic and that he cast a spell on one's speech and thinking faculties. Above all, they argued that he was only a mortal, unable to bring the divine message. They asked that he should produce angels or palpable miracles, which should set him apart from fellow human beings. They found it beyond them as to why he, not some outstanding member of the Quraysh, was selected for this august office. The Qur'ān takes up each of these baseless charges one by one and demolishes these superbly. It exposed the unbelievers in their true colours, given only to mischief-making and evil-doing.[55] Their allegations were exposed further when people listened to the Qur'ān, observed the Prophet's excellent conduct and his glorious face with halo and instantly recognized him as a genuine Messenger. For a liar could not possess such remarkable features or laudable traits.

Objection Against the Acceptance of Islam by the Poorer Sections of the Society

It has been an old practice to carry out the propaganda against the bearers of truth that their message is followed only by such who lack any position, authority or rank. As in the case of earlier Messengers, the Muslim community was dismissed as a motley of weaker, poorer people of the society. It was alleged that the community consisted only of poor, helpless and resourceless people. Given this, no member of the nobility could ever join it. The weapons of social disparity, class distinctions, material superiority, class conflict and political rivalries were used against Islam. The Quraysh chiefs condemned Islam as being the faith of only slaves, freed slaves and people belonging to weaker sections. They were dismissed as a backward people, without any social status or economic stability or cultural excellence.[56] Many Qur'ānic verses and *aḥādīth* make it plain that piety alone is the criterion of superiority and excellence. Social class does not confer greatness on anyone.[57]

The falseness of the Qurayshī propaganda against the Makkan Muslim community came to surface soon. For the majority of the Prophet's earliest followers were the Makkan Quraysh or members of other leading tribes. The Prophet (peace be upon him) himself came from a highly respectable and most outstanding family of Makkah. Shāh Walīullāh makes the point that Allah always selects His Messengers from noble families so that they are acceptable to the local people. Their higher social rank facilitates the spread of faith and the cause of truth.[58] The Muslim community represents mercy for the entire mankind. Members of noble families did accept it. People from weaker sections were also the members of the Muslim community. Men have divided themselves into noble and low classes and families. In Allah's sight the most respectable and beloved is he who is a true believer and a prominent bearer of truth.

CHAPTER 6

Defence Agreement

It was an important tradition in the Arabian tribal way of life that tribes entered into alliance with other tribes of their choice. They concluded political and military agreements. This organizing principle of the *Jāhiliyyah* period was followed in the Islamic era. For it ensured the safety of the life and property of weaker sections and tribes. In contrast, the law of the jungle is that the powerful usurp and devour weaker sections. Morally degenerate groups brazenly follow this practice of beasts. In the absence of any code of conduct the mighty ones oppress the weak. The same held true of Arabian tribal society. Tribal solidarity alone ensured their security. Each tribe made it a point to defend its members. An attack on the entire tribe however, posed a serious threat. To resolve this, tribes entered into agreements with one another. Some tribes formed an alliance which worked for their safety and security. By the same token, individuals or weak people sought a family's protection. As a result, each tribe had many patrons and allies. Political units were formed as parallel power structures against strong and large tribes.

As the Quraysh faced a formidable foe, they formed a political and military alliance with the powerful tribe of Banū Kinānah. As opposed to this, their foe was the ally of Qays ʿAylān and Hawāzin.

As ʿAbd al-Muṭṭalib ibn Hāshim faced a difficult situation, he had an alliance with Banū Khuzāʿah. He, however, did not include the other three members of the greater, united family of ʿAbd Manāf, namely Banū ʿAbd Shams/Banū Umayyah, Banū Nawfal and Banū Muṭṭalib. At a later date when the Prophet (peace be upon him) renewed this agreement in the Madīnan period after the Ḥudaybīyah treaty, he made all Muslims a party to it whereas the Quraysh established their alliance with Banū Bakr ibn ʿAbd Manāt. Such political and military agreements were the order of the day. Some of these were permanent, others casual and temporary. They easily changed their allies. Geo-political conditions and selfish interests played a key role in these agreements. Generally, however, these formed a permanent arrangement.[1]

The protection of life and property undergirded the Arab *Jāhiliyyah* tradition. Islamic society followed the same principle. The Prophet (peace be upon him) held dear the ideal of the security and safety of the community. He never compromised on this principle. The Qur'ān prescribes the norm that killing an individual amounts to killing the whole mankind and saving someone's life is equivalent to protecting the life of the entire humanity. The Qur'ān makes this point in the following instance: *al-Mā'idah* 5:32. The Prophet adopted this code of Arab tribal society for ensuring the safety of Muslim lives and property. In his personal capacity he secured the protection of Banū Hāshim. With Abū Ṭālib's death and loss of this protection, he got help and support from another family of Banū ʿAbd Manāf, Banū Nawfal. He enjoyed its protection all along his Makkan phase. Makkan Muslims generally had the support of their respective families. When they lost it, they secured it from other Quraysh families.[2]

Efforts for Alliance with Arabian Tribes

Sources on the *sīrah* indicate that on his return from the journey to Ṭā'if in 619 CE the Prophet, (peace be upon him) apart from presenting the message of Islam to Arab tribes, included this demand that they should take him to their territory and pledge to support and protect him. It was his intention for emigration. He aimed at selecting a place away from Makkah so that with the help of a powerful tribe he could preach Islam without any obstruction. It had the additional dimension of political and military significance. He was clearly guided in this matter by divine revelation. Even the astute tribal chiefs grasped its implications, as is evident from their response.[3]

It was not simply an issue of moving to another place or changing the headquarters of Islam. It was a step towards establishing the house of Islam, a centre, a political axis and a military base which would encompass not only the Makkan Quraysh, but also the whole of Arabia. Implicit in it was his plan to strike a severe blow to the might of the Quraysh. This point is borne out by the response given by the tribal chiefs. The Prophet's clarifications reinforce the point further. Significantly enough, the Prophet (peace be upon him) made the above proposal only to the most powerful tribes. Ibn Isḥāq endorses the above point.[4] Ibn Isḥāq, Ibn Hishām and other writers on the *sīrah* list the following strong Arab tribes whom the Prophet (peace be upon him) approached: 1) Kindah 2) Banū Ḥanīf 3) Banū Kalb/Quḍā'ah 4) Banū 'Abdullāh/Banū Kalb 5) Banū 'Āmir ibn Ṣa'ṣa'ah/Hawāzin/Qays 'Aylān 6) Banū al-Bakkā' 7) Banū Bakr ibn Wā'il 8) Banū Tha'labah ibn 'Ukābah 9) Banū Ḥanīfah/Banū Bakr ibn Wā'il 10) Banū al-Ḥārith ibn Ka'b/Banū Tamīm 11) Banū 'Abs/Qays 'Aylān 12) Banū 'Udhrah 13) Ghassān 14) Banū Salīm/Qays 'Aylān 15) Banū Fuzārah 16) Banū Muḥārib ibn Khaṣfah 17) Banū Shaybān.

We have already taken note of the Prophet's meeting with a leader of Banū 'Āmir ibn Ṣa'ṣa'ah. He had frankly expressed himself to the Prophet: 'What do you say? If we follow you in our faith and Allah makes you dominant over the enemies, would we get it after you?' He replied: 'The matter rests with Allah. He places it wherever He wills.' To this Shaykh al-'Āmirī replied: 'Even if we expose ourselves to the Arabs in protecting you, yet the position may go to someone else when you gain domination, thanks to

Allah. In this case we have no interest in your faith.'[5] Reports state that when the Shaykh returned to his tribe and one of the chiefs asked him about events in the Pilgrimage season, he mentioned the Prophet's offer and his response. That chief deeply regretted missing that offer and hailed the Prophet's message as truth.[6]

Ḥāfiẓ Yaḥyā ibn Saeed has recounted the Prophet's meeting with Banū Bakr ibn Wā'il. When the Prophet (peace be upon him) asked him about Persia's military power, the chief replied that they were no match to it. Nor could they offer any help in battle against Persia, for they were too weak. The Prophet (peace be upon him) told him: There would be a time when you would own their houses, marry their females and enslave their prisoners of war. Yet they did not respond positively to the Prophet's offer.[7] Almost the same happened in the Prophet's meeting with the Arab tribe Banū Shaybān ibn Tha'labah, that lived close to the Persian border: Their chiefs appreciated his message and thought of helping and supporting him. They, however, sought some time for considering seriously the offer to them. They realized that a clash with both the Persians and Makkan chief was likely in this event. They were not worried much about the Arabs. However, they already had an agreement with the Persians and they could not reach an independent decision. The Prophet (peace be upon him) had not asked their conditional help and support. He had given them glad tidings of the freedom from Persia. They decided to give their response after consultation. They declined the offer, though together with the Muslims they glorified and praised the Prophet (peace be upon him).[8] Banū 'Abs, a powerful tribe, was contacted every year by the Prophet (peace be upon him) in the Pilgrimage season. However, they never took his mission seriously. During his contact programme with leading Arab tribes the Prophet (peace be upon him) approached them again, seeking their help and support. Their chiefs refused to offer any help. One of them, Maysarah ibn Masrūq, however, told his fellow chiefs: 'You must help and support him and welcome him in your headquarters. For his mission is bound to be successful and ascendant.' They persisted in their refusal. At a later date, Maysarah accepted Islam and was appointed an official of Islamic state. However, his tribe could not attain any distinction. Nor did they help the Islamic state.[9]

War Agreement with Madinans

Early steps: It is against this political, military and religious backdrop that the Prophet's meeting with six Khazraj chiefs should be viewed. It was an ordinary event that six members of Khazraj tribe had accepted Islam. Rather, it signified their pledge for helping and supporting the cause of Islam. Conventional writers on the *sīrah* do not attach much significance to their acceptance of Islam.

In the eleventh year of the Prophet's mission i.e. in 620 CE the Prophet (peace be upon him) met the following six Khazraj chiefs:

1. Asʿad ibn Zurārah: Banū Taym Allāh ibn Banū Mālik. Al-Najjārī. Khazrajī.[10]
2. ʿAwf ibn Ḥārith ibn ʿAfrā': Banū Taym Allāh ibn Banū Mālik al-Najjārī. Al-Khazrajī.[11]
3. Rāfiʿ ibn Mālik: Banū Zurayq. Al-Khazrajī.[12]
4. Quṭbah ibn al-ʿĀmrī: Banū Salamah. Al-Khazrajī.[13] The Prophet later appointed him the head of an expedition against Khathʿam family.[14]
5. ʿUqbah ibn ʿĀmir: Banū Ḥizām. Al-Khazrajī[15]
6. Jābir ibn ʿAbdullāh: Banū ʿUbayd ibn ʿAdiyy. Al-Khazrajī.[16]

All the above were leading members of the community. Especially Asʿad ibn Zurārah who was reckoned as a very prominent chief. He enjoyed a top position in the social, political, tribal, community and military life of the day. It must also be borne in mind that the Aws and Khazraj chiefs were keen on entering into some agreement with the Quraysh. Their delegations arrived in Makkah for this purpose. The Khazraj delegation under discussion was part of the same design.[17] It is on record that when they met the Prophet (peace be upon him), the latter asked them whether they were the allies of Jews, a point acknowledged by them. On learning about the message of Islam they related the weakness of their tribe and their social divisions. Nonetheless, they expressed the hope that Allah might develop unity and solidarity amongst them through the Prophet's agency, which would save them from disgrace. This was stated also in their agreement with the Prophet (peace be upon him).[18] The above account does not project them in very good light. Yet they were chiefs of their respective families and tribes. Ibn Saʿd points to the weakness of the above report, though al-Wāqidī regards it as authentic and unanimous. Another report on the same subject relates that the Prophet (peace be upon him) had met the following eight persons of Madīnah – Muʿādh ibn ʿAfrā'; Asʿad ibn Zurārah (Banū al-Najjār); Rāfiʿ ibn Mālik and Dhakwān ibn ʿAbd Qays (Banū Zurayq); ʿUbaʿdah ibn al-Ṣāmit and Yazīd ibn Thaʿlabah (Banu Sulaym) and Abū al-Haytham ibn al-Ṭayhān al-Balwī (Banū ʿAbd al-Ashhal). When the Prophet (peace be upon him) presented before them the message of Islam, they accepted it. He asked them whether they would stand by him in carrying out his mission as the Messenger of Allah. They replied in the affirmative adding: 'You know that we fight among ourselves. At the beginning of the year we were engaged in a war. We are given to mire in civil war. If you visit us now, we would not be able to forge unity. Grant us one year's respite so that we persuade our family elders. May Allah bring peace among us. We promise to meet you the next year.'[19]

As part of this strategy the Prophet (peace be upon him) asked these chiefs both to accept Islam and extend him help and support. The latter demand provides internal evidence that they were tribal chiefs. For ordinary people were not in a position to pledge it. Nor did the Prophet (peace be upon him) ever approach commoners for such help and support.

The agreement was concluded at the second meeting at ʿAqabah and help was promised to the Prophet (peace be upon him). It was solemnized by seventy Madinan chiefs, not by ordinary persons. Ibn Saʿd clarifies that around five hundred members of Aws and Khazraj tribes had performed pilgrimage that year. Of them, seventy took the pledge. They were representatives of Aws and Khazraj tribes. The Prophet (peace be upon him) had secretly fixed a date and venue for this meeting. They were asked to visit him, without letting anyone know it.[20]

Asʿad ibn Zurārah was a prominent leader of Banū al-Najjār. Accordingly, the Prophet (peace be upon him) had appointed him the first chief of Madīnah. Such a position could not be conferred on an ordinary person. After his death, his office of Naqīb al-Nuqabā' was not granted to anyone. Rather, the Prophet (peace be upon him) himself held it. At the ʿAqaba pledge, when help and support was promised to the Prophet, Asʿad ibn Zurārah took a leading part. He was the first chief to enter the war agreement. ʿAwf ibn Mālik was the chief of Banū Mālik ibn Ghanam. His two brothers, Maʿūdh and Muʿādh are famous figures in Islamic history. All the three of them took part in the battle of Badr. In this battle between Islam and unbelief ʿAwf attained martyrdom in his bid to kill the Makkan chiefs Abū Jahl ibn Hishām al-Makhzūmī while the other two brothers succeeded in killing him. Maʿudh also became a martyr. This incident also indicates their prominent position.[21]

Although Rāfiʿ ibn Mālik was not a participant in the battle of Badr, his two sons, Rifāʿah and Khallad took part in it. They were known as al-Kummalah in view of their expertise as scribes and warriors. In the report recorded by Ibn Isḥāq and al-Wāqidī, Rāfiʿ features among the six earliest members of Khazraj who had called on the Prophet (peace be upon him). He was appointed the Naqīb of his tribe. The Prophet (peace be upon him) had selected Saʿīd ibn Zayd al-ʿAdawī, son of Zayd al-Ḥanīf and brother-in-law of ʿUmar, as his brother-in-faith. He attained martyrdom in the battle of Uḥud.[22]

Quṭbah ibn ʿĀmir too, took part in the battle of Badr. He was an outstanding warrior and a prominent chief. On the day of the conquest of Makkah he carried the banner of his family, Banū Salamah. He was appointed head of an expedition in 9 AH against Banū Khaytham. His leadership was widely acclaimed.[23]

ʿUqbah ibn ʿĀmir was the chief of Banū Hārāmand a participant in the battle of Badr. He participated in other battles as well. According to *ḥadīth,* the Prophet had appointed him as *Zakāh* official. He performed many other duties in the Prophet's day.[24]

Jābir ibn ʿAbdullāh al-ʿUbaydī was the chief of his family, Banū ʿUbayd. He took part in the battle of Badr, was the Prophet's close associate and well-versed in the Qur'ān and *ḥadīth. Aḥādīth* works contain a wealth of details about him and also throw light on his social rank, scholarship and religious fervour.[25] The significance of his visit to Makkah and of his acceptance of Islam is underlined by his major role and his study of its implications. He was an ally of the Jews. His rival Banū Aws used to visit Makkah for seeking alliance with the Quraysh of Makkah or someone else. The Khazraj resolved to counter this alliance activity of the Aws and their delegations tried to secure the Quraysh help and support. These six Khazraj chief had the same objective in mind. On coming across the Prophet's message, their response had military, political and religious overtones. They had alliance with the Jews because the latter were entrenched deep in their home town and enjoyed an all-round supremacy. They were reduced to be dependents upon the Jews and suffered oppression at their hands. The Jews had provoked them into fighting against their own brethren, the Aws and both the tribes were after each other's blood. It caused disunity among them. They realized all along the Jewish hegemony. Having lived in the company of Jews they were aware of the Jewish belief about the promised Messenger. They had come across the Jewish threat that after the advent of the promised Messenger, they would destroy Arabs in the manner the people of ʿĀd and Iram were extirpated earlier. They therefore had the mutual consultation: 'You know well that he is the honoured Messenger against whom Jews threaten you. Let them not precede you. Let you accept Islam first.' Accordingly they embraced Islam and submitted to the Prophet (peace be upon him): 'We have left behind our people who are given to mutual rivalry and evil. We hope Allah would enable you to bring peace among them. We would return to them and invite them to your message which we have already accepted. If Allah unites them on this, you would enjoy great honour among us.'[26]

These six or eight Khazrajī chiefs of Madīnah perceived clearly the universal dimensions of Islam and its potentials as a social, political and military force. On preaching Islam in Madīnah, they highlighted all these features. Apart from addressing their own tribesmen they contacted their foe, Banū Aws and conveyed to them the message of a religious and political alliance. They sought to unite all Arabs round the banner of Islam. Notwithstanding all their differences with Khazraj, Banū Aws responded positively and accepted the offer. Were they to act only on their tribal instincts, they must have rejected it outright. For they would not have paid any heed to their enemy's proposition and would have preferred to form their own front. Far from acting thus, they entered into a social, political and religious alliance with their foe and as a result, the whole of Madīnah extended help and support to the Prophet (peace be upon him). The next year, among the twelve representatives of Madīnah, three Aws chiefs also figured.[27]

Agreement for War and Support

In 621 CE twelve chiefs of both Aws and Khazraj called on the Prophet (peace be upon him) in Makkah after Pilgrimage. Of them, ten were chiefs of Khazraj and two of Aws.

A. Khazrajī chiefs
   1. Asʿad ibn Zurārah, Abū Umāmah, chief of Banū al-Najjār/Banū Mālik.
   2. ʿAwf ibn al-Ḥārith ibn ʿAfrā', chief of Banū al-Najjār/Banū Mālik.
   3. Muʿādh ibn al-Ḥārith ibn ʿAfrā', Banū al-Najjār/Banū Mālik.
   4. Rāfiʿ ibn Mālik, chief of Banū Zurayq.
   5. Dhakwān ibn ʿAbd Qays, chief of Banū Zurayq, emigrant to Madīnah who stayed in Makkah until the emigration.

6. ʿUbādah ibn al-Ṣāmit, head of Banū Ghanam ibn ʿAwf/ Quwāqil.
7. Yazīd ibn Thaʿlabah, Abū ʿAbd al-Raḥmān, chief of Banū Ghanam ibn ʿAwf/Quwāqil, Balawī Ḥanīf.
8. Al-ʿAbbās ibn ʿUbādah, chief of Banu Sulaym ibn ʿAwf.
9. ʿUqbah ibn ʿĀmir, chief of Banū Salamah/Banū Harim ibn Kaʿb.
10. Quṭbah ibn ʿĀmir, chief of Banū Sawād ibn Ghanam/ Banū Salamah.

B. Aws Chiefs

11. Mālik ibn al-Ṭayham, Abū'l-Haytham, chief of Banū ʿAbd al-Ashhal.
12. ʿUwaym ibn Sāʿidah, chief of Banū ʿAmr ibn Awf/Aws.

Significantly enough, five of these twelve Madīnan chiefs had pledged their support to the Prophet (peace be upon him) earlier. The rest had representatives from Aws as well. They too, pledged their allegiance to him. Included in this pledge of Nisa was the observance of morals, goodness and obedience.[28] The actual agreement was concluded the next year in 622 CE when seventy-five Madīnan representatives pledged their help and support to Islam and the Prophet (peace be upon him). They promised the following: 1) They would take the Prophet to their town 2) They would obey him in every matter 3) They would defend him as their own family members 4) They would fight against those whom the Prophet engages in war. They would be a party also to his peace agreements.

The Aws and Khazraj, however, apprehended like other Arab chiefs, that after gaining power, the Prophet (peace be upon him) would return to Makkah. They were more concerned, for by then their alliance with the Jews would have ended and after the Prophet's return they would have to face the Jews in war. The Prophet (peace be upon him), however, assured them of his total help and cooperation thus: 'Your blood is my blood. I would be bound by your peace agreements. My alliance with you is firm. I am ours and you are mine. I would fight against him with whom you war. I would enter into a peace treaty with your allies.'[29] Prior to the conclusion of the agreement some Madīnan chiefs vented their apprehension, saying that it amounted to waging war against everyone. In other words, they pledged their support to the Prophet (peace be upon him) in the full knowledge of its consequences and implications.[30] Among those who were a party to this agreement were Usayd ibn Ḥuḍayr al-Awsī, Salamah ibn Sulāmah al-Awsī, Abū Tayham al-Awsī, Zuhayr ibn Rāfiʿ al-Awsī, Saʿd ibn Khaythamah al-Awsī, Rifāʿah ibn ʿAbd al-Mundhir al-Awsī and ʿAbdullāh ibn Jubayr al-Awsī. The prominent Khazrajī chiefs were: Abū Ayyūb al-Anṣarī, Asʿad ibn Zurārah, sons of Afrā', Sahl ibn ʿAtiq, Khārijah ibn Zayd, ʿAbdullāh ibn Rawāḥah, Bashīr ibn Saʿd, Abū'l-Nuʿmān ibn Bashīr, Ziyād ibn Labīd, al-Barā' ibn Maʿrūr, Bishr ibn al-Barā', Kaʿb ibn Mālik, ʿAbdullāh ibn Harim, al-ʿAbbās ibn ʿUbādah, Saʿd ibn ʿUbādah etc.[31]

Ibn Saʿd's report makes it plain that all of them were influential persons. The meeting opened with the following words by al-ʿAbbās ibn ʿAbd al-Muṭṭalib al-Hāshimī: 'Muḥammad is honoured and safe in his family, irrespective of the point that his family members may not have accepted his message. However, he has preferred you to others. If you have power, military machinery and the resolve to fight, and can take the risk of a united attack by all the Arabs, you may take him to Madīnah. Have mutual consultation and think carefully. Do not fall prey to disunity.' Al-Barā' ibn Maʿrūr al-Khazrajī was the first to respond: 'O Messenger of Allah! We have taken the pledge. We do have arms which we have inherited for generations.'[32] The Prophet (peace be upon him) had discussion with select chiefs, including the twelve nuqabā'.[33]

The right to live in one's home town has been universally recognized. One is free to live in the town and country of his birth and of his parents and grandparents. This concept of motherland has less to do with one's faith or language. For these might vary. The deciding factor is one's birth place.

The idea of birth place was central to the concept of nationalism in Makkan and Madīnan societies and the tribal network of the Prophet's day. It is worth stating, however, that Bedouins being nomads did not have any home town. They moved from place to place in search of food and water. They settled down wherever they managed to get both of these. Their nomadic way of life was recognized. Often did these Bedouins clash with each other over a suitable spot of settlement. Whoever won had control over the place while the defeated party moved to some other spot or contracted a truce with the stronger party.

The Arabs settled in towns, however, did not face any such problem. As they were blessed with sufficient supply of food and water, they lived in their respective villages or towns. Makkah had been founded by Prophet Abraham. Prophet Ishmael and his mother Hājirah had lived there. Banū Jurhum and other tribes settled in Makkah and took it as their home town in view of their kinship with Prophet Abraham. Banū Ismāʿīl were entrusted with the custody of the Kaʿbah and the zamzam well.

The Quraysh's claim to Makkah as their home town rested on the fact that they had lived there for ages. Other tribes, guilty of evil deeds, were removed from office and expelled from Makkah. However, the Quraysh did not drive away any of their members or family, regardless of the crime they committed. Quraysh al-Ẓawāhir were, no doubt, settled at some distance from the Kaʿbah while al-Baṭḥā' were closer to it. However, it was in relation to their relative political power, especially of the Quraysh al-Baṭḥā' chief, Quṣayy ibn Kilāb. This arrangement was political and reflected the ascendancy of Quraysh al-Baṭḥā'.

The Prophet (peace be upon him) was a distinguished member of Quraysh al-Baṭḥā' and a descendent of the family entrusted with the custodianship of the Kaʿbah. Like any other member of the Quraysh he had every right to live in Makkah. Even some non-Arabs had secured the right to live there by dint of their agreements with the Quraysh. Some of them had been there for generations. Take for example, Bilāl, a non-Makkan who was a resident there.

Even after the public call to Islam the Prophet (peace be upon him) and Companions had the right to live in Makkah, which was not challenged by the enemies of Islam.

As some foreigners accepted Islam, the Prophet (peace be upon him) adopted the strategy of sending them back to their territories, though some of them loved to stay in Makkah. There were many considerations behind the decision to send back these new Muslims. It would not delink them from their own people. Otherwise, it would have created many social problems. They could face emotional and psychological complexities in addition to political, social and cultural problems. Moreover, staying in another town on account of the change in faith could give rise to further complications. Being cut off from their home land they would have been deprived of their right to live in their birth place. They would not have enjoyed such economic opportunities which were available to them in their ancestral country. They would have to structure their economy anew. Culturally too, they would have been separated from their language, customs and family traditions. More importantly, the Prophet (peace be upon him) sent them back after imparting them necessary knowledge and training for preaching Islam directly and indirectly in their respective areas. As a result, a new community of Muslims came into existence, as is borne out by the acceptance of non Makkans or Bedouin Arab tribes.

After Abū Dharr al-Ghifārī accepted Islam, the Prophet (peace be upon him) directed him to return to his people and instruct them until the Prophet gave him another directive.[34] According to Ibn Ḥajar, he was directed to join the Prophet (peace be upon him) on learning about the ascendancy of Islam. The Prophet's directive is interpreted in the above sense by some scholars.

ʿAmr ibn ʿAbasah Al-Azdī accepted Islam at an early date. He was also directed by the Prophet (peace be upon him) to return home and rejoin him when Islam is triumphant. Accordingly he returned and kept on preaching Islam. He was in constant touch with the Prophet (peace be upon him) so that he could rejoin him at a suitable time.[35] Ḍamād ibn Thaʿlabah, an influential member of

Azd tribe was the Prophet's friend in the *Jāhiliyyah* period and his trade partner. According to reports, he came to Makkah after several years and learnt about the Prophet's mission and called on him. In accordance with the Prophet' advice he went back to his people and invited them to Islam.[36] That he returned after several years or that he came to know of the new message is not plausible. For, being a trader he often visited Makkah and being the Prophet's friend, he kept on meeting him. Ibn Kathīr adds that he had given the pledge to the Prophet (peace be upon him) on behalf of his people.

In the Makkan period Ṭufayl ibn ʿAmr al-Dawsī embraced Islam and returned to his tribe on the Prophet's advice. He preached Islam among them and converted many individuals and groups. However, as his tribe was reluctant to embrace Islam *en masse*, he called on the Prophet (peace be upon him) in Makkah and requested him to pronounce a curse upon his tribe. However the Prophet, being a mercy unto the worlds, prayed to Allah that his whole tribe be guided to Islam. Allah accepted his supplication and around eighty families entered the fold of Islam.[37]

Ashajj and his nephew of ʿAbd al-Qays tribe accepted Islam in Makkah and returned home.

Emigration

At the time of the Prophet's advent, leaving home and emigration were not on his agenda. While bearing out the divine revelation sent down to the Prophet, (peace be upon him) Waraqah ibn Nawfal predicted that Makkans would expel him. This had astonished the Prophet that one day his own people would drive him away.[38]

While recounting al-Suhaylī's elucidation of the above report Ibn Ḥajar relates that Waraqah's observation had disturbed the Prophet (peace be upon him) that he would be driven away from his home town. Waraqah's prediction makes mention of the emigration undertaken by earlier Messengers. This point was not very clear to the Prophet (peace be upon him) in the early stage of his career. As *sūrahs* were revealed to him in Makkah, recounting the stories of earlier Messengers and their emigration, he realized that he and his Companions were destined for it. The stories of Prophets reinforced his conviction.

The account of Messengers' Emigration in Makkan Sūrahs

- Prophet Abraham's emigration (*Ibrāhīm* 14:37 and *al-Anbiyā'* 21:71).
- Prophet Lot's emigration (*al-ʿAnkabūt* 29:26).
- Prophet Moses's emigration (*al-Qaṣaṣ* 28:21; *al-Aʿrāf* 7:138; *Yūnus* 10:90; *al-Shuʿarā'* 26:52 and other verses).

Emigration to Abyssinia

The first role model of emigration is afforded by the emigration to Abyssinia in the Makkan period. Its geographical and religious significance is that the Makkan Muslim minority was asked to move to a non-Muslim territory, delinking itself from the Makkan Quraysh society. In other words, Muslims were allowed to live as a minority in a non-Muslim country. These emigrants had the unenviable status of the minority in both Makkah and Abyssinia. Yet there was one marked difference. In their birth place they were not free to practise the faith of their choice. Rather, they were subject to persecution at the hands of their own kith and kin. They did not have any social security or status. The minority community had made their life miserable. It was hard for them to practise their faith. In contrast, in the just and peaceful state of Abyssinia ruled by the Christian king they enjoyed the protection of life, honour and property. They were not subject to any harassment in discharging their religious duties. In the company of strangers they were fully secure and blessed with social justice.

The consideration behind the emigration to Abyssinia was that the Muslim minority, which is not free to act on its faith, should emigrate to a just, non-Muslim country. This was the Prophet's directive to the Makkan Muslims and emigrants to Abyssinia.[39]

Bukhārī cites the following *ḥadīth* on 'Ā'ishah's authority. When people asked her about emigration, she replied: 'Today there is no longer any emigration. Earlier, a Muslim emigrated in the cause of his faith and Allah lest he may fall prey to some mischief.'[40]

Elucidating the above, Ibn Ḥajar states that emigration is conditional, subject to the fear of mischief. Every command has a cause. Therefore, if one is able to worship at his place, he is not obliged to emigrate. Imām al-Māwardī brings home the same point thus: 'If one is able to express and practise his faith in a town of the land of unbelief, that town constitutes for him the land of Islam. Therefore, it is better to stay there than emigrate. For it is expected that others would embrace Islam there.' Imām al-Khaṭṭābi maintains: 'In the early period of Islam it was desirable to emigrate towards the Prophet (peace be upon him). After his emigration to Madīnah it was obligatory on Muslims to join him, participate in fighting and killing along with him and learn Islamic practices and commands.' With reference to many Qur'ānic verses and *aḥādīth* Ibn Ḥajar explicates the above point.[41]

Let this point be realized regarding the emigration to Abyssinia that the Prophet (peace be upon him) had allowed the distressed Muslims to emigrate. It was not his command. Rather, it was a way out, for saving his family members against the persecution unleashed by the Quraysh. Those who availed themselves of this leave left for Abyssinia and lived in peace under the patronage of the justice-loving Christian king of Abyssinia. They stayed there until their condition improved. Despite the Prophet's permission many Muslims, both Quraysh and non-Quraysh, did not opt for the emigration and preferred to bear with the oppression along with the Prophet (peace be upon him). It would be unrealistic to assume that the Muslim population of Makkah had reduced considerably after the emigration to Abyssinia. Many Muslims, outnumbering the emigrants, still stayed in Makkah along with the Prophet (peace be upon him).

Another significant point implicit in the emigration was that it was a temporary move. They had not gone there to settle down. It was the Prophet's advice, which the emigrants had imbibed, that they should move for the time being and return home as soon as conditions improve. This point is evident in the reports of the day and was confirmed by later events.

A few months after the emigration, these emigrants received the report that the Makkan chiefs had accepted Islam. Immediately they returned home. On reaching Jeddah they realized that it was a false report. Many of them returned to Abyssinia. However, a large number of them secretly made their way into Makkah and they started living under the Quraysh's protection. This was, no doubt, of much relief for them. However, it did not put an end to their persecution. They still suffered on account of professing their faith. Even their return to Makkah makes their emigration no less desirable. Some of these emigrants later emigrated to Madīnah. Reports state that many of them returned from Abyssinia to Makkah and then emigrated to Madīnah while some went directly from Abyssinia to Madīnah. For by then the Prophet too had emigrated to Madīnah.

Emigration to Madīnah

In contrast to the emigration to Abyssinia, the emigration to Madīnah is much more important and of far-reaching social, cultural and religious implications. The first and foremost point is that Allah had directly revealed the command for emigration to Madīnah. The leave for migrating to Abyssinia, no doubt, rested on the Prophet's advice which he had derived from revelation. Yet it did not point to Allah's sovereignty. Regarding the emigration to Madīnah the Prophet (peace be upon him) pointedly spoke of divine command. Bukhārī and other *ḥadīth* scholars report that the Prophet (peace be upon him) said: 'I saw in a dream emigrating from Makkah to a land full of date palm trees. I thought it was an allusion to Yamāmah or al-Ḥijr. However, it turned out to be Madīnah.'[42] It is important to establish the date of this divine command. For it is central to the concept of emigration and the divine command for it. Reports indicate that this dream was shown to the Prophet (peace be upon him) after the emigration to Abyssinia. He saw in the dream the new land of emigration, which was certainly different from Abyssinia. Writers on *sīrah* generally hold that it happened after the second pledge of ʿAqabah, as is evident from Ibn Saʿd's report.[43] However, it appears from a report cited by Ibn Kathīr that after Abū Dharr al-Ghifārī's acceptance of Islam, the Prophet (peace be upon him) said that he was sent towards a land full of date palm trees, which can only be Madīnah. He asked Abū Dharr: 'Would you preach, on my behalf, Islam among your people so that they benefit from you and you earn reward for them.'[44]

Balādhurī clarifies that this divine command was received after the return of the seventy Madīnans. For Makkan Muslims had sought the permission for emigration on account of the persecution they faced from the Quraysh. He, however, asked them to wait until a divine command was issued. Soon after that he mentioned the above dream of his. The report makes the additional observation that the Companions' emigration to Madīnah had lasted for a year. Another clarification, based on historical evidence, is more significant. Muṣʿab ibn ʿUmayr al-ʿAbdarī had emigrated to Madīnah after the ʿAqabah pledge. All reports describe him as the first emigrant. The next in order were Ibn Umm Maktūm and Abū Salamah al-Makhzūmī, who had gone there, one after another, in quick succession. About Mukarram, Ibn Isḥāq reports that he had emigrated a year before the ʿAqabah pledge. For on his return from Abyssinia, his Qurayshī relatives tormented him. Since his brother was in Madīnah, he went there. He left in such haste that he did not take his family, who joined him later. Umm Salamah's account also refers to the one year period of emigration.[45]

Ibn Ḥajar further clarifies that Abū Salamah had emigrated after the return of the twelve Anṣār coinciding with the first pledge. Ibn Ḥajar also maintains that Muṣʿab had emigrated for settlement in Madīnah and for educating Muslims there at the Prophet's command. In contrast, Abū Salamah had gone there, fleeing from the polytheists. This distinction is academic. The fact of the matter is that both of them had emigrated. It is unthinkable that Abū Salamah went without the Prophet's leave. His intention was not to secure settlement in Madīnah. This point comes out from several *aḥādīth*. He is reckoned as one of the earliest emigrants.[46]

One should therefore take the Prophet's dream about emigration and about Madīnah as their destination at a time before the first pledge of ʿAqabah i.e. around 620 CE. It is likely that he was shown the dream much earlier about emigration while the one specifying Madīnah was shown in the period of the ʿAqabah pledge. This view is more plausible and in line with historical records.

The issue of the land of emigration was linked with the demand for providing help and support to the Prophet (peace be upon him). The Arab tribes paid no heed to it. Those who responded set their own conditions. However, the Khazraj chiefs accepted the demand and sought some respite for consulting their tribesmen. The next year they endorsed the agreement. This was the deciding factor regarding the specification of the land of emigration. The Prophet (peace be upon him) had seen the dream earlier, perhaps after his return from Ṭā'if when he demanded of the Arab tribes help and support.

Chronologically, the first divine suggestion for emigration was made to the Prophet (peace be upon him) in 615 CE. Accordingly the emigration to Abyssinia was experimented. It was not, however, a fit place for permanent emigration for many reasons. First of all, it was a foreign land whereas the emigration was to be sited somewhere in Arabia. Through his true dream the Prophet (peace be upon him) was shown the place of emigration, full of oases. He first thought of Yamamah or al-Ḥijr. However, both of these were border areas remotely linked with Arab tribes. They were not central locations while a central place was essential for striking a deadly blow to the arrogant Quraysh. Madīnah was suited best for it. Madīnah was identified as the place in the Prophet's dream in the tenth year of the Prophet's career after his agreement with Khazrajī chiefs about their help and support.

In seeking help and support from Arab tribes, specifying Madīnah as the land of emigration and in the gradual unfolding of these events the same considerations were at work which lie at the heart of the gradual revelation of the Qur'ān and phases of the Prophet's mission. It was not easy for Makkan Muslims to leave their birth place and go somewhere else. They were not emotionally prepared for it. Apart from their natural attachment to their home town, they were bound to Makkah because of the Kaʿbah. They were, however, trained gradually for this eventuality to sacrifice their homeland in the cause of Allah. The temporary emigration to Abyssinia readied them for it, reinforcing their desire to sacrifice.

The most serious complication involving the emigration to Madīnah was that it spelled, permanent settlement at another place, far away from their home town. This was not so in the case of the emigration to Abyssinia. It had the prospect of returning home. And this came true as well. However, the emigration to Madīnah was a permanent move. There was no chance of returning home. At most, they could return as pilgrims in a strange land as strangers. The Prophet (peace be upon him) was so much overwhelmed by these emotions that he uttered the following moving words: 'O Makkah! There is no town dearer than you for me. However, your chiefs do not let me live here.'[47] According to Imām Bukhārī, while praying for the end to an epidemic in Madīnah the Prophet (peace be upon him) made this touching supplication: 'O Allah! Endear Madīnah to us as Makkah was dear to us. Rather, make it dearer for us.'[48] This emotional tie was not special to the Prophet (peace be upon him) and Qurayshī Muslims in view of their centuries – long association with Makkah. Even a foreigner like Bilāl was closely attached to Makkah. He found it hard to reconcile to the thought of leaving Makkah. He composed sorrowful couplets, cried and expressed his anguish. Unable to bear with it, he exploded against the Quraysh chiefs for forcing him to leave Makkah. Bukhārī has cited some of his couplets: 'I wish I had known that I would never spend a night in a valley abounding in such fragrant grass. Would I ever be able to reach the Majannah spring? Would I ever again see the Shāmah and Ṭufayl hillocks?'[49] On the authority of "*Kitab al-Haj*", Ibn Hajr has cited Bilal's curse: 'O Lord! Drive them away from Your mercy as they have expelled us from our home town.' Ibn Ḥajar's interpretation is sound that Bilāl uttered these words on feeling the pain of exile. However, it refers also to the land of epidemics i.e. Madīnah. With the Prophet's supplication the epidemics ended, restoring Madīnah as a clean, healthy town. The persecuted emigrants naturally lamented their exile. Even the oppressive Quraysh were sad over it, as it was expressed by them on various occasions. Since the victims were their own kith and kin, they felt it strongly; Muslims had bright prospects about their emigration. It could help them attain ascendancy and victory. Having undergone subjugation and persecution for long, Muslims saw a glimmer of hope. Implicit in it was the possibility that they would be able to accomplish their faith and Sharia'h. They could freely uphold there the word of Allah and work for their political, social and military strength. They were promised by Allah their return to Makkah as victors. Yet, their permanent departure from Makkah saddened them. It always tormented them. They reconciled to it out of deference to Allah's command, for the sake of their faith and out of their love for the Prophet (peace be upon him). For these goals, they could sacrifice even what was dearest to them.

CHAPTER 7

Muslim Mionorities After the Formation of the Islamic State

After the Prophet's emigration to Madīnah, the Islamic society in Madīnah was reorganized and a dominant Muslim majority emerged there.[1] Established between 622 and 632 CE the Islamic state of Madīnah gradually embraced the entire Arabian Peninsula and gained control over the whole of Arabia. All Arab tribes acknowledged, one after another, its political, religious and military supremacy. The Muslim community emerged as the ruler, ascendant, sovereign and strong.[2]

Until the control over the Peninsula, Muslim minorities lived as usual in their respective areas, as was the case in the Makkan phase. The most telling instance is of the Muslim minority in Makkah. It is generally believed in the light of observations made by some writers on *sīrah* that after the Prophet's emigration no Muslims were left in Makkah and all of them had emigrated. This is not true. This Muslim minority had been studied little. Scant information is available about its role and activities. Some speak in a general sense of their plight, as reported in primary sources.[3] Since even Makkah the Muslim minority has not been studied by conventional writers on *sīrah*, little is reported about the Muslim minority groups in other Arabian towns. The truth is that there flourished Muslim minorities in various regions, villages, towns, tribes, families and nooks and corners of Arabia. They had this status until their areas became part of the Islamic state. They were forced, prior to this, to live as helpless, dependent minorities in a non-Muslim region.[4] The same holds true for the Muslim minority in Abyssinia. Writers on the *sīrah* have paid little attention to it. Only a few incidents related to it, as featuring in primary sources, are recounted. One, however, gets no idea as to how this minority managed to survive in a non-Muslim dominated society.

Makkan Muslim Minority after the Prophet's Emigration

From Monday, 12 Rabīʿ al-Awwal 53rd year of the Prophet's birth, corresponding to 24 September 622, the day of his emigration to Madīnah, to 20 Ramaḍān 8/11 January 630, the day of Makkah's conquest, a large number of Muslims stayed on in Makkah. They represented a Muslim minority, closely akin to the one that was the lot of the Prophet (peace be upon him) and his Companions before the emigration. Rather, the former were in a worse condition as they were reduced in number. For around eight years they had to face a very difficult life there.

What demoralized them most was that they were deprived of the company and guidance of their master and leader. It was an irreparable loss politically, socially and religiously. It was a severe psychological blow. They had to bear also the loss of the company of other Muslims, their love and affection and the sense of security. When they were more in number and had been united by their strong bond of fraternity, they enjoyed the fruits of community life, solidarity and social order. They had gained some social ranking. Likewise, they were somewhat politically important. Their economy had improved. In summary, in religious and cultural domains they were better placed. With the Prophet's emigration they lost all of it. Religiously they were reduced to a miserable lot. The tribal instincts of the Quraysh and their stiff opposition to Islam wreaked havoc on them. They were exposed to numerous challenges. Notwithstanding all this, the Makkan Muslim minority survived and strove for its existence. It was due to their religious fervour. They maintained their identity until the conquest of Makkah and the establishment of Islamic state. It was an enviable achievement on their part. There were many factors responsible for it. The Makkan protection system as followed by the Quraysh society helped them greatly.

The Makkan Muslim minority of the post-emigration period had several groups and sections. Tribal divisions were at work among them. They were divided in various social groups. Sections among them had emerged for a variety of reasons. They differed from one another in terms of their practising faith. All Muslims of Makkah were not placed in an identical situation. It would be rather unrealistic to assume so. It is important to analyze their different sections for a better appreciation of their problems and condition.

Muslim Prisoners

The worst was the lot of those Muslims who had been taken as prisoners by their own kith and kin. They were confined to prisons or cells inside houses, often in fetters and handcuffs. Sources on *sīrah* indicate that such imprisonment had started in the middle of the Makkan phase and in the Prophet's presence. However, it was often a temporary step as Muslims or even non-Muslim chiefs helped secure their release. Some of them escaped and migrated to Abyssinia.[5] Khālid ibn Saʿīd al-Umawī was imprisoned by his father. It was not an isolated case. Works on *sīrah* and *ḥadīth* cite many instances of the injustice inflicted by the Quraysh chiefs on Muslims.

Some Abyssinian emigrants faced the same ordeal on their return. However, they were imprisoned or placed under house arrest for a short time. After the emigration to Madīnah, however, the situation changed altogether. Many members of the Muslim community were forced to suffer imprisonment at the hands of their own relatives. For there was no one to look after them. Abū Jandal al-Sahmī was imprisoned for years by his father, Ṣuhayl ibn ʿAmr, an influential Makkan chief. For seven years he had no protector. Apart from other sufferings, he was kept in fetters and was denied food and drink. While discussing the conditions of the Ḥudaybīyah peace treaty Imām Bukhārī writes about Abū Jandal that he was severely persecuted in Allah's way. Somehow he fled from his prison and appeared before the Muslims in a miserable condition while the clauses of the treaty were being drafted. It was a moving scene that shook the Muslims. Even ʿUmar, otherwise a brave and well-poised person, lost balance on witnessing his plight. For years Abū Jandal had been facing his father's cruelty.[6] According to Ibn Ḥajar, Abū Jandal was confined to Makkah and prevented from emigrating to Madīnah. He was punished mercilessly for having embraced Islam. Ibn Isḥāq clarifies that Abū Jandal's own father had made him a captive. ʿUrwah and Abū al-Aswad too, relate that Ṣuhayl ibn ʿAmr had put fetters on his son for his crime of accepting Islam. He somehow fled and joined the Muslims. This was not, however, the end of his ordeal. In line with the clause of the Ḥudaybīyah treaty the Prophet (peace be upon him) had to return him, for his father Ṣuhayl ibn ʿAmr had drawn this condition. It was an intensely painful situation. He had to suffer captivity for some more time.[7]

ʿAbdullāh, a brother of Abū Jandal ʿAmr ibn Ṣuhayl ibn ʿAmr al-Sahmī, was also imprisoned for some time. He, however, managed to migrate to Abyssinia. However, when he returned to Makkah on getting the report that the Makkans had accepted Islam, his unbelieving father imprisoned him along with Abū Jandal. Until the battle of Badr in 2/624 he was in his father's captivity.[8]

Abū Baṣīr ʿUtbah ibn Usayd al-Thaqafī was an ally of Banū Zahrah of the Quraysh. After accepting Islam he parted ways with his people and the Quraysh, and this landed him into serious trouble. He too, was imprisoned. He had no supporter in Makkah. No authentic details are on record about his acceptance of Islam and the period of his imprisonment. What is certain is that like Abū Jandal he too, was in prison a little after the Ḥudaybīyah treaty in 6/628.[9]

Many Muslims, who were allies to the Quraysh, had to face imprisonment for long in Makkah. Some of them were those

Muslim men and women who had been arrested during the Prophet's emigration to Madīnah. Some were the Abyssinian emigrants who were imprisoned on their return to Makkah. It is quite a task to compile an account of all these captives. Some of them, however, deserve mention in order to indicate the hardship these representatives of the Muslim minority had to suffer in the captivity of the Quraysh after the Prophet's emigration.

Abū Jahl al-Makhzūmī's real brother Salamah ibn Hishām was imprisoned by his brother on his return from Abyssinia. For more than six years until the battle of the Trench in 5/627 he suffered imprisonment.[10] Abū Jahl's other brother, ʿAyyāsh ibn Rabīʿah al-Makhzūmī was forced into returning to Makkah on the false report of his mother's illness while he was on his way to Madīnah. He was imprisoned in Makkah and treated unjustly. Reports indicate the deceit employed in imprisoning him. His captivity too, lasted for many years. He secured his freedom in the battle of Uḥud in 3/625.[11]

Hishām ibn al-ʿĀṣ al-Sahmī, a friend of ʿUmar ibn al-Khaṭṭāb al-ʿAdawī, intended to emigrate. Like ʿAyyāsh al-Makhzūmī, he too, was prevented from doing so by the Quraysh chiefs and was put in a prison along with ʿAyyāsh. He was fettered for three to four years.[12] According to a report, he was arrested on his return from Abyssinia by his own father. He was the younger brother of ʿAmr ibn al-ʿĀṣ al-Sahmī.[13] His father al-ʿĀṣ ibn Wā'il al-Sahmī had granted protection to ʿUmar. However, he did not allow his son to accept Islam. Even after his father's death Hishām did not get his freedom, as other family members kept him in prison. As reports suggest, he was released only after the battle of Uḥud or the Trench. His arrest lasted for seven to eight years.[14]

Apart from men, even Muslim women and children faced the Quraysh persecution, imprisonment and separation from their immediate families, as they were in captivity in Makkah. They might not have faced such harsh conditions as the men had. Some enjoyed relatively little freedom. Yet they could not escape the Quraysh embargo and emigrate to Madīnah. Among them was the

Prophet's eldest daughter, Zaynab, who was detained in Makkah notwithstanding the Prophet's plea, by her unbelieving husband Abū'l-ʿĀṣ ibn Rabīʿ al-Abshamī and his family. They did not let her emigrate to Madīnah. In the battle of Badr, her husband was part of the Makkan army and was taken as a captive by the victorious Muslims. As ransom he offered and promised to send her to Madīnah. He made arrangements that his brother should send her yet the Quraysh chiefs erected many obstacles in this arrangement.[15]

Another arrested woman was Umm Salamah bint Umayyah al-Makhzūmī, who was separated forcibly from her emigrant husband, Abū Salamah ibn ʿAbd al-Asad al-Makhzūmī. She stayed in Makkah for long. According to Bukhārī, she faced this agony for a year.[16] Her believing sister, Umm Kulthūm bint ʿUqbah ibn Abī Muʿīṭ al-Umawī was the daughter of a Makkan Quraysh chief. She had embraced Islam in the early Makkan period. However, she was not allowed to emigrate. Rather, her family put her under house arrest.[17]

Sincere Makkan Muslims

Many sincere Muslims faced all sorts of hardships, including imprisonment yet it did not deter them from following the way of Islam. Some secured release, as is detailed below. However, some died within prison. For example, Saʿd ibn Khawlah al-ʿĀmirī al-Qurashī died in captivity. The Prophet (peace be upon him) used to invoke Allah's grace and mercy for those suffering Makkan Muslims.[18] Saʿd's wife, Sabʿah bint Ḥārith al-Aslamī gave birth to a daughter after his death. The Prophet (peace be upon him) let her marry soon after delivery. The child was born only a month after Saʿd's death. There are contradictory reports about the true identity of Saʿd. According to al-Wāqidī, he was the freed slave of Wahb ibn Saʿd ibn Abī Sarḥ of Banū ʿĀmir ibn Lu'ayy. Others take him as a resident of Yemen. Some reports speak of him as a freed slave of Abū Ruḥm and his mother as the female slave of Saʿd ibn Abī

Sarḥ. Both Ibn Isḥāq and al-Wāqidī describe him as an emigrant to Abyssinia. This is not contested by Mūsā ibn ʿUqbah and Abū Mashhar. Al-Wāqidī adds that he had emigrated to Madīnah and taken part in the battle of Badr while he was only fifteen and also in the battle of Uḥud and the Trench. He died in Makkah as he had gone there on some business. Another report, however, states that he could not emigrate to Madīnah and died in Makkah. Ibn Saʿd includes him among those who participated in the battle of Badr. For him, he was twenty-five years old at the time of that battle. The Prophet (peace be upon him) did not approve that the emigrants return to their home town. He regretted that Saʿd had died in Makkah. It emerges from Ibn Ḥajar's account that he had gone to Makkah after his emigration to Madīnah. In Makkah death overtook him. However, some reports insist that he could not emigrate, as is asserted in Imām Bukhārī's work.

Muʿammar ibn ʿAbdullāh al-ʿAdawī is another obscure figure. For Ibn Saʿd, he was one of the earliest Muslims and emigrants to Abyssinia. Then he returned to Makkah and settled down there. He kept on deferring his emigration to Madīnah and did so at a later date. Some suggest that he had joined the Prophet (peace be upon him) at Ḥudaybīyah. Contradictory reports are found about Khirāsh ibn Umayyah al-Kaʿbī.[19] Balādhurī, however, states that he had returned from Abyssinia to Madīnah along with Jaʿfar ibn Abī Ṭālib al-Hāshimī, and had not gone at all to Makkah.[20]

Ibn Isḥāq includes both Saʿd ibn Khawlah and Muʿammar ibn ʿAbdullāh among the emigrants to Abyssinia. For him, Saʿd had returned to Makkah while Muʿammar had not.[21]

There is no such controversy about Sakrān ibn ʿAmr ibn ʿAbd Shams, an emigrant to Abyssinia who died in Makkah after his return. The Prophet (peace be upon him) married his widow, Sawdah bint Zamʿah, as is reported by Ibn Isḥāq and Ibn Hishām.[22] It is on record that some Muslims who had settled in Makkah died there after the Prophet's emigration. Some of them had to undergo imprisonment and persecution. For certain reasons they could not emigrate to Madīnah.

The Free Yet Helpless Muslims of Makkah

Weaker Muslims formed an independent section of the society. Owing to the lack of resources and having no social rank they were unable to emigrate. They were too unimportant to be imprisoned by the Quraysh. They are described thus in the Qur'ān: 'And why should you not fight in the cause of Allah and of those who being weak are ill-treated? Men, women and children whose cry is: "Our Lord! Rescue us from this town, whose people are oppressors."'[23] These helpless Muslims prayed for their release from the clutches of their Makkan oppressors. Notwithstanding their freedom they did not have resources to emigrate. They were weak and helpless. In his *tafsīr* Ibn Kathīr quotes ʿAbdullāh ibn ʿAbbās to the effect that he regarded himself and his mother among such resourceless Muslims. Imām Bukhārī adduces the same in a report.[24] Imām Bukhārī in his '*Kitāb al-Tafsīr*' has cited *Ḥadīth* Nos. 4587 and 4588 related to *Sūrah al-Nisā'* on the authority of ʿAbdullāh ibn ʿAbbās. Ibn Ḥajar, quoting Imām Sufyān ibn ʿUyaynah, says that both the young Ibn ʿAbbās and his mother Lubābah bint al-Ḥārith al-Hilālī were weak Muslims. For Abū Dharr, no male features in this list. Ibn Ḥajar has not added any name to this list.[25]

The Qur'ān commentators of a later date, however, have provided further details. Mawlānā Ashraf ʿAlī Thānvī maintains: 'Such weak Muslims were left behind in Makkah that they could not emigrate on account of the lack of strength and resources. The unbelievers did not let them go either and persecuted them in a variety of ways.' Works on *ḥadīth* and *tafsīr* name some of them – Ibn ʿAbbās and his mother, Salamah ibn Hishām, al-Walīd ibn al-Walīd and Abū Jandal ibn Sahl.[26] For Mawlānā Syed Abu'l Aʿlā Mawdūdī, some Arab tribes also belonged to the same category, which is stated in the Qur'ān.[27] Mawlānā Amīn Aḥsan Iṣlāḥī extends the point further in making the following observations: 'At the time of the revelation of this verse[28] in certain towns many men, women and children had accepted Islam and were victims of persecution at the hands of their unbelieving guardians or tribes.'[29]

Some of these Muslims had the freedom of movement and were capable of emigration. Their laziness, cowardice and inaction, however, stopped them from emigrating. As a result, they fell prey to temptations. In this world they were subject to violence and killing and in the next life they would meet with divine punishment, as is clarified in verses 97-98 of *al-Nisā'*, and reported by Ibn Hishām and Ibn Isḥāq.

Persecuted Muslims

During the period of intense persecution some Muslim prisoners faltered and could not adhere to their faith. Among them were al-Ḥārith ibn Zamʿah al-Asdī, Abū Qays ibn al-Fukayh al-Makhzūmī, Abū Qays ibn al-Walīd al-Makhzūmī, ʿAlī ibn Umayyah al-Jumaḥī and al-ʿĀṣ ibn Munbih al-Sahmī. These youths had embraced Islam in Makkah at the Prophet's hands and formed part of the Makkan Muslim minority. After the Prophet's emigration their own family members imprisoned them and forced them into reverting to their ancestral faith. They joined the Quraysh army in the battle of Badr and were killed there. It was regarding them that verses 97-99 of *Sūrah al-Nisā'* were sent down. They could not preserve their faith in the face of persecution. Owing to their weakness they did not emigrate and were punished for colluding with their wicked community. They are destined for punishment in the Hereafter in that they did not adhere to faith and emigrate to Madīnah.[30] Imām Bukhārī adduces *Ḥadīth* No. 4594 regarding them.[31] On Ibn ʿAbbās's authority Ibn Ḥajar has listed their names, including the following not found in Ibn Isḥāq's list: Qays ibn al-Walīd ibn al-Mughīrah, Abū Qays ibn al-Fatḥ ibn al-Mughīrah, al-Walīd ibn ʿUtbah ibn Rabīʿah, ʿAmr ibn Umayyah ibn Sufyān. The five names in this list differ from those in Ibn Isḥāq's account. It is said about them that when they set out for Badr and thought that the Muslims were few in number, they recanted their faith in Islam and were killed on the battleground.[32] Ibn Ḥajar cites Ṭabarī's report to the effect that some Makkan Muslims used to conceal their faith. The polytheists forced them into joining the battle and some of them were killed. Muslims held that these helpless Muslims were forced into fighting. Therefore, forgiveness from Allah should be sought for them. It was against this backdrop that the above verses of *Sūrah al-Nisā'* were sent down. The same verse was communicated to the Muslims still staying in Makkah. It left them with no excuse.[33]

The Sincere Settled Muslims of Makkah

A section of Makkan Muslims, who had wealth and rank, did not emigrate to Madīnah for certain considerations. They stayed there by choice and with the Quraysh chiefs' leave. They may be divided into two broad groups. To one group belonged those who were personally asked by the Prophet (peace be upon him) to stay put. Others were those who were not allowed to leave by the Quraysh in view of their social and welfare work. They were treated as equal citizens. Their adherence to Islam was not some secret. Rather it was public knowledge.

Among the first group were the Prophet's uncle, al-ʿAbbās ibn ʿAbd al-Muṭṭalib al-Hāshimī, his family members and his freed slaves. Reports insist that he was one of the earliest Muslims and that the Prophet (peace be upon him) had directed him to keep on staying in Makkah for finding out about the plans of Quraysh chiefs and for protecting the interests of Muslims. He therefore stayed in Makkah for long.

On al-Kalbī's authority a report is related by his son, ʿAbdullāh ibn ʿAbbās to the effect that some members of Banū Hāshim had embraced Islam. However, they did not declare it lest the Quraysh and Abū Lahab al-Hāshimī might arrest them, as in the case of Salamah ibn Hishām and ʿAyyāsh ibn Rabīʿah. It was in line with this that the Prophet (peace be upon him) had instructed his Companions not to kill al-ʿAbbās, Ṭālib, ʿAqīl, Nawfal or Abū Sufyān on the battle ground because they had been forcibly brought there.[34] According to Ibn Isḥāq, al-ʿAbbās ibn ʿAbd al-Muṭṭalib, as stated by his slave Abū Rāfiʿ, had accepted Islam at an early date.

His wife, Umm al-Faḍl and his slave, Abū Rāfiʿ too, had become Muslims. However, he apprehended the Quraysh's reprisal and did not want to antagonize them. Therefore, he concealed his new faith. His trade was spread in Makkah among the Quraysh. Under compulsion he joined that battle of Badr.[35] Ibn Saʿd has cited several reports of the same import.[36] Some reports indicate that al-ʿAbbās was taken as a captive in the battle of Badr and secured his release by paying ransom money and returned to Makkah, a point featuring in many sources.[37] During his stay in Makkah he regularly informed the Prophet (peace be upon him) of the Makkan chiefs' moves.[38]

However, some reports make the point that since important public offices were entrusted to al-ʿAbbās, he was ordered to stay in Makkah. Later on, he emigrated to Madīnah.[39] Some reports state that al-ʿAbbās, along with some members of Banū Hāshim had emigrated to Madīnah during the battle of the Trench.[40] It is also held that he was in Abū Hurayrah's group and emigrated at the time of the battle of Khaybar or later.[41]

On analyzing these divergent reports it is clear that irrespective of al-ʿAbbās's early conversion to Islam, he emigrated after the conquest of Makkah. The date of his accepting Islam and emigration is yet to be established.[42] According to Balādhurī, during the journey to Makkah the Prophet (peace be upon him) met al-ʿAbbās at Dhū'l-Ḥulayfah. It was then that he declared himself as a Muslim and told that he was on his way to Madīnah as an emigrant. The Prophet (peace be upon him) directed him to proceed.[43]

Some incidents indicate that he had not accepted Islam in the Makkan period. Rather, he did so a little before the conquest of Makkah. However, some members of his family, as for example, his wife, Lubābah and son, ʿAbdullāh had entered the fold of Islam earlier. Reports differ widely on al-ʿAbbās's conversion to Islam and his emigration. It calls for a detailed study.

To the other category belong Nuʿaym ibn ʿAbdullāh al-Naḥḥām al-ʿAdawī and his family. He was a Qurayshī who accepted Islam at an early date yet he did not make it public for the fear of his people.[44] He did invaluable social work for the widows, orphans and the poor, Muslims and non-Muslims alike. For this reason the Quraysh did not let him emigrate. They did not imprison him either. They only requested him not to leave Makkah so that the needy ones were not deprived of his help and support. He obliged the Quraysh and stayed in Makkah until the Ḥudaybīyah treaty. He served everyone alike and earned their gratitude. The Prophet (peace be upon him) had probably granted him this leave for the larger interests of the Muslim community.[45]

Some reports put the number of Nuʿaym's family or of Banū ʿAdiyy ibn Kaʿb at forty. This points to the large number of Muslim minority in Makkah. Even if all of them were not early Muslims, they had certainly embraced Islam before the emigration to Madīnah. One also notes the rising number of Muslim community in Makkah. In the post-Ḥudaybīyah treaty period many Makkan Quraysh accepted Islam and kept on emigrating to Madīnah until the conquest of Makkah. Among them were such Quraysh chiefs as Khālid ibn al-Walīd al-Makhzūmī, ʿAmr ibn al-ʿĀṣ al-Sahmī and ʿUthmān ibn Ṭalḥah al-ʿAbdarī.[46] Ibn Saʿd has provided an extensive account of the Companions who had accepted Islam prior to the conquest of Makkah. Included among them are many Quraysh and non-Quraysh figures.[47] These 150 persons belong to the Quraysh, Banū Sulaym, Aslam, Daws, Ashjaʿ, Juhaynah, Balī and Ḥaḍramī.[48] Some opted for staying in Makkah until its conquest and later joined the larger Muslim community.

The Secret Group of Makkan new Muslims

Even after the Prophet's emigration, Islam spread in Makkah, though at a slower pace. The pace was much slower before the Ḥudaybīyah peace treaty. Later on, it picked up fast. Many young Quraysh accepted Islam, though secretly. Even those of leading families did not declare it. Nor did they emigrate to Madīnah. For this would have divulged their secret.

According to a report at least, two sons – Yazīd and, Muʿawiyah of the Makkan chief and Quraysh commander in chief, Abū Sufyān, had embraced Islam after the Ḥudaybīyah treaty. Yet they kept it as a secret, fearing reprisal.[49] In the two years between the Ḥudaybīyah treaty and the conquest of Makkah the number of new Muslims was higher than those in the earlier twenty years. For it was by then common knowledge that Islam was the true faith. The Arabs could clearly see the truth, unhampered by tribal prejudice.[50] Khālid ibn al-Walīd, ʿAmr ibn al-ʿĀṣ al-Sahmī and ʿUthmān ibn Abī Ṭalḥah al-ʿAbdarī accepted Islam after the Ḥudaybīyah treaty. However, they emigrated soon to Madīnah. There were many such Makkan Muslims who stayed in Makkah and then emigrated. A large number of Makkan Muslims did not openly present themselves as Muslims. Ibn Saʿd describes those who continued to stay and did not emigrate to Madīnah.

The Prophet and the Makkan Muslim Minority

Traditional writers on *sīrah*, especially the *ʿulamāʾ* convey the impression that the Prophet (peace be upon him) instructed the helpless, persecuted Makkan Muslims to bear with their plight and kept on supplicating for their release yet he never took any practical step. He was prevented by the local conditions to do anything. However, internal evidence suggests that he did everything possible for their release. Nor did Makkan Muslims sit idle. They resorted to many strategies for their liberation and often got success. True, the Prophet (peace be upon him) invoked Allah's help for the suffering Makkan Muslims, exhorted them to emigrate to Madīnah and comforted and consoled the victims in every way.

The Prophet's Efforts for the Release of Muslim Prisoners

The Prophet (peace be upon him) tried his best to secure the release of the Makkan Muslims in captivity. With the help of Madīnan Muslims and brave souls he was successful in getting them released from Makkan captivity. Reports state that he was very concerned for the release of ʿAyyāsh ibn Abī Rabīʿah al-Makhzūmī and

Hishām ibn al-ʿĀṣ al-Sahmī and planned for their release. Al-Walīd ibn al-Walīd al-Makhzūmī was the younger brother of Khālid ibn al-Walīd who was taken a prisoner in the battle of Badr. During the same period he was drawn towards Islam and after paying ransom he returned to Madīnah and accepted Islam. Yet his family arrested him and took him to Makkah. Somehow he fled back to Madīnah. There he heard the Prophet's invocation: 'Who would get the helpless Makkan Muslims released?' While putting his own life at risk he secured the release of ʿAyyāsh and Hishām and brought them to Madīnah.[51]

Efforts for Liberating Muslims

Makkan Muslims were constantly engaged in efforts for their release. ʿAbdullāh ibn al-Suhaylī al-ʿĀmirī gave the impression to his father that he had reverted to his ancestral faith. His father therefore took him along with the Makkan army to Madīnah. However, ʿAbdullāh joined the Prophet (peace be upon him) and thus secured his release.[52] Al-Walīd ibn al-Walīd al-Makhzūmī was imprisoned in Makkah along with Muslims of Banū Makhzum. The Prophet (peace be upon him) kept on praying for these three for three years. Somehow al-Walīd ibn al-Walīd al-Makhzūmī secured his release and reached Madīnah.[53]

Abū Baṣīr ʿUtbah ibn Usayd al-Thaqafī managed to escape from the Quraysh captivity and reached Madīnah. However, in line with the provisions of the Ḥudaybīyah treaty he was sent back to Makkah. On the way back he killed one of the guards and fled. Later on, he settled down in ʿAyṣ, in the vicinity of Madīnah and lived as a free person. This opened the way for the Makkan Muslims in Quraysh captivity. After fleeing from Makkah they joined Abū Baṣīr at ʿAyṣ. Abū Jandal ʿAmr ibn al-Suhaylī al-Sahmī was also one of them. He had been made to return to Makkah in line with the Ḥudaybīyah treaty. According to reports, around seventy Muslim prisoners assembled there, most of whom were Qurayshī. Another report puts the number of the Muslim minority at ʿAyṣ at three hundred.[54]

Resource Mobilization for Prisoners

Balādhurī makes this significant point about Abū Jandal which underscores the Prophet's effective strategy. In line with the provisions of the Ḥudaybīyah treaty and at the insistence of Abū Jandal's unbelieving father, the Prophet (peace be upon him), no doubt, sent him back to Makkah. However, in response to Abū Jandal's apprehension that the unbelieving Makkans would kill him on his return the Prophet (peace be upon him) made two Makkan chiefs Ḥuwayṭib ibn ʿAbd al-ʿUzzā al-ʿĀmirī and Mikraz ibn Ḥafṣ al-ʿĀmirī pledge to his protection. On the fulfillment of this condition he let Abū Jandal go. Both had pledged to protect Abū Jandal against his father's evil and the latter had to abide by it.[55]

Efforts of Madīnan Muslims

Apart from the Prophet, (peace be upon him) the Madīnan Muslims were in constant touch with their Makkan brethren in faith. They too, acted on ways and means for their release. They exhorted them as well to emigrate and comforted them for their plight. They kept them abreast of the latest Qur'ānic verses.

When the unbelievers arrested by deception two associates of ʿUmar ibn al-Khaṭṭāb – Salamah ibn Hishām and ʿAyyāsh ibn Rabīʿah, Qur'ānic verses were sent down regarding them. ʿUmar transcribed these verses and sent these to them for their consolation and inspiration. According to Ibn Ishaq, the following verses were revealed on this occasion. 'Say: O My servants who have transgressed against their souls! Do not despair of Allah's mercy. For Allah forgives all sins. He is Oft-Forgiving, Most Merciful. Turn to your Lord in repentance and bow to His will, before the penalty comes on you. After that you shall not be helped. And follow the best of the courses revealed to you from your Lord, before the penalty comes on you, of a sudden while you do not perceive.'[56]

ʿUmar, as stated by him, sent these to Hishām ibn al-ʿĀṣ who did not emigrate notwithstanding his professing Islam. According to Hishām, he could not comprehend when he got these at Dhū Ṭuwā. He prayed to Allah to enable him to follow these. As soon as it dawned on him that these applied to his case, he mounted a camel and went straight to the Prophet (peace be upon him).[57]

Verses 97-99 of *al-Nisā'* are related to those Makkan Muslims who did not emigrate and fell into mischief. Ibn Ḥajar clarifies that Madīnan Muslims had passed on these verses to Muslims in Makkah, requesting them to expedite their emigration. For after the promulgation of divine directive these Makkan Muslims could not resort to any pretext.[58] It is evident from *Tafsīr Ṭabarī* that Madīnan Muslims had, at least, thrice informed the Muslims in Makkah of these verses – after the revelation of verses 97-99 of *al-Nisā'* after *Sūrah al-ʿAnkabūt* and after *Sūrah al-Naḥl.* On other occasions too, they exhorted Makkan Muslims. In view of these reports it may be asserted that Madīnan Muslims used to apprise their brethren, both Muslim and non-Muslim, in Makkah of the Qur'ānic verses, Islamic commands and major events. It was done though correspondence, couriers, pilgrims or traders or perhaps all of these together.

The Assistance Rendered by Makkan Chiefs

There were many noble souls in Makkah. They had love and concern for fellow community members. Some of them had sympathy owing to their kinship. They found it hard to reconcile to separation from them, especially women and children. Their tribal code of conduct urged them to treat well this minority group. They played an important role in their release from unlawful confinement.

Umm Salamah and her young son had been detained by her family while they were about to emigrate. They were not allowed to accompany their husband and father. Abū Salamah's family separated the young son from his mother. For about one year Umm Salamah underwent this agonizing experience. Every morning she would be on the road leading to Madīnah and cried there until evening. One of her cousins took pity and reunited her son with her. She was allowed also to emigrate. She rode a camel and left for Madīnah alone. At Tanʿīm she was spotted by the Makkan chief and the key bearer of the Kaʿbah, ʿUthmān ibn Ṭalḥah al-ʿAbdarī, who was kind enough to accompany her to Madīnah and then returned to Makkah. Umm Salamah always felt grateful to him, saying that he was the kindest person known to her.[59]

Another noble Makkan chief was Abū Sufyān ibn Ḥarb al-Umawī, full of love for his family. He had assisted in the freedom and travel of the Prophet's eldest daughter Zaynab to Madīnah. In the battle of Badr her unbelieving husband Abū'-lʿĀṣ ibn Rabīʿ al-Abshamī was released on the condition that he would send Zaynab to Madīnah. When Hind bint ʿUtbah, wife of Abū Sufyān learnt about it, she offered to help her. However, Zaynab did not trust her. Finally, when she sought to leave along with her husband's brother, Kinānah ibn al-Rabīʿ al-Abshamī, some Quraysh chiefs forcibly stopped her. Kinānah vowed to fight and it could lead to bloodshed when Abū Sufyān reached on the spot along with Quraysh chiefs and persuaded Zaynab and Kinānah to return to Makkah. As things cooled down, he helped them leave for Madīnah.[60]

Muslim Minorities Among Arabian Tribes

Apart from Makkah, Muslim settlements had come up in many towns in the Arabian Peninsula. Their lot was similar to that of the Muslim minority under the Quraysh in the Prophet's Makkan phase. In some instances they were in a worse condition. After the emergence of the Islamic state in Madīnah, they continued to exist as minorities and their rank did not register any improvement. Leaving aside some variation in their status, as a minority they were subservient in their respective areas to the non-Muslim minority. This holds true of ʿAbd al-Qays of Bahrain, Ashʿar and Daws. The only exceptions were the tribes of Ghifār and Aslam. For Muslims in these tribes had assumed majority and were akin in status to Madīnan Muslims. Being the majority community in their respective areas they were not obliged to emigrate, for they could practise their faith without any hindrance. Yet many of them had emigrated to Madīnah in order to be blessed with the Prophet's company there.

Imām Bukhārī has related at length the following report about ʿAbd al-Qays tribe. When their delegation called on the Prophet (peace be upon him), he enquired after them. On being introduced to Rabīʿah he welcomed him. They told the Prophet: 'We can only enter the blessed city. For the unbelieving families of Midr hinder us from visiting you. Instruct us in something which would transport us to Paradise, if we preach it.'[61] While elucidating it, Ibn Ḥajar states that al-Qays comprised fourteen riders, who were the leaders of the tribe. They were headed by Ashajj. His full name was al-Mundhir ibn ʿĀ'iḍ. The other members of the delegation were: Munqidh ibn Ḥibbān, Muzaydah ibn Mālik, ʿAmr ibn Marḥūm, Ḥārith ibn Shuʿayb, ʿUbaydah ibn al-Humām, al-Ḥārith ibn Jundub, Siḥār ibn al-ʿAbbās. While tapping other sources Ibn Ḥajar has identified the names of the rest: ʿUqbah ibn Jurwah, Qays ibn al-Nuʿmān al-ʿAbdī, Jahm ibn Qutham, al-Rustum al-ʿAbdī, Juwayriyyah al-ʿAbdiyyah and al-Zarrāʿ ibn ʿĀmir al-ʿAbdī. They had a guide as well. According to another they were forty in number.

The Muslim minority of Arabian tribes had the following two ways open to them:

1. They could either continue living in the midst of their non-Muslim tribes and while benefiting from their tribal norms they could practise Islam. This was the practice of most of these minority groups. Until the conquest of their region by Muslims or the merger with the Islamic state through a treaty, they flourished as a minority. Their non-Muslim tribes observed their tribal norms and offered them peace and security. Another alternative open to them was to emigrate to Madīnah on facing obstructions in practising their faith. This was adopted by Muslims of Ashʿar, Daws and some other tribes. Some of them, however, did not have the means to emigrate. They were forced to face persecution, as it emerges from verse 75 of *Sūrah al-Nisā'*. Amīn Aḥsan Iṣlāḥī is correct in not taking this verse as specific to Makkah. For other Muslim minorities existed amid various tribes, villages and towns.[62]

The Muslim Minority in Abyssinia and the Post-emigration Madīnah

A number of Makkan Muslims had migrated to Abyssinia in the face of the anti-Islam stance of the Makkan Quraysh, especially their chiefs. Of them, thirty-three had returned within two years. However, seventy of them stayed there. On coming to know of the Prophet's emigration, some moved to Madīnah via Makkah. Such were few in number. The majority went to Madīnah, in twos or threes over a long period. Ibn Hishām provides a list of Makkan Muslims family-wise. Their total was forty. However, sixteen preferred to stay in Abyssinia for long i.e. at least seven years until the battle of Khaybar. Reports suggest that they did so by the Prophet's leave hence they cannot be reproached. Yet there is no denying the fact that a group of Muslim emigrants to Abyssinia was reconciled to its status as a minority in a non-Muslim country and even in the face of congenial conditions it did not opt for the Islamic state headquarters. They did so at a time when the Muslims in Madīnah, the Islamic state and the Prophet (peace be upon him) were surrounded by enemies and were in adversity. Until the battle of the Trench in 5/627 the Islamic state and a hard time. Muslims in Madīnah, under the Prophet's leadership, were exposed to the Quraysh onslaught. In such circumstances the *en masse* emigration of the Abyssinian emigrants to Madīnah could boost the morale of the Muslims and comfort the Prophet (peace be upon him). Yet they did not emigrate and in the safe haven provided by King Negus they led life. During this period they lost for ever the distinction of participating in the battles of Badr, Uḥud, the Trench, Ḥudaybīyah and Khayber and of earning reward. Nor did they play any role in the evolution of Islamic society and state in Madīnah and thus deprived themselves of numerous blessings. They, no doubt, had the Prophet's leave to stay there yet it was, at most, an allowance, not a brave course of action. They returned to the Islamic state at a time when their help was not at all needed. They had a minority status, as was the case with many Muslim minorities across the Arabian Peninsula.

CONCLUSION

The Prophet's Role Model for the Muslim Minority

1. The Prophet's illustrious life provides the role model for the Muslim minority. In the backdrop of divine directives and Qur'ānic teachings the Prophet (peace be upon him) drew up an elaborate design for the construction and development of the Makkan Muslim minority. The norms for the Makkan Quraysh, particularly of their elite, added another dimension to the presence of the Muslim minority there. The Prophet helped Muslims evolve within the constraints imposed by the tribal system and the prevalent social values and customs. He raised the middle community of Muslims amid the Arab cultural traditions and civilizational evolution.

Shāh Walīullāh has identified the following principle behind the Prophet's construction and development of the Makkan Muslim community. For him, Islam was not determined to extirpate fully the *jāhiliyyah* Arab culture and civilization. It was not after demolishing each and everything. Rather, it opted for the middle way by way of reforming, adapting, restoring and reconstructing the existing order. The Prophet reformed such Arab social practices which were injurious to morals, health and faith. Yet he retained noble traditions and introduced, keeping in mind the changing needs, new practices, rites and rituals and deeds.[1]

That is the very essence of Islam and the Prophet's practice. Muslims believe that Islam is the eternal way of life. It is in this sense that Islam came to this world with Prophet Adam's advent. All Messengers preached the same faith of Islam to their respective communities and in line with the demands of their times they accomplished reform, construction and development. Muḥammad ibn ʿAbdullāh laid the final brick, marking the completion of this faith at his blessed hands. The middle community of Muslims was raised and until the Last Day, the way of Islam has been pronounced as the way to salvation for Muslims and non-Muslims alike. The Prophet's illustrious example embodies the quintessence of the ways and conduct of all the Messengers.

The division of Islam into Makkan and Madīnan phases underscores a far-reaching divine strategy. Allah knew it well that the Muslims' lot would change with time. Like other believing communities they would be reduced to a weak, despised, resourceless and helpless minority. At times they would be a dominant, powerful majority, able to enforce their way of life. Allah has laid down some eternal principles for both of these eventualities. These are known as the way of Allah. Its observance, adherence to the laws of nature, strictly following the Prophet's model would accrue to Muslims power, authority and sovereignty. This is Allah's promise. Any violation of it is bound to cause disaster in terms of ignorance, subjugation, decline and disintegration. Faith and good deeds alone ensure success and felicity. It can make or mar prospects in varying degrees.

In accordance with this law of nature it is the essential principle that Muslims would make their beginning as a minority. If they follow divine laws and the Prophet's guidance this minority would gradually register growth. After passing through several stages they would attain majority status. In the Makkan phase the same philosophy of life was adopted by the Muslim minority. This brought to them exaltation and glory. An individual commenced the gigantic task of constructing an Islamic community and within thirteen years managed to create a considerable Muslim community in and around

Makkah. This was the nucleus of the larger community, with the Prophet (peace be upon him) at the centre stage. Other Muslim minorities were the offshoots of the same Islamic headquarters. They looked forward to growth and success by way of maintaining the linkages with the core community.

A strong bond underlies the Makkan and Madīnan phases of the Prophet's career. These two phases bring out in full the strategy at work. This is the connecting link also between Makkan and Madīnan Surahs. Through a series of effective, hard and long-term steps the Prophet steered the minority Muslim group to the path of growth and success. Ultimately, it culminated in the majority community that assumed power. This transformation could take place in Makkah while Muslims were overwhelmed by the Quraysh. However, it could not clearly demonstrate the two diametrically opposite behaviour patterns of subjugation in Makkah and power and rule in Madīnah. The two could not appear as so distinct and different. In its absence the Muslim minority would not have received such a plan of action. Muslims would have been otherwise unable to find the way.

2. Both faith and good deeds were prescribed as the essential prerequisite for the formation and evolution of the Muslim minority in Makkah. Generally speaking, both the Muslim masses and *ʿulamā'* in particular, entertain a narrow view of faith and deeds. The range of deeds is equally limited to the body and the soul. Muslim individuals together constitute the larger community. The objective is same - to restore gloriously the link between all individuals. It encompasses the entire community of mankind.

Islamic faith and practices are not restricted to some rituals. Apart from having conviction in Islam, deeds should be performed sincerely for Allah's sake. Both these components are equally valid and important. It helps build the character of Muslims and they grow as members of the Muslim community. In Islam individual life does not have much significance. In the absence of the community, however, an individual Muslim stands out as the middle community. It is imperative for every Muslim to forge and maintain close relations with brethren in faith. Various theories and systems urging collectivity and the unified society appeared on the scene at a much later date. The Scriptures and Messengers of Allah instructed mankind long ago in the dual role of man as individual and as a member of the larger community. They imprinted this truth on man's mind and heart that every member of the community should participate actively in the collective life. The Prophet raised the Muslim community to perform both these roles. On the one hand, a Muslim is a sincere, loyal servant of Allah and on the other, a dedicated member of the Muslim community. This is required of every Muslim.

It may be termed as the psyche of the minority or of collectivity or of Muslim character or Muslim community that there exists a deep, unbreakable link between individuals and the community. It goes without saying that individuals constitute a group. However, what binds them as a community is their commitment and attachment. They are united by their religious fraternity. If this brotherhood is not reflected in the social life of the community and appears only as a mere slogan, it betrays the lack of fraternity and collective spirit in the community.

The above point is illustrated at its sharpest in the Prophet's word and deed. He remarked that the Muslim community is like a single body. If part of the body is hurt, the pain is felt in the entire body. Only when that part is cured, does the body attain relief. However, it is only one dimension of the love obtained between the individual member and the community. The Qur'ān and *ḥadīth* speak of the perfect structure and solid foundation to describe the above relationship. As the number of interconnected bricks together constitute and support a structure and ensure its durability. The Prophet had infused a strong collective spirit into the Makkan Muslim minority. Individual interests were secondary to the community welfare. All Muslims were brethren and friends to one another. Mutual love, respect and fraternity characterized them. Above all, they were blessed with divine mercy which supported them.

The spirit of collectivity in the Makkan Muslim minority began with the profession of faith in the One True God. Islamic commands and teachings made Muslims fully subservient to Allah. Their devotion to Allah united them also as members of the same religious community. They were imbued with a strong sense of being members of a single community. Monotheism and the worship of Allah provide the basis of the collectivity in Islam. Muslims are bound and sustained by mutual help and cooperation. The Prophet encouraged this spirit among them in the Makkan phase.

This religious bond transformed their entire society and way of life. Blood ties dominated so far social relations and aspects of faith and culture. The Prophet (peace be upon him) accorded priority to the tie of religious fraternity, placing it above kinship. Let this be clarified that he did not abolish the sacredness or significance of blood ties. However, he placed it at its proper place in the wider context of Islam. Blood ties have importance in their own way. Even in the Makkan period, kinship was highlighted and the Prophet (peace be upon him) accorded it its due place. Yet a balance was achieved between kinship and religious fraternity. Islam provided the larger context and ties of kinship were subordinated to it. The two do not cancel out each other. Rather, these affirm one another. By placing check and balance on the absolute nature of kinship, Islam utilized it for broader objectives. This helped it play a more effective role in achieving collectivity and serving the cause of humanity.

The formation of the Makkan Muslim community took place in two spheres – inner building and outward development. Deeds emanated from faith and developing a strong pious character and related to the inner sphere whereas one's devotion to the community as its member is reflective of the other. This blending marked the psyche of the Makkan Muslim minority. The Prophet and his Companions worked around the twin pivots. Faith, prayer and other modes of worship and rituals were essential for developing the character as a Muslim. These were equally indispensable for their growth as a distinct community. The Prophet's steps for educating and training Muslims, setting up Islamic centres, construction and expansion of mosques etc. went a long way in inculcating the collective spirit among Muslims.

3. However, preaching was the most effective strategy. It was the key to developing the collective spirit among Muslims. The same holds true even today. Within a short period of only thirteen years the Prophet expanded Islam from a single person to a hundreds strong Muslim community in Makkah. As time passed and preaching was intensified, Islam spread far and wide across the Arabian Peninsula. Eventually it grew into the Muslim majority state of Madīnah. In Abyssinia the universal dimension of Muslim community came into light. The entire growth owed only to the preaching of Islam. Without the Prophet's sincere efforts and the valuable cooperation of the Companions, the Muslim community would not have grown so deep and wide. It is evident from history that Arabs gave priority to preaching Islam. As is pointed out by Daniel Pipes, wherever Muslims ruled, they grew into a majority community, with Arabic as the national language and Islamic civilization in ascendancy. Only in such countries where preaching was neglected, Muslims remained as a minority group. For the Muslim rulers paid no heed to their basic duty. These Muslim communities were responsible, in equal measure, for it.

What is not only some magical formula for converting a minority into a majority, but ensures also the survival and identity of the minority is that faith should be preached vigorously. This is demanded by the concern and love for humanity that if one regards his faith as the key to success in this world and the means for deliverance in the next, he should convey it to everyone, especially his countrymen. For one's success in both the worlds should not blind him to the welfare of his own friends, kith and kin and men and women at large. He should not let them be consigned to Hellfire.

The Prophet's main strategy in Makkah was preaching Islam. The methods he adopted for it are equally valid and effective today. His preaching in private was not special to the Makkan minority phase. The same is useful for all such societies. Rather, it is all the more relevant in view of the prevalent psyche of people. It was an outstanding feature of Arabs that once the truth dawned on them, they unhesitatingly preached it actively to others. Other people lacked this feature for a variety of reasons. They did not accept truth even when it became manifest before them. We are not concerned here with its causes. The important point is that preaching is highly effective. Constant efforts move mountains. The divine message is bound to influence people, provided it is carried out consistently.

Doing something consistently has its specific psychological value and effectiveness. It strengthens both individuals and community. It introduces a collective spirit in their faith and thought. With deference to the milieu of the day the Prophet (peace be upon him) consistently preached. It was the scenario of the minority phase. The same was not adopted in the Madīnan period . For other factors were at work, which did not exist earlier.

Preaching privately has its universal effectiveness. The Prophet's strategy was undoubtedly eternal. His main activity was to approach his addressees directly. He conveyed his message to individuals, groups and gatherings, regardless of time and place. As the range of preaching widened, and the truth spread, many seekers of the truth themselves approached the Prophet (peace be upon him). Their quest was not however, part of preaching. The Prophet's other main principle was that the message of Islam be conveyed to everyone by every conceivable means. Along with the Companions he went door to door and informed people through caravans. They won over the hearts by their worship. New Muslims were sent back as preachers to their respective home towns. They were asked to stay there, which opened the way for the spread of Islam. For thirteen years the Prophet (peace be upon him) followed all such methods for preaching Islam and attained success. Implicit in it is the guidance for Muslims, be they in minority or majority, that they should draw upon all means of communication – oral, written, radio, television, computer to which everyone has access today. Their use for preaching faith is significant and may accrue far reaching consequences. For the message of Islam can thus reach everyone.

Preaching privately is important for the Muslim minority today, for unnecessary publicity evokes a strong reaction, obstructing people from embracing truth. The opponents resort to propaganda for intensifying the reaction which ultimately poisons the minds of unsuspecting people and they disregard the message altogether. In preaching Islam the principle of conveying the message in an appropriate way is of great importance. Once the community emerges, the truth may be preached even publicly. However, it is not obligatory to do so. If public preaching is useful, it may be adopted. Otherwise it should be avoided. For preaching Islam is the goal, not a particular mode of doing so.

In the Prophet's preaching mode the Qur'ān was an integral part. Other sources may, no doubt, be tapped. For some readers may be conversant with other thought patterns. However, the Qur'ān being the word of God has its own impact, which is felt, at best, in the original Arabic. Let this misperception not cloud our minds that non-Arabic speaking people may not benefit at all from the Qur'ān in Arabic. This is owing to our ignorance of the effectiveness of the Qur'ān. If the need arises, we should, of course, utilize a translation of the Qur'ān so that the target readers fully understand the Qur'ānic message. However, the impact of the Qur'ān is innate in its Arabic idiom and its divine order. The Qur'ānic text is marked by its own impact. History bears it out that many individuals and groups embraced Islam on listening to the Qur'ān. It was the Qur'ānic recitation which opened their hearts, influenced their minds and eventually resulted in their conversion to Islam. The Qur'ān is capable of winning over the hearts and minds of every group of human beings, including an average person and a genius. The Muslim community cannot survive, if it severs its link with the Qur'ān. Bereft of the Qur'ānic guidance it would be reduced to a crowd which may be swayed in any direction.

There is the problem of differences, divisions and disintegration within the community which eats into its vitals. Notwithstanding its appearance, it is no longer a united community, fragmented into numerous sects that are after one another's blood. They are vulnerable to sectarian, jurisprudential, social, regional, linguistic and many other differences. These obstruct the unity and collectivity of the community. Regrettably this problem afflicts the Muslim minority. Without checking this, nothing can be done for its welfare, what to say of its progress. It is the duty of Muslim minority leaders to reflect and devise a way out. Internal and sectarian differences should not be overblown into a battle between truth and falsehood itself. Everyone who recites the creedal statement of Islam should be taken as a Muslim and part of the Muslim community. According to the Qur'ān, a single creedal statement is common to the People of the Book. The same should be followed for achieving unity in the community. Otherwise, Muslims cannot enjoy the fruits of collective life. They would find it hard to survive. It would be pointless to invite others to Islam, for they would be unable to form part of any community. Others would not be prepared to join a group that is on the brink of destruction. In the Makkan phase when the Prophet (peace be upon him) united the community, they did not suffer from hypocrisy or inner conflicts. They were united on their faith and practice. They enjoyed also social unity. Their fervour for spreading the message of Islam saved them against hypocrisy. One of the advantages of preaching faith is that it protects against inner differences. Moreover, it helps increase the number and strength of the minority group.

4. For maintaining their identity and for preaching faith among the majority community it is essential for the Muslim minority to set up local centres of education and training for making the call to faith. This was the Prophet's glorious practice in his Makkan phase. They should not be content with just one or two centres. Rather, in accordance with needs they should establish these in every locality, village and town. These centres may be affiliated with mosques and other institutions. Local centres are more active, effective and wide ranging. For these can attract community members at least five times a day at the time of obligatory Prayers. This opportunity should be utilized for religious training and for preaching among others. These centres are likely to work energetically for the cause of faith. Let this be realized that local centres provide guidance and promote collectivity. In both Makkan and Madīnan phases the real task was accomplished by local persons. Today they can again perform the same role.

There is no denying the fact that there should be mutual cooperation amid various centres within a locality or village or town. For this reinforces the local initiative and strengthens the efforts for education, training and preaching. In the absence of such cooperation these centres do not lose their effectiveness. Nor do they face any obstruction. The same holds true for the cooperation and linkages at national level. As already indicated, others are less helpful, as compared to local centres. Their performance alone is the deciding factor. Regrettably the Muslim minority has overlooked this highly important point. Far from absorbing the new Muslims as part of the Makkan Muslim community, the Prophet, in his Makkan phase, had directed them to their respective areas for training and preaching. As a result, Muslim groups emerged in different towns and countries.

5. Another principle of the Makkan phase was that wherever a Muslim minority was unsafe, in terms of its faith and life and property, it was asked to join another Muslim group or to a safer place. This is known as *Hijrah* (emigration). The emigration to Abyssinia stands out as its first example. Makkans, especially believing members of the Quraysh were asked to emigrate in that they were not safe in the existing social system. Emigration assumed different forms in the Makkan period. Some Muslims from adjoining areas had merged with the Makkan Muslim community. Some went to a non-Muslim country to lead life under the protection of a just state. Some moved to safer places within the region. Some Makkans had entered into alliance with their Madīnan coreligionists who offered them help and support. Finally the Makkan Muslim community merged with the Madīnan Muslim majority, paving the way for the emergence of a dominant Muslim community.

All these forms of emigration may be emulated by Muslims today. It would be unlawful for Muslims to live in a locality, town or village where they are not free to practise their faith or face a constant threat to their life and property. It is imperative for them to move to a safer place, where they have the freedom of faith. Likewise, it is important to have Muslim pockets in a town. This does not entail emigration. Rather, moving from an unsafe place to a safer one accrues all the advantages of emigration. This movement from one locality to another within a town or village protects against many dangers. In today's world it is not easy to emigrate to a foreign country. For the laws of the land and social justice system have now become relatively better.

6. It is evident from the Prophet's social life in Makkah that he utilized fully the prevailing Arab social security system both for himself and other Muslims. He lived under the protection extended to him by Banū Hāshim. When this cover was violated by the reproachable conduct of the head of the family, he secured protection from another Quraysh family, Banū Nawfal. Other Muslim individuals too, availed themselves of the protection offered by their respective families and on losing it they took others' help. Those unable to get any cover felt compelled to emigrate. All modern political systems and societies promise the safety and security of individuals and sections. Their rights are enshrined in state constitutions. So are they assured of social rights and civil liberties. The law of the land protects their life and property and their faith. As citizens they are entitled to all of this. Every minority should make the most of its state constitution, its protection system and its provision for safety and security. It is therefore, essential that they should be familiar with their constitutional rights and be able to benefit from these as a minority. Obviously individual efforts cannot be so fruitful in this regard in comparison to a sustained move at the collective level. As a minority group Muslims in all countries should mobilize themselves for their civil liberties and their rights. They should develop initiative and dynamism. Such groups and communities cannot be helped by any constitution or security system who do not defend themselves. If they fail to secure rights, they cannot achieve anything. Today minorities and human rights commissions are there in every country. They should make the most of these. However, these cannot be as effective as Muslims themselves, provided they pursue their case vigorously and collectively.

Another way out for a Muslim minority in today's world is to forge a coalition with secular and patriotic groups and political organizations. However, the identification of a Muslim minority with a particular political party may cause some problems, especially when the latter is politically not so strong. Commonsense demands that they should be associated with two or three political parties. Their joining many parties may harm their interests, for they would then lose their strength as a group. The linkage of the Muslim community with two or three leading secular parties may prove highly useful. Generally speaking, minorities take little interest in political life, betraying indifference and disillusionment. Their attitude is largely negative and cynical. This is a dangerous trend for the minority community. For it renders them as light and unimportant in national politics. More seriously, it poses a threat to their security.

Members and leaders of the Muslim community should be closely associated with social organizations. It could provide them with security. They may develop love and understanding with non-Muslims. Such social organizations operate at local and state level. In the same vein, Muslims' participation in public life at *Panchayat*, *Parishad*, Municipality and other levels may have far-reaching results. Muslims must realize that their welfare as a community is contingent upon their association with political social, cultural institutions and organizations. The Prophet's role model on this count is illustrated by his being party to the *Ḥilf al-Fuḍūl* and his leading role in the construction of the Kaʿbah. Even the pre-Prophetic deeds of his have great Sharīʿah value, a point established by *ḥadīth* scholars. Equally important for Muslim minorities is their cooperation and interaction with the ruling party and political order of the day. Wherever it is possible to cooperate with states and political organizations, provided that it protects the interests of the Muslim community, Muslims should join hands with them. In proportion with their population they should demand positions in the government. For it is their right to get these. This point comes out from the cooperation of Muslim position holders such as Abū Bakr al-Taymī, ʿUmar al-ʿAdawī, ʿUthmān al-ʿAbdarī, Khālid al-Makhzūmī and al-ʿAbbās al-Hāshimī with the Makkan ruling class. The Prophet, needless to add, endorsed this arrangement. It does not amount to joining hands with *Ṭāghūt*. Rather, it constitutes an effort to clip the wings of *Ṭāghūt*. Such a strategy would be helpful for Islam and Muslim minorities in every respect.

7. Proper training and education may play a crucial role in imbuing Muslims with collective spirit, especially the pursuit of modern education. Religious education is undoubtedly the axis around which the Muslim minority exists. It is like a blood-line without which a minority cannot maintain its identity, particularly in competition with others. At the same time, the Muslim community should be fully grounded in modern knowledge. In the Middle Ages there was not such a yawning gap between religious and current knowledge, as it exists today. Even at that time the current knowledge was employed for organizing and developing the Muslim community. Muslims today must draw upon science and technology. Rather, it is important that selected Muslims should excel on this count. For their merit equivalent to that of the majority community would not bring them anything because of their numerical disadvantage. The majority community would be in an advantageous position.

They would not need any help or support from minorities. Even if they draw upon Muslims' talent with reference to the principle of social justice Muslims would still not be able to reap any benefit. It is therefore imperative for the Muslim minority to gain competence in both religious and current knowledge. They should be on the top which alone would help them become part of the national polity. Islam places great emphasis on education for every Muslim. They should possess working knowledge of faith. As compared to them, *ʿulamā'* should be characterized with deep, specialist knowledge. A thorough familiarity with modern knowledge is essential today for the survival of Muslim scholars. This alone can accrue to them social security. It can help them face the challenges posed by the majority. So doing, they can demonstrate that they are indispensable for the country. Jews in the world over and Sikhs in India have proved their utility, though both happen to be minorities. Their excellence has earned them many advantages.

8. Like any minority, Makkan Muslims had to defend their faith, their community members and their entire community. This defence was both ideological and physical. Under the Prophet's leadership the Makkan Muslim minority successfully managed to discharge this duty. In the words of the great Urdu poet, the opponents remain the same. So are the servants of Allah true to their nature. Muslims had to vindicate that the Qur'ān is the word of God. They had to face the Quraysh attacks, both intellectual and physical, directed against the Prophet (peace be upon him) and the weak Muslims. The Quraysh too, provided many rejoinders, refuting the allegations. The Qur'ān enabled Muslims to vindicate their faith and practices. Muslims resorted to literature, in both prose and poetry, in order to defend their faith, the Prophet and the community. It goes without saying that it was not possible without premising themselves on a particular worldview and thought pattern. They could mount this ideological, religious, social and cultural defence with the help of their scholarship. Nor is it possible to do so without this today.

Minorities in general and the Muslim minority in particular, are obliged to answer these charges. Surprisingly enough despite the change in the format, the charges remain the same in spirit. Their refutation may be carried out with the help of the latest knowledge. For all allegations are now hurled, laced with the latest technique and under the garb of modern scholarship. Muslim intellectuals of the Makkan phase studied the religious and social traditions and cultural elements and offered a fitting rejoinder. Muslim minorities in our times should master languages, especially polemical, modern critical idiom and methodology. Otherwise, they would not be able to comprehend the charges against them and would not be in a position to refute these. One of the ways of preaching Islam is to silence the critics with cogent arguments. This can be achieved only with the help of appreciating modern sensibility.

Both the Prophet (peace be upon him) and the Makkan Muslim minority resorted to the physical defence of Islam as well. Undoubtedly Islam does not recommend aggression. It prescribes perseverance for its followers and asks them to preach Islam in a peaceful manner. It deters them against violence and bloodshed. Through peaceful means and mutual understanding the Muslim community should be raised while military option should be avoided. However, there is a limit to it. If the opponents are given to fighting and violence in violation of all treaties and resort to persecuting Muslims which might extirpate them, the Muslim minority stands obliged to defend itself. It cannot be a passive victim to the violence perpetrated against it. This issue, which is crucial, stared the Makkan Muslim minority in the face. This situation is faced by every minority.

The Muslim minority has the following three responses to this injustice done by the majority (1) They might surrender, resigning to subjugation which might satisfy the majority. (2) They might emigrate in order to escape persecution and settle down in some foreign country. (3) They might utilize legitimate means for their defence and security. The Makkan Muslims employed all the above three options. When life became too difficult for them and they were not allowed to practise their faith, they took up the third option. During the Makkan phase every one acquired military skills and was trained in weapons. This was true of every Makkan Muslim and non-Muslim alike. It was part of masculine glory and aimed at defence and security.

Often did the Prophet (peace be upon him) opt for perseverance in the face of the worst provocation. At times, however, he took up arms. His Companions did not feel shy of drawing on defensive tactics. Included in these were fighting and even killing.

In our times wherever state, law of the land, constitution and institutions fail to protect minorities for any reason, the latter make their own arrangements for self-defence. This is both natural and legitimate. It is part of history, as is illustrated also by the Makkan phase of the Prophet's career. In doing so, the Muslim minority does not necessarily have to take recourse to unlawful means. A whole array of legitimate means are available. In every country and town there are institutions for civil defence. Take for instance, home guards, NCC and other outfits that train citizens, irrespective of their faith or colour in self defence so that they may render useful service in times of peace. They are called to assist the army in war conditions. In some countries civil defence training is compulsory for all adult citizens, including women. Modern educational institutions have included martial arts as part of their curriculum, imparting this training to both male and female students. Included amid these are Judo, Karate and archery etc. Some of these involve weapon training as well. The Muslim minority should draw fully on this, especially the youth. The other Muslims should also receive this training, as part of the Makkan model. Islam does not approve of weak Muslims. It instructs them to gain strength and be not a prey to oppressors.

9. For the survival and growth of the Muslim minority it is important to have educational excellence, religious superiority, collectivity, strong economy and sound financial condition. Rather, it is their religious duty to achieve all this. It is a pity that poverty is preferable to affluence in Muslim psyche. They regard poverty as the means for attaining deliverance. *ʿUlamāʾ* and Sufi masters have given general currency to the above notion. Based on a handful of reports and *aḥādīth,* they represent poverty as the sign of faith and piety. This position is absolutely untenable. Contentment is the real value. Islam recommends the possession of resources. Affluent members may be a source of strength for the community. Lack of resources is utterly deplorable. Wealth underlines the order prescribed by Islam. It looks down upon neediness, misery and weakness.

In the Makkan phase the Prophet (peace be upon him) was blessed with many divine favours. The Qur'ān lists his affluence as one of the favours bestowed upon him. Some myopic *tafsīr* writers misconstrue it as the wealth of the heart. Such an interpretation is not borne out by the context. More serious is the misperception of those scholars who ascribe the Prophet's wealth to others. In Arab or any other society the wife's wealth may help support the husband. However, it cannot turn him into a rich person. The Prophet (peace be upon him) earned his wealth by dint of his expertise as a trader. The resources provided by Khadījah and Abū Bakr, no doubt, helped the cause of Islam. However, this was not the wealth possessed by the Prophet. ʿUmar al-ʿAdawī, ʿAbd al-Raḥmān al-Zuhrī, Ṭalḥah al-Taymī, al-Zubayr al-Asdī, and above all, ʿUthmān al-Ghanī took an active part in the economic life of the Makkan Muslim community and helped its business and trade. Khabbāb ibn al-Arat al-Tamīmī, an ironsmith and Ṣuhayb ibn Sinān al-Rumi, a craftsman, earned wealth with their skills. Some of the Makkan Muslims were rich and many had enough income. According to the Quraysh, ʿUmar ibn al-Khaṭṭab was one of the richest among the Quraysh. Through his word and deeds the Prophet (peace be upon him) tried to make the community rich. This wealth was imperative for the community welfare. It was the lifeline for its growth. No head of the community could disregard the importance of wealth in community life. Given this, no such motive was ascribed to the Prophet which does not befit him.

For the Muslim minority today, better economy, stable finance and wealth are essential. Many religious duties cannot be performed without wealth. Reference may be made to the construction of mosques and madrasas, payment of *zakāh*, performance of Ḥajj, charity work and numerous collective projects. In summary, certain Islamic duties cannot be discharged in its absence. The security and progress of the community cannot be achieved either. Muslims have to be more active than non-Muslims in economy, for they have to stand on a strong base. They are pitted against the fabulous wealth of others. In all fields of human activity, be it business, agriculture, industry or craft, Muslims have to work harder as their religious duty. Their private wealth is equally important. For it contributes to the economic welfare of the entire community.

Today, Muslims, no doubt, face many obstructions in the economic field. One of these is the mindset of *ʿulamāʾ* and *fiqh* scholars. Many of their prohibitions arise from their own inferences, having little to do with Allah's or the Prophet's commands. They are ignorant of modern economics. Worse, they do not wish to gain this important knowledge. Their starting point is prohibition. Contrary to it, Islam regards everything wholesome as lawful. Furthermore, they are guilty of equating the medieval *fiqh* scholars' rulings with the eternal divine commands and the Prophet's directives. Let this be realized that the former's views were very much governed by the milieu of their own times. Leaving aside the basic category of the lawful and unlawful, economic laws should be formulated afresh with regard to the exigencies of our times. We cannot go into its further details in this work. Nor am I competent to deal with this subject.

Yet this point must be made that the Muslim community should be asked to draw upon available resources, provided these are lawful and not unlawful in the sight of Sharīʿah, for their economic well being and progress. All resources must be tapped in the light of the above principle. For a community cannot achieve all-round progress without wealth and financial resources. For Muslims it is all the more important for preserving their identity. Apart from *'ulamā'* and *fiqh* scholars, modern scholars should also take up this important issue. For it is a matter of life and death for the entire community. *Fiqh* academies of the day have been carrying out important academic work. These should turn their attention to the organization of the Muslim minority, especially its economy and for activating its institutions.

Like other departments of life, the economic life of Muslim minorities is in a shambles. Muslims may not be affluent. However, there is no death of rich Muslims who are willing to spend on the cause of the community. Some of them have a strong desire to do so. They generously donate to the religious and community cause. However, all this is without any organization. They give individually and at their discretion. It helps run some religious educational institutions and support some individuals. However, the community as a whole does not benefit much.

Individual donations should, no doubt, be given. Yet a conscious effort must be made for setting up *Bayt al-Māl* (public funds). It is an important duty of the community. For it helps meet many needs of the community. Some Muslim groups and sections manage funds. As a result, they are relatively more prosperous, better organized and deeply religious-minded. If *Bayt al-Māl* are set up in every village and town by local organizations, it can help solve the economic problems of Muslims. The whole community may grow self-independent. Local centres may merge into a central one. If every earning member sets aside only one percent of his income for *Bayt al-Māl*, it would change the fortune of the community. Such a system exists among some sections of Muslims. As a result many benefit from it.

10. Identity is a crucial issue for a community, especially for minorities. It has been a complicated problem for the Muslim minority. Their identity is central to their survival and an integral part of their social life, fraternity and unity. For they are deluged by cultural invasions. At the same time, many problems arise on account of their identity. For it is perceived as the sign of their assertion and refusal to surrender to the mainstream culture. It is Islam which invests them with identity, both inwardly and outwardly. Notwithstanding all the adjustments, Islam adopts a particular code in all spheres of life, ranging from food and drink to lifestyle, social norms, intermixing of men and women, education and training, political and economic order and all cultural matters.

It demands the believers to display their identity. It is not therefore, surprising that the Muslim minority holds its identity very dear.

Majority communities and dominant civilization are liable to accept the identity of minorities only up to an extent. For demonstrating their political strength or social and cultural supremacy, for asserting their numerical advantage, for introducing cultural integration and for a variety of social and psychological complexes, the former often seek to deprive minorities of their identity. The Muslim minority has been their prime target. For their distinct culture is inextricably interlinked with their faith. As a result, they are often persecuted at the hands of the majority. The Prophet's role model for them is that they should preserve their identity at any cost. This alone is the way to fight against evil forces.

11. Finally there is the issue of the social relations which the Muslim minority should have with the majority community. Let this be realized at the outset that Islam does not approve total separation from the non-Muslim society. At the social, humanitarian level Muslims are directed to forge cordial social relations with all. Islam is, no doubt, firmly opposed to polytheism and all that is injurious to morals and health. It, nonetheless, exhorts Muslims to have social, cultural and economic interaction and maintain friendly ties with non-Muslims. Keeping in mind the Islamic principle of supporting the ties of kinship they should treat non-Muslims well.

It is evident from the Prophet's practice in the Makkan period that he and his Companions maintained social relations with their non-Muslim society and made every allowance for them, except in religious matters. They had close economic terms, ties of kinship and social interaction with non-Muslims. They would visit them at their homes, meeting places and other social forums. They shared their joys and sorrows. They called on the sick, attended their funerals, weddings and other family occasions. Likewise, they joined their market place, fairs, seasonal gatherings and other social groups. They fulfiled their obligations to their polytheistic parents and friends and relatives. Marital ties with them were in place until the Qur'ān forbade it. Their kindness towards them, at times, exceeded their generosity towards Muslim brethren. More importantly, they played a leading role in rendering social welfare work, irrespective of caste, creed or colour.

For Muslim minorities all over the world in general, and for the Indian Muslim minority, in particular, the Prophet's above role model is of immense appeal, relevance and emulation. For it is characterized by pragmatism, wisdom and far-sightedness. With its help Muslims may defend themselves best and preach their faith as well. More importantly, it can enable them to realize the ideals of world peace and unity, which lie at the heart of Islam and its culture and civilization. Serving mankind was the Prophet's outstanding feature. On this Khadījah's remark is insightful, when she comforted the Prophet (peace be upon him) on receiving the divine revelation for the first time. What is amazing is that the same distinct quality is ascribed to Abū Bakr on the authority of Ibn al-Daghnah. Other prominent Muslims are also known for their social service. ʿAbdullāh al-Naḥḥām al-ʿAdawī's example is equally illustrious. For the enemies of Islam put up with his new faith yet in view of his philanthropy they did not want to lose him.

This concern and love for humanity at large is born of one's appreciation of and sharing others' sufferings. The Prophet (peace be upon him) was prompted constantly by the same urge for serving mankind in calling them to Islam. For, out of his boundless mercy he could not bear the thought that anyone be consigned to loss in this world and punishment in the Hereafter. He and his Companions were keen on saving everyone against divine penalty and on driving them to Paradise. They helped people in their suffering and brought them joy and comfort in this life. They tried to provide everyone with relief, convenience and happiness. Little wonder then that the Qur'ān designates Muslims as the best community. For serving mankind elevates it to an exalted rank.

Muslims all over the world, especially Muslim minorities have to prove that they are the best community, devoted to the cause of protecting mankind against suffering and blessing everyone with happiness, regardless of caste, colour or creed. Their position is of the best community and their duty is to serve mankind. Muslims have failed to live up to this ideal. By serving their coreligionists they must illustrate that they are bearers of public service and goodness. Their presence must guarantee help for everyone, especially of their non-Muslim country. However, this cannot be affirmed merely verbally or by recounting old stories. They have to prove it by their conduct.

There is a vast ground for Muslims' social relations as a minority with non-Muslims. Broadly it is at two levels: (i) Excellent social relations with non-Muslims and establishing centres for social welfare. Both these steps are inter-dependent. For these are rooted in the mindset produced by Islamic teachings. If this is realized that a Muslim is obliged to serve everyone, without any discrimination, it would motivate us to share the sorrows of the suffering humanity and helping those in need. Muslims would be thus mentally prepared for assisting others in an active manner. It would help eradicate such negative traits such as selfishness, greed, and self-centeredness and promote values such as sacrifice, self-abnegation, spending on others, generosity, treating others well, maintaining ties of kinship, love, affection and concern for others. This would prompt them to treat others on a preferential basis.

Many points are involved in the social relations with non-Muslims. The obligations due to neighbours necessitate that Muslims should regularly visit their non-Muslim friends at their homes, workplace and other platforms. Their interaction would promote good will, culminating in close friendship. For example, the Prophet's practice of calling on the sick has many far-reaching considerations. Sharing one's sorrow brings people closer. The advantages of visiting the sick are common knowledge. It infuses mutual love. Leaving participation in non-Muslims' festivals, seasonal gatherings, weddings, funerals and other gatherings is important. It is especially useful for the Muslim minority.

Equally important it is for Muslim minority to invite non-Muslims to parties at home and invite them for Idd and other social and religious get together. They should be cordially invited to marriage parties and other socio-cultural occasions. In summary, they should be welcomed at home, in the work place, shops and public places. It would produce good results within a short time. Wherever such social relations have existed, riots have not affected much the Muslim minority.

Gifts are the key to inculcating and developing mutual love, as is stated by the Prophet (peace be upon him). One cannot deny this self-evident truth. The Prophet accepted the gifts of non-Muslims. This practice was faithfully followed by his Companions. For they sent presents on a regular basis to their friends, relatives and acquaintances. This naturally endeared them to non-Muslims.

The above practice of the Prophet (peace be upon him) has much to offer to the Muslim minority. If they regularly send presents to both Muslim and non-Muslim friends and relatives, they would discharge an important social obligation and follow an Islamic principle that promotes mutual love. Another important institution for serving others and doing valuable service is education. Non-Muslims can obviously benefit only from modern educational institutions. The Muslim minority should pay special attention to it. They should establish a network of these institutions, of which the doors should be open for everyone. Rather, non-Muslims should be treated better and be awarded discount in fees. If students of poor families are provided with quality education, it would attract students from wealthier sections. Renowned Muslim educational institutions are an instance in point. The most telling example is of the Muslim University, Aligarh which caters for higher education and moral training. It is a vast ground for guiding both Muslim and non-Muslim students. Through this avenue, religious duty may be performed as well.

It is important for the Muslim minority to establish institutions of public welfare such as hospitals, poor people's homes, children's homes, orphanages, centres for the disabled, travelers' lodges, coaching centres for students etc. These are essential not only for the survival of the Muslim minority but also for attracting non-Muslims. Keeping their doors open for non-Muslims would have manifold advantages. This would ensure not only the welfare of the minority but also endear the non-Muslims and serve the cause of helping humanity.

We often complain of the lack of resources. Obviously resources are needed for setting up such institutions. However, arranging for funds for these is not so difficult. The Muslim community which has already been sponsoring hundreds of thousands of madrasas can easily set up these welfare institutions. What is really needed is the deep realization to take up such projects. These could not be obviously run without competent managers. The only thing missing is to realize community and national obligations and to establish institutions which are suited best in the given circumstances. There is a pressing need for taking up this project with single-minded devotion. For this sincere intention Allah promises that He provides ways and means for all the good projects aimed at His cause: 'And those who strive in Our cause, We will certainly guide them to our paths. For verily Allah is with those who do right.'[2]

12. Muslims, be they in majority or minority, stand obliged to adhere to their faith and devote themselves fully to Allah regardless of the directive for them to draw upon material resources. Islam prescribes spiritual growth as a prerequisite for material prosperity. Logically speaking, if a Muslim is not committed fully to Allah, His Messenger and Islam, his claim to faith cannot be taken seriously.

Allah's help and support is contingent upon the proximity with Allah and observance of the Qur'ān and *sunnah* and love for faith. The more these qualities are, the greater divine help would be. On the same basis many small groups have registered victory over numerically bigger groups. The Makkan minority by Allah's grace alone grew into a majority in Madīnah and eventually prevailed over the Quraysh and Arabs.

Muslims in general and Muslim minorities in particular must intensify the efforts for their spiritual development. It would accrue to them material prosperity and bless them with stability and constant evolution. Without spirituality and religious fervour even non-Muslims scale heights of progress. What is then so special about Muslims? Notwithstanding all material efforts the Muslim minority must strive to gain spiritual power. It is by dint of supplicating to Allah invoking Him for help, commitment to faith and practising it in its fullness and adhering to the Prophet's excellent example that they may be blessed with true spirituality. On its quintessential evolution depends the destiny of the Muslims. For the allegiance to the Prophet draws one closer to Allah.

To Allah be praise at the first and at the last. For Him is the command. And to Him all of you shall be brought back.[3]

Bibliography

Primary Sources

The Glorious Qur'ān

Abū ʿUbayd Qāsim ibn Sallām (224/836), *Kitāb al-Amwāl*, Cairo, 1934.

Abū Dāwūd (Sulaymān ibn al-Ashʿath 275/888), *al-Sunan,* Cairo, 1922.

Abū Ḥanīfah al-Dīnawarī (Aḥmad ibn Dāwūd 282/895), *Kitāb al-Akhbār al-Ṭiwāl*, Leiden, 1888).

Abū Nuʿaym al-Iṣfahānī (Aḥmad ibn ʿAbdullāh 430/1039), *Dalā'il al-Nubuwwah*, Hyderabad, 1950.

Abū Yūsuf (Yaʿqūb ibn Ibrāhīm 182/898), *Kitāb al-Kharāj*, Cairo, 1933.

Abū Zarʿah al-Dimashqī (ʿAbd al-Raḥmān ibn ʿĀmir 282/895), *Sīrat al-Rasūl wa Ta'rīkh al-Khulafā' al-Rāshidīn*, Damascus, 1980.

Abū'l-Faraj al-Iṣfahānī (ʿAlī ibn Ḥusayn 356/969), *Kitāb al-Aghānī*, Leiden, 1900; *Maqātil al-Ṭālibīn,* Najaf, 1934.

Al-Ashʿarī (ʿAlī ibn Ismāʿīl 330/941), *Maqālāt al-Islāmiyyīn wa Ikhtilāf al-Muslimīn*, Istanbul, 1930.

Al-Azraqī (Muḥammad ibn ʿAbdullāh 244/858), *Akhbār Makkah al-Musharrafah*, Beirut, 1964.

Al-Baghdādī (ʿAbd al-Qāhir ibn Ṭāhir 429/1037) *al-Farq bayn al-Firaq*, Cairo, 1910.

Al-Baghdādī (Muḥammad ibn Ḥabīb 245/849), *Kitāb al-Muhabbar*, Hyderabad Deccan, 1942; *Kitāb al-Munammaq*, Hyderabad Deccan, 1964.

Al-Balādhurī (Aḥmad ibn Yaḥyā ibn Jābir 279/892), *Ansāb al-Ashrāf*, Cairo, 1959 (I); Jerusalem, 1938 (IV), 1936 (V); *Futūḥ al-Buldān*, Cairo, 1932.

Al-Bukhārī *al-Jāmiʿ al-Ṣaḥīḥ*, Cairo, 1955.

Al-Dhahabī (Muḥammad ibn Aḥmad 748/1347), *Ta'rīkh al-Islām*, Cairo, 1973; *Tadhkirat al-Ḥuffāẓ*, Hyderabad, Deccan, 1914-1915; *Mīzān al-Iʿtidāl*, Cairo, 1910.

Al-Diyārbakrī (Ḥusayn ibn Muḥammad 966/1559), *al-Khamīs fī Aḥwāl Anfās al-Nafīs*, Cairo, 1885.

Al-Fakīhī (Muḥammad ibn Isḥāq 272/886), *al-Muntaqā fī Akhbār Umm al-Qur'ān*, Beirut, 1964.

Al-Ḥalabī (ʿAlī ibn Burhān al-Dīn 1044/1634) *Insān al-ʿUyūn fī Sīrat al-Amīnwa'l-Ma'mūn,* Cairo, 1964

Al-Ḥimyarī (Sulaymān ibn Mūsā 634/1236), *al-Iktifā fī Maghāzī al-Muṣṭafā wa al-Thalāthah al-Khulafā'*, Cairo 1970.

Al-Jāḥiẓ (ʿAmr ibn Baḥr 255/868), *al-Bayān wa al-Tabyīn*, Cairo, 1948; *Risālah fī Tafḍīl Banī Hāshim*, Cairo, 1931; *al-ʿUthmāniyyah*, Cairo, 1958; *Kitāb al-Bukhalā'*, Cairo, 1958.

Al-Jaḥshiyarī (Muḥammad ibn ʿAbdūs 331/942), *Kitāb al-Wuzarā' wa'l-Kuttāb*, Cairo, 1938.

Al-Jumḥī (Muḥammad ibn Salām 231/845), *Ṭabaqāt Fuḥūl al-Shuʿarā'*, Cairo, 1952.

Al-Kashshī (Muḥammad ibn ʿUmar 4th/10th Century), *Maʿrifat Akhbār al-Rijāl*, Karbalā', 1962.

Al-Kindī (Muḥammad ibn Yūsuf 350/961), *Kitāb al-Umarā' wa'l-Wulāt wa'l-Quḍāt*, Leiden, 1912; *Wulāt Miṣr*, Beirut, 1959.

Al-Maqrīzī (Aḥmad ibn ʿAlī 845/1442), *Imtāʿ al-Asmāʿ*, Cairo, 1941.

Al-Masʿūdī (ʿAlī ibn Ḥusayn 345/956), *Kitāb al-Tanbīh wa'l-Ashrāf*, Leiden, 1894; *Murūj al-Dhahab*, Cairo, 1927.

Al-Māwardī (ʿAlī ibn Muḥammad 450/1058), *al-Aḥkām al-Sulṭāniyyah*, Cairo, 1880.

Al-Nasāʾī (Aḥmad ibn Shuʿayb 203/915), *al-Sunan*, Kanpur, 1882.

Al-Nawawī (Yaḥyā ibn Sharaf al-Dīn 676/1277), *Riyāḍ al-Ṣāliḥīn*, Damascus, 1976; *Sharḥ Ṣaḥīḥ Muslim*, Cairo, 1928.

Al-Samhūdī (ʿAlī ibn ʿAbdullāh 911/1505), *Wafāʾ al-Wafā bi-Akhbār Dār al-Muṣṭafā*, Cairo, 1908-1909.

Al-Shāmī (Muḥammad ibn Yūsuf al-Dimashqī 942/1535), *Subul al-Hudā wa'l-Rashād fī Sīrat Khayr al-ʿIbād*, Cairo, 1975.

Al-Suhaylī (ʿAbd al-Raḥmān ibn ʿAbdullāh 581/1185), *al-Rawd al-Unf* , Cairo, n.d.

Al-Ṭabarī (Muḥammad ibn Jarīr 310/923), *Ta'rīkh al-Rusul wa'l-Mulūk*, Cairo, 1960; *Tahdhīb al-Āthār*, Riyāḍ, 1982' *Jāmiʿ al-Bayān ʿAn Ta'wīl Āy al-Qur'ān*, Cairo, 1960.

Al-Tirmidhī (Muḥammad ibn ʿĪsā 279/892), *al-Jāmiʿ al-Ṣāḥīḥ,* Ḥimṣ, 1969-1971; *al-Shamā'il al-Nabawiyyah*, Cairo, 1863.

Al-Wāqidī (Muḥammad ibn ʿUmar 207/822), *Kitāb al-Maghāzī*, London, 1966.

Al-Zubayrī (Mūsā ibn ʿAbdullāh 236/851), *Nasab Quraysh*, Cairo, 1953.

Ibn ʿAbd al-Barr (Yūsuf ibn ʿAbdullāh 463/1260) *al-Istīʿāb fī Maʿrifat al-Aṣḥāb*, Hyderabad, 1900.

Ibn ʿAbd al-Ḥakam (ʿAbd al-Raḥmān ibn ʿAbdullāh 259/870), *Kitāb Futūḥ Afrīqiyyah wa'l-Andalus*, Algeria, 1947.

Ibn ʿAbd al-Ḥakam (ʿAbdullāh 214/829), *Sīrat ʿUmar ibn ʿAbd al-Azīz*, Cairo 1927.

Ibn ʿAbd Rabbih (Aḥmad ibn Muḥammad 328/940), *al-ʿIqd al-Farīd*, Cairo, 1940.

Ibn ʿAsākir al-Dimashqī (ʿAlī ibn Ḥasan 571/1176), *Ta'rīkh Madīnat Dimashq*, Damascus, 1951 *Tahdhīb al-Ta'rīkh al-Kabīr*, Damascus, 1911-1932.

Ibn Abī al-Ḥadīd (ʿAbd al-Ḥamīd ibn Hibat Allāh d. 655/1259), *Sharḥ Nahj al-Balāghah*, Cairo 1959.

Ibn Abī Iyās (Muḥammad ibn Aḥmad d. 930/1524), *Badā'iʿ al-Zuhūr fī Waqā'iʿ al-Duhūr*, Bulaq, 1311 AH.

Ibn al-ʿArabī (al-Qāḍī Muḥammad ibn ʿAbdullāh 546/1148), *Aḥkām al-Qur'ān*, Cairo, 1957.

Ibn al-ʿImād al-Ḥanbalī (ʿAbd al-Ḥayy ibn Muḥammad 1089/1687), *Shajarat al-Dhahab fī Akhbār man Dhahab*, Cairo, 1350 H.

Ibn al-Aʿtham al-Kūfī (Aḥmad ibn ʿUthmān 314/926), *Kitāb al-Futūḥ*, Hyderabad, 1968.

Ibn al-Athīr (ʿIzz al-Dīn ʿAlī ibn Muḥammad d. 630/1233), *Usd al-Ghābah*, Tehran, 1938; *al-Kāmil fī al-Ta'rīkh*, Beirut, 1965.

Ibn al-Jawzī (ʿAbd al-Raḥmān ibn ʿAlī 597/1200), *Sīrat ʿUmar ibn ʿAbd al-ʿAzīz*, Cairo, 1912; *Ṣifat al-Ṣafwah*, Hyderabad, 1936; *al-Muntaẓam fī al-Ta'rīkh*, Hyderabad, 1938.

Ibn al-Kalbī (Hishām ibn Muḥammad 204/816), *Kitāb al-Aṣnām*, Leipzig, 1941.

Ibn al-Murtaḍā (Aḥmad ibn Yaḥyā 840/1437), *Ṭabaqāt al-Muʿtazilah*, Beirut, 1961.

Ibn al-Nadīm (Muḥammad ibn Isḥāq 235/849), *al-Fihrist*, Cairo, 1968. Urdu translation, Lahore, 1988.

Ibn al-Ṭiqṭaqā (Muḥammad ibn ʿAlī ibn Ṭabaṭabā'ī 709/1309), *Kitāb al-Fakhrī*, Cairo, 1899.

Ibn Durayd al-Azdī (Muḥammad ibn Ḥasan 321/933), *Kitāb al-Ishtiqāq*, Gottingen, 1854; Cairo, 1958.

Ibn Ḥajar al-ʿAsqalānī (Aḥmad ibn ʿAlī 852/1448) *al-Iṣābah fī Tamyīz al-Ṣaḥābah*, Cairo, 1938; *Tahdhīb al-Tahdhīb*, Hyderabad, 1911; *Fatḥ al-Bārī fī Sharḥ al-Bukhārī*, Bulaq, 1882; Riyadh, 1997; *Lisān al-Mīzān*, Hyderabad, 1911.

Ibn Ḥajar al-Haythamī (Aḥmad ibn Muḥammad 974/1566), *Taṭhīr al-Janān*, Cairo, n.d.; *al-Ṣawāʿiq al-Muḥriqah*, Beirut, 1965.

Ibn Ḥanbal (Aḥmad ibn Muḥammad 241/855), *al-Musnad*, Cairo, 1949.

Ibn Ḥazm (ʿAlī ibn Aḥmad 456/1064), *Jamharat Ansāb al-ʿArab*, Cairo, 1948; *Jawāmiʿ al-Sīrah*, Cairo 1956; *Kitāb al-Fiṣal fī Milal wa'l-Niḥal*, Cairo, 1899-1902.

Ibn Hishām (ʿAbd al-Malik ibn Hishām 218/333), *al-Sīrat al-Nabawiyyah*, Cairo, 1925.

Ibn Isḥāq (Muḥammad ibn Isḥāq d. 150/767), *al-Sīrah al-Nabawiyyah*, Rabat, 1967.

Ibn Kathīr (Ismāʿīl ibn ʿUmar 774/1373), *al-Bidāyah wa'l-Nihāyah*, Cairo, 1932; *al-Sīrah al-Nabawiyyah*, Beirut, 1983; *al-Fuṣūl fī Sīrat al-Rasūl*, Damascus, 1402-1403 AH.

Ibn Khaldūn (ʿAbd al-Raḥmān ibn Muḥammad 804/1406), *Kitāb al-ʿIbar*, Beirut; *al-Muqaddimah*, Maṭbaʿat Muṣṭafā Muḥammad, Cairo, n.d.

Ibn Khallikān (Aḥmad ibn Muḥammad 681/1281), *Wafayāt al-Aʿyān*, Bulaq, 1859.

Ibn Mājah (Muḥammad ibn Yazīd 273/886), *al-Sunan*, Cairo, 1952.

Ibn Manẓūr (Muḥammad ibn Mukarram 711/1311), *Lisān al-ʿArab*, Beirut, 1955-56.

Ibn Qayyim al-Jawziyyah (Muḥammad ibn Abī Bakr 751/1350), *Iʿlām al-Muwaqqiʿīn ʿAn Rabb al-ʿĀlamīn*, Cairo, n.d.; *Zād al-Maʿād,* Cairo 1971; *al-Manār al-Munīf*, Aleppo, 1970.

Ibn Qutaybah (ʿAbdullāh ibn Muslim al-Dīnawarī 276/889), *al-Shiʿr wa'l-Shuʿarā'*, Leiden, 1920; *ʿUyūn al-Akhbār*, Cairo, 1925; *Kitāb al-Imāmah wa'l-Siyāsah*, Cairo, 1925.

Ibn Saʿd (Muḥammad ibn Saʿd 230/1334), *ʿUyūn al-Athar fī Funūn al-Maghāzī wa al-Shamā'il wa'l-Siyar*, Cairo, 1937.

Ibn Taymīyah (Aḥmad ibn ʿAbd al-Ḥalīm 652/1254) *Jāmiʿ al-Kalām al-Ṭayyib*, Beirut, 1976; *Kitāb (ʿIlm al-Salūl)*, 1398 AH; *Majmūʿ Fatāwā Shaykh al-Islām Aḥmad ibn Taymīyah*, edited by ʿAbd al-Raḥmān ibn Muḥammad al-Ḥanbalī; *al-Muntaqā min Akhbār al-Muṣṭafā* Cairo, 1931; *Minhāj al-Sunnah*, Cairo, 1958.

Ibn Ṭūlūn (Muḥammad ibn ʿAlī 953/1546), *Quḍāt Dimashq al-Shām*, Damascus, 1956

Khalīfah ibn Khayyāṭ (240/854) *Kitāb al-Ta'rīkh*, Damascus, 1967; *Kitāb al-Ṭabaqāt*, Damascus, 1966-67.

Mālik ibn Anas (179/795), *al-Muwaṭṭa'*, Cairo, 1951.

Muslim ibn al-Ḥajjāj al-Qushayrī (261/875) *al-Jāmiʿ al-Ṣaḥīḥ*, Cairo, 1955.

Qāḍī ʿIyāḍ (ibn Mūsā Yaḥsubī 542/1147), *al-Shifā'*, Cairo, 1950.

Walīullāh al-Dihlavī (1176/1762), *Izālat al-Khafā' ʿan Khilāfat al-Khulafā'*, Maṭbaʿat Siddiqui, Bareilly, 1286/1869; Suhayl Academy, Lahore, 1976; *Ḥujjatullāh al-Bālighah*, Maṭbaʿat Siddiqui, Bareilly, 1286, Kitāb Khānah Rashīdiyyah, Delhi, 1953, al-Maktabah al-Salafiyyah, Lahore, n.d.; *Fatḥ al-Raḥmān*, Lahore.

Yaʿqūbī (Aḥmad ibn Abī Yaqʿūb 284/897), *Ta'rīkh al-Yaʿqūbī*, Beirut, 1960; *Kitāb al-Buldān*, Leiden, 1860, Cairo, 1955.

Yaḥyā ibn Ādam (203/818), *Kitāb al-Kharāj*, Leiden, 1896.

Yāqūt al-Ḥamawī (626/1229), *Irshād al-Arīb*, Leiden, 1907-1931; *Muʿjam al-Buldān*, Beirut, 1956.

Some Important Secondary Sources

Ali, Saleh Ahmad, *Tanẓīmāt al-Rasūl al-Idāriyah fī al-Madīnah*, Baghdad, 1960.

Ali, Syed Ameer, *A Short History of the Saracens*, London, 1951.

Amīn, Aḥmad, *Fajr al-Islām*, Cairo, 1964; *Ḍuḥā al-Islām* Cairo, 1964.

Azad, Abul Kalam, *Rasūl-i Raḥmat*, Delhi, 1982.

Dennet, D.C., *Conversion and Poll-Tax in Early Islam*, Cambridge, 1950. Urdu translation by Ghulam Rasul Mehr, Lahore, 1971.

Dūrī, ʿAbd al-ʿAzīz, *Baḥth fī Nash'at ʿIlm al-Ta'rīkh ʿInd al-ʿArab*, Beirut, 1960.

Gabrielli, Francisco, *A Short History of the Arabs,* London, 1965

Hamidullah, Muhammad, *ʿAhd-i Nabawī kā Niẓām-i Ḥukmrānī*, Hyderabad, 1949, *Muḥammad Rasūl Allāh*, Lahore, 1982 (in both English and Urdu); *Nabī Akram kī Siyāsī Zindagī*, Karachi, 1949.

Haykal, Muḥammad Ḥusayn, *Ḥayāt Muḥammad*, Cairo, 1952.

Hitti, Philip K., *The History of the Arabs*, London, 1969.

Kāndhalwī, Muḥammad Idrīs, *Sīrat al-Muṣṭafā*, Deoband, n.d.

Levy, Ruben, *The Social Structure of Islam*, Cambridge, 1950.

Manṣūrpūrī, Shāh Muḥammad Sulaymān, *Raḥmat lil-ʿĀlimīn*, Delhi, 1980.

Margolouith, D.S. *Mohammed and the Rise of Islam*, London 1905.

Muir, William, *The Life of Muhammad*, Edinburgh, 1923; *The Caliphate*, Beirut, 1963.

Nadvi, Shāh Mueenuddin Ahmad, *Ta'rīkh-e-Islām*, Azamgarh, 1953.

Nadvī, Syed Suleyman, *Sīrat al-Nabī*, Dār al-Muṣanifīn, Azamgarh, 1976. Vols. 3-7.

Nuʿmānī, Shiblī, *Sīrat al-Nabī*, Azamgarh, 1976, Vols. 1-2; *al-Fārūq*, Azamgarh, 1993.

Pipes, Daniel, *Slave Soldiers and Islam*, (242) Yale University Press, 1981.

Rosenthal, Franz, *History of Muslim Historiography*, Leiden, 1952.

Siddiqi, Muhammad Yasin Mazhar, *Ta'rīkh Tahdhīb-i Islāmī*, New Delhi, Vol. 1, (1994), Vol. 2 (1998); *ʿAhd-i Nabawī mayn Tanẓīm-i Riyāsat wa Ḥukūmat*, Delhi, 1988; *Organization of Government under the Prophet*, Delhi, 1987, Lahore, 1988; A number of articles on *Sīrah* in various journals.

al-ʿUmarī, Akram Ḍiyā', *al-Mujtamaʿ al-Madanī fī ʿahd al-Nubuwwah*, Madīnah, 1983.

Watt, W.M., *Muhammad at Mecca*, Oxford, 1953; *Muhammad at Madina*, Oxford 1956.

Wellhausen, J., *Arab Kingdom and Its Fall*, London, 1973.

NOTES

CHAPTER I

1. Balādhurī 1,51; Ibn Hishām 1, 136-138; al-Baghdādī, *Kitāb al-Mahbir* 167-169.
2. Azraqī 66-71; Ibn Hishām 1, 141-142; Zubayrī 14-15; Shiblī 1, 164-165; Idrīs Kāndhalwī, 1, 27-29 For further details see Yasin Mazhar Siddiqi, 'Banū ʿAbd Manāf – Azīm Tar Muttaḥidah Khāndān-i Risālat', *Maʿārif*, Azamgarh Feb 1996, 85-106 and March 1996, 96-187.
3. Ibn Hishām 1, 141-142; Shiblī 1, 211-213 and my above-mentioned article on ʿAbd Manāf.
4. Azraqī 66-71; Shiblī 1, 211-213; Balādhurī 1, 55-57; 'Banū ʿAbd Manāf Muttaḥidah Aẓīm Tar Khāndān-i Risālat'.
5. Balādhurī 1, 56, Ibn Hishām 1, 143-44; 'Banū ʿAbd Manāf – Muttaḥidah ʿAẓīm Tar Khāndān-i Risālat'.
6. Ibn Hishām 1, 144-45 and 398; 'Banū 'Abd Manāf'.
7. *Kitāb al-Munammaq*, 94-21; 'Banū ʿAbd Manāf'.
8. For details see the article 'Banū ʿAbd Manāf– ʿAẓīm Tar Muttaḥidah Khāndān-i Risālat'.
9. Ibn Hishām 1, 123-126.
10. Ibn Hishām 1, 131 and 135-136.
11. Ibn Hishām 1, 151-153 and 155; *Kitāb al-Munammaq* 42-93, 217-223 and 275-335 passim.

12. Ibn Hishām 1, 269-274; Mawdūdī, *Sīrat* 2, 155-161.
13. Balādhurī 1, 291.
14. Ibn Hishām 1, 337-338; Suhaylī 3, 196 and 320.
15. Balādhurī 1, 231.
16. Balādhurī 1, 228.
17. *Fatḥ al-Bārī* 7, 291; Ibn Hishām 1, 406.
18. Balādhurī 1, 237 and Ibn Sayyid al-Nās 1, 179.
19. Balādhurī 1, 211.
20. Ibn Hishām 1, 309 and Suhaylī 3, 77
21. Ibn Hishām 1, 395-396; Suhaylī 3, 352; Bukhārī, 'Kitāb Manāqib al-Anṣār, Bāb al-Hijrah ilā al-Madīnah'; *Fatḥ al-Bārī* 7, 287-292 and Balādhurī 1, 205-207.
22. Ibn Hishām 2, 240-241 passim, al-Suhaylī 5, 63-65, 79-80 and 85-90 passim; Shiblī 1, 314-319 passim, particularly 333-364.
23. Ibn Hishām 4, 102-104; al-Suhaylī 4, 186-188 and 217 and 5, 88; *Fatḥ al-Bārī* 7, 297-303.
24. Ibn Hishām 2, 98.
25. Ibn Hishām 3, 359-368.
26. Ibn Hishām 1, 339-340; al-Suhaylī 3, 199-200; al-Balādhurī 1, 184-185. For details see the chapter, The Abyssinians.
27. al-Balādhurī 1, 180-184.
28. Ibn Hishām 2, 30-31; al-Suhaylī 4, 35-36 and 56-57.
29. Ibn Hishām 1, 420; Mawdūdī, *Sīrat* 2, 317-318.
30. Shāh Walīullāh Dihlawī, *Ḥujjatullāh al-Bālighah*, al-Maktabah al-Salafiyah, Lahore, n.d., 1, 60-64 passim.
31. Shiblī, 1, 118-123.
32. Ibn Hishām 1, 81-90; Shiblī 1, 118-121; The Qur'ān: *Sūrah al-Najm* 53-19-21.
33. Ibn Hishām 81-82; Shiblī 1, 120-121.
34. Ibn Hishām 1, 91 passim; Shiblī 1, 120; The Qur'ān:*Sūrah Luqmān* 31:25, *al-'Ankabūt* 29:61-62 and *al-Zukhruf* 43:9 and 87.
35. *Ansāb al-Ashrāf* 1, 113.
36. The Qur'ān: *Sūrah al-Mā'idah* 5:55, *al-Baqarah* 2:125, *al-Ḥajj* 22:26.
37. *Fatḥ al-Bārī* 7, 186 passim especially 188.
38. Ibn Hishām 1, 82 passim, al-Suhaylī 2, 1; Balādhurī 1, 34 passim. For *Ḥimṣ* see *Fatḥ al-Bārī* 7, 188 passim especially 196-203. For a detailed discussion see *Ḥujjatullāh al-Bālighah* 1, 124, 128.
39. Balādhurī 1, 191; *Kitāb al-Munannaq* 129-130.

40. The Qur'ān, *Sūrah al-Baqarah* 2:135, *Āl ʿImrān* 3:67 and 95, *al-Aʿnām* 6:79 and 161, *Yūnus* 10:105, *al-Naḥl* 16:120 and 123, *al-Rūm* 30:30, *al-Ḥajj* 22:31 and *al-Bayyinah* 98:5.
41. *Kitāb al-Munammaq* 531-532; *Kitāb al-Muḥabbar* 171-172 and 237-241; Ibn Hishām 1, 242; al-Suhaylī 2,1; Shiblī 123-126.
42. Ibn Saʿd 4,222.
43. Ibn Saʿd 4,216.
44. Ibn Saʿd 2, 217-218.
45. Ibn Isḥāq and Ibn Hishām 1, 244; Balādhurī 1, 116-117.
46. Ibn Hishām 1, 243; Suhaylī 2; Balādhurī 1, 106-107; Bukhārī, '*Kitāb Bad' al-Waḥy*'. Ibn Sayyid al-Nās 1, 115. For more details see Yasin Mazhar Siddiqi's article '*Jāhilī ʿAhd mayn Ḥanīfiyat*'.
47. Ibn Hishām 1, 28-40.
48. Ibn Ḥajar, *Fatḥ al-Bārī* 1, 30, and 1, 256-257; al-Suhaylī 2; Balādhurī 1, 106-107; Ibn Sayyid al-Nās 1, 115-117.
49. Ibn Hishām 2, 31.
50. Balādhurī 1, 111.
51. Ibn Hishām 1, 256.
52. *Fatḥ al-Bārī* 7, 236-240.
53. Ibn Saʿd 4, 76-77; On the debate with the Christian delegation of Najrān on the accretions in Christianity see al-Suhaylī 5, 5-16 passim.
54. al-Suhaylī 5, 9 passim.
55. Ibn Hishām 2, 31.
56. Balādhurī 1, 475-489; Ibn Saʿd 4, 75-82 passim.
57. al-Balādhurī 1, 72-73.
58. Ibn Hishām 1, 277-279 and 283-284 passim.

CHAPTER 2

1. The Qur'ān, *Sūrah Muḥammad* 47:38.
2. Balādhurī, *Ansāb al-Ashrāf* 1, 133.
3. Ibn Hishām 1, 246-247; Ibn Sayyid al-Nās *ʿUyūn al-Athar* 1, 125. The latter is based purely on Ibn Isḥāq's report.
4. Ibn Hishām, 349; al-Suhaylī, *al-Rawḍ al-Unf* 3, 270; Ibn Isḥāq 1, 280. See the comment on it is al-Suhaylī's work and in Ibn Sayyid al-Nās,

ʿ*Uyūn al-Athar* 1, 163 passim; Bukhārī, *Kitāb Manāqib al-Anṣār, Bāb Islām ʿUmar, Fatḥ al-Bārī* 7, 23-229.

5. This is endorsed by Ibn Isḥāq and Ibn Hishām, 1, 264; al-Suhaylī, al-*Rawḍ al-Unf* 3, 43-44 on the authority of Ibn Isḥāq.
6. Ibn Saʿd 1, 199.
7. *Āl ʿImrān* 3:19.
8. The Qur'ān: *Sūrah al-Baqarah* 2:97; *Āl ʿImrān* 3:3, 39 and 50; *al-Mā'idah* 5:46 and 48; *Fāṭir* 35:31 and *al-Aḥqāf* 46:30.
9. The Qur'ān, *Al-Baqarah* 2:256.
10. The Qur'ān, *Yūnus* 10:99.
11. The Qur'ān, *Hūd* 11:28.
12. The Qur'ān, *al-Naḥl* 16:125.
13. The Qur'ān, *al-Kahf* 18:6.
14. The Qur'ān, *al-Shuʿarā'* 26:3.)
15. Ibn Hishām 1, 264-276; Balādhurī 1, 115-118 and 123-124. For further details see the article: Yasin Mazhar Siddiqi, 'Daʿwat-i Nabawī ke Ṭarīqe'.
16. Ibn Hishām 1, 268-270 passim; Balādhurī 1, 123-124 and the article 'Daʿwat-i Nabawī ke Ṭarīqe'.
17. Ibn Hishām 1, 407-410; Ibn Saʿd 4, 105 passim and the article, 'Daʿwat Nabawī ke Ṭarīqe'.
18. Ibn Hishām 1, 262; *al-Rawḍ al-Unf* 3, 42 passim; Ibn Saʿd's work, al-Zuhrī's report appears also in Ibn Sayyid al-Nās's ʿ*Uyūn al-Athar* 1, 131 on Ibn Isḥāq's authority. For further details see Yasin Mazhar Siddiqi, ʿ*Ahd-e Nabawī mayn Tanẓīm-i Riyāsat wa Ḥukūmat*, especially chapters 1-2.
19. For a detailed analysis of the views of Ibn Hishām, Balādhurī, Ibn Ḥajar, Bukhārī, and Ibn Saʿd see Yasin Mazhar Siddiqi's ʿ*Ahd-e Nabawī mayn Tanẓīm-i Riyāsat wa Ḥukūmat*, especially chapter 2.
20. See also ʿ*Ahd-e Nabawī mayn Tanẓīm-i Riyāsat wa Ḥukūmat*, especially chapter 2.
21. See also the article, Yasin Mazhar Siddiqi, 'Daʿwat-i Nabawī ke Ṭarīqe'.
22. The Qur'ān, *al-Kāfirūn* 109:6.
23. Ibn Hishām 1, 275-290 passim and 371. See also the ʿ*Ahd-e Nabawī mayn Tanẓīm-i Riyāsat was Ḥukūmat*, especially chapter 2 and 'Daʿwat-i Nabawī ke Ṭarīqe'.

24. Bukhārī, Kitāb al-Wuḍū'; Kitāb al-Ṣalāt and other Chapters *Fatḥ al-Bārī* 306-307; Ibn Hishām 1, 243-245; al-Suhaylī al-*Rawḍ al-Unf* 3, 11-15. Its editor ʿAbd al-Raḥmān al-Nabīl has cited Ibn Ḥajar's remark that before the night journey the Prophet (peace be upon him) is on record leading the Companions in prayer.
25. al-Suhaylī 3, 11-12.
26. Ibn Hishām 1, 263-265 and 275; See also Balādhurī, Bukhārī, Ibn Saʿd and other sources as cited above.
27. Ibn Hishām 1, 275-276; Balādhurī 1, 112-113 and 117-118.
28. Balādhurī 1, 117.
29. Ibn Hishām 1, 216-221; Shāh Walīullāh Dihlawī, *Ḥujjatullāh al-Bālighah* 124-128; Mawdūdī, *Sīrah*, Chapter on Tawḥīd awr Islamī Daʿwat.
30. *Ḥujjatullāh al-Bālighah* 124-128.
31. Ibn Hishām 1, 229-230; 276-278 and 386 etc; 'Daʿwat-i Nabavī ke Ṭarīqe'; Kāndhlawī 1, 116-120.
32. Ibn Hishām 1, 163; al-Suhaylī 3, 6-7; reports on the authority of Ibn Isḥāq and Ibn ʿAbbās.
33. Ibn Hishām 1, 337-338; al-Suhaylī 3, 196-197.
34. Ibn Hishām 2, 25.
35. *ʿUyūn al-Athār*. On observing ʿAlī praying along with the Prophet (peace be upon him) Abū Ṭālib directed Jaʿfar to join the Prayer. *Usd al-Ghābah* 1, 187 and al-*Iṣābah* 1, 237.
36. Ibn Hishām 1, 263 and al-Suhaylī 3, 8.
37. Ibn Hishām 1, 265 and al-Suhaylī 3, 9.
38. Ibn Saʿd 3, 171-172; Ibn Hishām 1, 263 and al-Suhaylī 3, 43.
39. Al-Suhaylī 3, 54.
40. Ibn Hishām 1, 394-396 and al-Suhaylī 3, 337.
41. *Fatḥ al-Bārī* 7, 287-291.
42. Ibn Hishām 2, 9-10; al-Suhayli 3, 401.
43. Balādhurī, 1, 162.
44. Ibn Hishām 4, 221.
45. Bukhārī, *Kitāb al-Jumuʿah*; *Fatḥ al-Bārī* 2, 488-489.
46. *Usd al-Ghābah*; *al-Iṣābah*. See also *ʿAhd-i Nabawī mayn Tanẓīm-i Riyāsat was Ḥukūmat*, chapter 2 on the ʿAbd al-Qays tribe.
47. Ibn Hishām 2, 242-243.
48. *Fatḥ al-Bārī* 7, 331 and Ibn Hishām.
49. *Fatḥ al-Bārī* 7, 306.

50. For details see *ʿAhd-i Nabawī main Tanẓīm-i Riyāsat was Ḥukūmat*, chapter on the religious system.
51. *Fatḥ al-Bārī* 7, 324-325.
52. Ibn Saʿd. *Ṭabaqāt*; Ibn al-Athīr *Usd al-Ghābah*; Ibn Ḥajar *al-Iṣābah*; Ibn ʿAbd al-Barr *al-Istīʿāb* and Yasin Mazhar Siddiqi, *ʿAhd-i Nabavī* chapter on the religious system. Further discussion appears in the chapter on Islamic centres in Makkah, in this book.
53. See *ʿAhd-i Nabawī* chapters 1 and 2 and the last chapter.
54. Ibn Hishām 1, 259, 263 and 264-265.
55. Ibn Hishām 1, 366.
56. Ibn Hishām 1, 274; Balādhurī 1, 118-119.
57. Ibn Hishām, 420. For further details see the article 'Nabawī Daʿwat wa Sīrat awr Qurayshi Majālis', *Taḥqīqat-i Islām*, Aligarh July – September 1995.
58. Ibn Saʿd 1, 200; Balādhurī, 1, 119-121.
59. Ibn Saʿd 1, 202-203.
60. Bukhārī, 'Kitāb Manāqib al-Anṣār, Bāb Islām Abī Dharr al-Ghifārī' Ibn Ḥajar, *Fatḥ al-Bārī* 7, 217-229; Balādhurī 1, 157, 176, 180, 194, 213 and 218-219.
61. Ibn Saʿd 3 and 4.
62. *Fatḥ al-Bārī* 7, 221; Ibn Saʿd 4, 219-221.
63. Ibn Saʿd 4, 214-218; *ʿAhd-i Nabawī mayn Tanẓīm-i Riyāsat was Ḥukūmat* Chapter 2.
64. Ibn Saʿd 4, 237-240; *ʿAhd-i Nabawī mayn Tanẓīm-i Riyāsat was Ḥukūmat* Chapter 2.
65. Ibn Saʿd 4, 241; *ʿAhd-i Nabawī mayn Tanẓīm-i Riyāsat was Ḥukūmat* Chapter 2.
66. Ibn Saʿd 4, 105-107 and *ʿAhd-i Nabawī mayn Tanẓīm-i Riyāsat was Ḥukūmat* Chapter 2.
67. *ʿAhd-i Nabawī mayn Tanẓīm-i Riyāsat was Ḥukūmat* Chapter 2.
68. *ʿAhd-i Nabawī mayn Tanẓīm-i Riyāsat was Ḥukūmat* Chapter 2.
69. Ibn Hishām 2, 51; al-Suhaylī 4, 83 and Ibn Sayyid al-Nās 1, 225.
70. *Fatḥ al-Bārī* 7, 287.
71. Ibn Hishām 2, 55.

CHAPTER 3

1. Muḥammad Mujībullāh Nadwī, *Ahl-i Kitāb Ṣaḥābah wa Tābiʿīn* 91-96.
2. Balādhurī 1, 59.
3. Balādhurī 1, 73.
4. Ibn Hishām 1, 339.
5. *Fatḥ al-Bārī* 7, 126 and 4, 520.
6. Masud Ahmad on the authority of *Ṣaḥīḥ Muslim*, 'Kitāb al-Jihād', 858 *Fatḥ al-Bārī* 7, 113; Ibn Saʿd 8, 223.
7. Ibn Sayyid al-Nās 2, 398-399.
8. Balādhurī 1, 471-473 and 476; Mawdūdī, *Sīrat*, 2, 95; For further details see, Yasin Mazhar Siddiqi, 'Ḥaḍrat Umm Ayman – Rasūl Akram kī Anna', *Maʿārif*, Azamgarh, February-March 2003.
9. Balādhurī 1, 482; Ibn Saʿd 3, 48-49.
10. *Ṭabaqāt* 3, 48-49.
11. Balādhurī 1, 484.
12. *Ṭabaqāt* 3, 49-50.
13. Ibn Hishām 1, 167.
14. Ibn Saʿd 1, 204; Ṭabarī 2, 329.
15. Ṭabarī 2, 328.
16. Ibn Hishām 1, 343-344; Balādhurī, 1, 198; Ibn Sayyid al-Nās 1, 151.
17. For geographical and historical details see the entry 'Ḥabashah' in *Urdū Dā'irah Maʿārif Islāmiyyah*, Lahore and *Muʿjam al-Buldān*.
18. Ibn Hishām 1, 321-330; al-Suhaylī 3, 203-215 and 222-230; Ibn Saʿd 1, 203-208; Balādhurī 1, 198-205; *Fatḥ al-Bārī* 7, 237-240.
19. Ṭabarī 2; Ibn Kathīr 3, 66-68; Shiblī, *Sīrat al-Nabī* 1, 231-240 and Muhammad Hamidullah, *Muḥammad Rasūl Allāh. Nuqūsh: Rasūl Number* 2, 557; *Muḥammad at Mecca.*
20. Ibn Hishām 1, 344-353; al-Suhaylī 3, 203-213 and 222-230; Balādhurī 1, 198-205.
21. Ibn Hishām 1, 353-357; al-Suhaylī 3, 213-215.
22. Ibn Hishām 1, 356, al-Suhaylī 3, 213 and 230-239.
23. Ibn Hishām 1, 356-364 and 2, 388; al-Suhaylī 3, 242-248, 252-263 and 330-333.
24. Al-Suhaylī 3, 253-255; Ibn Isḥāq on the authority of Yūnus ibn Bukayr and Abū al-Faraj al-Iṣfahānī; Musab Zubayri *Nasab Quraysh*, 322.

25. Ibn Hishām 1, 357-361; al-Suhaylī 3, 346-248 and 255-261.
26. Ibn Hishām 1, 361 and al-Suhaylī 3, 248-249.
27. Ibn Hishām 1, 388-394 and 336 and the article, Yasin Mazhar Siddiqi, ''Ahd-i Nabawī mayn Samaji Taḥaffuẓ kā Niẓām', *Taḥqīqāt-i Islāmī,* Aligarh, October-December 2002.
28. Ibn Hishām 2, 360-361; al-Suhaylī 3, 448 and passim. *Fatḥ al-Bārī* 7, 237-238; Mawdūdī, *Sīrat* 2, 360-361 only the authority of Ibn ʿAsākir and Ṭabarānī.
29. Bukhārī, 'Kitāb al-Maghāzī', Bāb Ghazwat Khaybar No. 38, ḥadīth no 4230; *Fatḥ al-Bārī* 7, 605-608.
30. Ibn Kathīr 3, 70-71 on the authority of Abū Nuʿaym's *Dalā'il al-Nubuwwah* and Bayhaqī's *Dalā'il al-Nubuwwah.*
31. See also the article, Yasin Mazhar Siddiqi, 'Kiyā Muhājirīn-i Makkah khālī hāth Madīnah Āye the?' in *ʿAhd-i Nabawī* Chapter – 5.
32. See our discussion above on this point.
33. Mawdūdī, *Sīrat,* 2, 569.
34. Ibn Hishām 1, 357 and al-Suhaylī 3, 244.
35. al-Suhaylī 3, 223.
36. Ibn Hishām 2, 346; al-Suhaylī 3, 27; Ibn Hishām 3, 414 and 423; Bukhārī, 'Kitāb Manāqib al-Anṣār, Bāb Hijrat al-Ḥabashah'; *Fatḥ al-Bārī* 7, 236-239.
37. Ibn Hishām 2, 348 and 3, 423.
38. Ibn Hishām 2, 416 and 3, 423.
39. Ibn Hishām 2, 349.
40. Al-Suhaylī 3, 241-242.
41. Ibn Hishām 3, 423; Balādhurī 1, 200-201 and 430; al-Suhaylī 3, 223 passim.
42. Ibn Hishām 3, 414 and 423.
43. Balādhurī 1, 538.
44. Shiblī 2, 418; Kāndhalawī 3, 340; Ibn Hishām 3, 417 and 423.
45. See the entry 'Umm Ḥabībah', *Urdū Dā'irah Maʿārif Islāmiyyah,* Lahore.
46. Ibn Hishām 3, 423.
47. Ibn Hishām 3, 423.
48. Balādhurī 1, 202.
49. Balādhurī 1, 9.
50. Balādhurī 1, 202.
51. Al-Suhaylī 2, 230.
52. Ibn Hishām 3, 414.

53. Ibn Hishām 1, 416.
54. Ibn Hishām 2, 416 and 3, 422-423.
55. Ibn Hishām 3, 420.
56. Balādhurī 1, 217.
57. Ibn Hishām 3, 422.
58. Balādhurī 1, 202-203 and 216.
59. Balādhurī 1, 215.
60. Balādhurī 1, 199 and 226.
61. Ibn Hishām 3, 420.
62. Balādhurī 1, 199.
63. Balādhurī 1, 205-208, 214 and 226-227.
64. Ibn Hishām 32, 417 and 421; al-Suhaylī 6, 535-545.
65. Ibn Hishām 3, 417-418; Balādhurī 1, 199-200.
66. Ibn Kathīr 3, 70
67. The Qur'ān, *al-Ṣaff* 61:6.
68. Ibn Kathīr 3, 71-72.
69. Ibn Kathīr 3, 77.
70. Ibn Kathīr 377; Bukhārī, 'Kitāb Manāqib al-Anṣār, Bāb Mawt al-Najāshī'; *Fatḥ al-Bārī* 7, 240-241; Kitāb al-Janā'iz.
71. Ibn Hishām 1, 361 and 363-64; al-Suhaylī 3, 248-249 and 251-252.
72. See also the article, 'Hijrat Ḥabashah awr Daʿwat-i Islāmī', *Rāh-i Iʿtidāl*, Omarabad, November 2002.
73. Muḥammad Mujībullāh Nadwī, *Ahl-i Kitāb.*
74. Muḥammad Mujībullāh Nadwī 1,2.
75. Ibid, p.4
76. Balādhurī 1, 257.
77. Balādhurī 1, 257.
78. Al-Suhaylī 3, 260.
79. Al-Suhaylī 3, 226-227; Bukhārī, 'Kitāb al-Jihād'; *Fatḥ al-Bārī* 7, 236.
80. Ibn Hishām 1, 360; al-Suhaylī 3, 248 and 256. 'Shiyūm' is interpreted as an Abyssinian word or as a derivative of Arabic.
81. Muḥammad Mujībullāh Nadvī, *Ahl-i Kitāb Ṣaḥābah wa Tābiʿīn*, Azamgarh, 1951, p. 108.
82. Mawhūb ibn Aḥmad al-Jawālīqī, 465AH-540AH, *al-Muʿarrab*, edited by V. Abdur Raheem, Dār al-Qalam, Damascus, 1990, 62-63.
83. al-Suhaylī 3, 260.
84. Ibn Hishām 1, 353-357; al-Suhaylī 3, 230-239 and 3, 244 dealing respectively with grammatical points and Abū Ṭālib's poetry.

CHAPTER 4

1. Ibn Hishām 1, 265; al-Suhaylī 3, 45.
2. Ibn Hishām 1, 265; al-Suhaylī 3, 45.
3. Ibn Hishām 1, 265; al-Suhaylī 3, 46-47.
4. Ibn Hishām 1, 267-269; al-Suhaylī 3, 47-49.
5. (Ibn Hishām 1, 270-271 and Suhaylī 3, 61.)
6. Ibn Hishām 1, 293; al-Suhaylī 3, 120.
7. Ibn Hishām 1, 29; al-Suhaylī 3, 117.
8. Ibn Hishām 1, 344 and al-Suhaylī 3, 266.
9. Ibn Sayyid al-Nās 1, 264-265; Muḥammad ibn Ḥabīb al-Baghdādī, *Kitāb al-Muḥabbar* 70-71; Yasin Mazhar Siddiqi, 'Makkī Muwākhāt – Islāmī Mu'āshire kī Awwalīn Tanẓīm' *Ma'ārif*, Azamgarh, December 1997 – January 1998.
10. Ibn Hishām 1, 340-341; Balādhurī 1, 186; *Fatḥ al-Bārī* 7, 16-18.
11. Syed Suleyman Nadwī and Shiblī Nu'mānī *Sīrat* 1, 185-187 and 187-190; *Ta'rīkh Tahdhīb-i Islām* 1, 92-94.
12. Ibn Kathīr, *Sīrat* 1, 123-130; 'Ma'īshat-i Nabawī-Makkī 'Ahd mayn'.
13. Balādhurī *Ansāb* 4A, 12; Muḥammad Jāsim Ḥammādī Mashhadānī, *Mawārid al-Balādhurī*, Maktabat al-Ṭālib al-Jāī'ī, Makkah, 1986, 1, 197; 'Ma'īshat-i Nabawī Makkī 'Ahd mayn'.
14. Shibli 1, 185-188 on the authority of *Sunan Abī Dāwūd* 2, 326, 'Kitāb al- Adab, and 2, 317; *al-Iṣābah* 5, 253; *Nūr al-Nibrās fī Sharḥ Ibn Sayyid al-Nās*; *Musnad* of Aḥmad ibn Ḥanbal 4, 206; 'Ma'īshat-i Nabawī Makkī 'Ahd mayn'.
15. Ibn Hishām 2, 86.
16. *Fatḥ al-Bārī* 7, 298-303.
17. *Fatḥ al-Bārī* 7, 303 and 298.
18. *Fatḥ al-Bārī* 7, 313.
19. *Fatḥ al-Bārī* 7, 304 and Ḥāfiẓ Ibn Ḥajar al-'Asqalānī's discussion on the point.
20. Balādhurī 1, 171-172 and 182; Ibn Sa'd 3, 164 and 228-229. For further details see the article by Yasin Mazhar Siddiqi, 'Kiya Muhājirīn-i Makkah khālī hāth Madīnah Āye the?'.
21. Ibn Sa'd 3, 150-151.
22. Ibn Sa'd 3, 41-42.
23. Ibn Sa'd 3, 230.

24. Balādhurī 1, 118-119; Shiblī 1, 210 on the authority of Ṭabarī 3, 107, *Tafsīr* 16, 18 along with Syed Suleyman Nadwī's note; Ṭabarī 2, 319-320; it provides details of the meal.
25. Ibn Hishām 1, 250-252.
26. Balādhurī 1, 137-138.
27. Ibn Hishām 1, 353-354.
28. Ibn Kathīr 3, 87-88 and passim.
29. *Kitāb al-Munammaq* 206, 456; *Kitāb al-Muḥabbar* 174; Abū'l-Faraj al-Iṣfahānī *Kitāb al-Aghānī* 6, 195-199; Ibn Hishām 2, 402-403; al-Wāqidī, *Kitāb al-Maghāzī* 817-818; Balādhurī 1, 355; Ṭabarī 3, 53 and 'Banū Hāshim awr Banū Umayyah ke Taʿalluqāt' 16.
30. Ibn Saʿd 8, 44; Ṭabarī, 2 249 *Kitāb al-Aghānī* 4, 33; Ibn Hishām 1, 608.
31. Bukhārī; Ibn Hishām 2, 297-299; Ibn Saʿd 8, 30-36; Balādhurī 1, 397; Zubayrī 157-158; *Kitāb al-Muḥabbar* 99-100 and 451; Ibn Qutaybah, *Kitāb al-Ma'ārif* 141.
32. Ibn Saʿd 8, 58; Shiblī 2, 407; Syed Sulayman Nadwī *Sīrat-i ʿĀ'ishah*, 11 on the authority of the works of Aḥmad and Ḥākim.
33. Bukhārī, 'Kitāb al-Jihād wa'l-Siyar' Ḥadīth 2, 988; *Fatḥ al-Bārī* 6, 159-160 on the authority of ʿAbd al-Razzāq and Ṭabarānī.
34. The Qur'ān, *al-Nisā'* 4:58.
35. See Bukhārī, 'Kitāb al-Ḥajj' Ḥadīth 1634-1635 and also 1743-1745, *Fatḥ al-Bārī* 3, 620-622.
36. Muslim, 'Kitāb al-Ḥajj'.

CHAPTER 5

1. Ibn Hishām 1, 269 and 317; al-Suhaylī 3, 48; Ibn Saʿd 1, 203; Balādhurī 1, 156 and Ibn Kathīr 3, 57.
2. Ibn Hishām 1, 321 and 316; Balādhurī 1, 130-131, see also the commentary on *Sūrah al-Lahab*.
3. Balādhurī 1, 205-207.
4. *Fatḥ al-Bārī* 7, 223.
5. For details see Yasin Mazhar Siddiqi, 'ʿAhd-i Nabawī mayn Samājī Taḥaffuẓ ka Niẓām', *Taḥqīqāt-i Islāmī*, Aligarh October-December 2003.

6. Balādhurī 1, 156-158.
7. Ibn Hishām 1, 406; al-Suhaylī 3, 362; Balādhurī 1, 237; ''Ahd-i Nabawī mayn Samājī Taḥaffuẓ ka Niẓām'.
8. Balādhurī 1, 227. The same is reiterated by other writers on the *sīrah* and history. For further details see the article, Yasin Mazhar Siddiqi, 'Samājī Taḥaffuẓ ka Niẓām'.
9. Bukhārī, 'Kitāb al-Wakālah'; *Fatḥ al-Bārī* 4, 604-605.
10. Ibn Isḥāq/Ibn Hishām 2, 271-272; al-Suhaylī 5, 105-110; Ṭabarī 2, 451; Balādhurī 1, 191.
11. Ibn Hishām 1, 275; al-Suhaylī 3, 43; Balādhurī 1, 116.
12. *Fatḥ al-Bārī* 7, 209-214.
13. *Fatḥ al-Bārī* 7, 212-213.
14. Ibn Hishām 1, 413.
15. Ibn Hishām 1, 291-292.
16. *Ṭabaqāt* 3, 101.
17. Balādhurī 1, 228.
18. Ibn Hishām 1, 364.
19. Ibn Hishām 1, 364; Ibn Saʿd 3, 269-270; Ibn Kathīr 3, 33.
20. Ibn Kathīr 3, 31.
21. Ibn Kathīr 3, 31.
22. Ibn Hishām 1, 365.
23. Ibn Hishām 1, 368.
24. Ibn Hishām 1, 370.
25. Ibn Hishām 1, 370-371; *Fatḥ al-Bārī* 7, 222-229.
26. For discussion see Mawdūdī, *Sīrat* 2, Chapter 6 Sections 1-5; Ibn Hishām 1, 2.
27. Ibn Hishām 1, 310-311; al-Suhaylī 3, 117-118; *Fatḥ al-Bārī* 7, 212-214 on the authority of Ibn Isḥāq and *ḥadīth* scholars such as Abū Yaʿlā, Ibn Ḥibbān, al-Bayhaqī etc., Ibn Kathīr 3, 46.
28. Balādhurī 1, 131.
29. Balādhurī 1, 148-149.
30. Ibn Kathīr 3, 46; Bukhārī, 'Kitāb Faḍā'il', Ḥadīth No. 3678: *Fatḥ al-Bārī* 7, 129.
31. Ibn Kathīr 3, 44-45 on the authority of Aḥmad, Bukhāri and Muslim; Bukhārī, 'Kitāb al-Ṣalāt', Ḥadīth No. 520; *Fatḥ al-Bārī* 1, 776-876.
32. See 'Kitāb al-Maghāzī'; *Fatḥ al-Bārī* 7, 365; 'Kitāb al-Wuḍū'', *Fatḥ al-Bārī* 1, 454-458, Ḥadīth No. 240.
33. The Qur'ān, *al-Ṣāffāt* 37:171-173.

34. Ibn Kathīr 3, 10.
35. Ibn Kathīr 3, 13.
36. Ṭabarī 2, 311; Ibn Kathīr 3, 25.
37. Ibn Kathīr 3, 60.
38. Ibn Hishām 2, 27; al-Suhaylī 4, 17.
39. Mawdūdī, *Sīrat* 2, 523-525; Ṭabarī 2, 324.
40. Ṭabarī 2, 325.
41. Ibn Hishām 2, 33; al-Suhaylī 4, 39 and 59; Ṭabarī 2, 350.
42. Ibn Hishām 2, 95.
43. Al-Suhaylī 4, 179.
44. Ibn Hishām 1, 335.
45. Ibn Hishām 1, 313-314; al-Suhaylī 3, 120-121.
46. Ibn Hishām 1, 319-320; al-Suhaylī 3, 127.
47. Ibn Hishām 1, 335 and al-Suhaylī 3, 141-142.
48. Al-Suhaylī 3, 146-147.
49. See *tafsīr* of *Sūrah al-Rūm* in various *tafsīr* works; Gibbon *The Decline and Fall of the Roman Empire* 2, 788.
50. *Al-Baqarah* 2:4; *al-Mā'idah* 5:48; *Banū Isrā'īl* 17:82 and 105; *al-Kahf* 18:27; *al-Zumar* 39:42; *al-Shūrā* 42:7; *al-Aḥqāf* 46:9-10; *Ṣād* 38:29; *al-Naml* 27:6; *al-Shuʿarā'* 26:192-195; *al-Qiyāmah* 75:16-19; *al-Aḥzāb* 33:20; *al-Anʿām* 6:106; *al-Aʿrāf* 7:203; *Yūnus* 10:15; *al-Ḥāqqah* 69:44-47; *al-Ḥijr* 15:9; *al-Burūj* 85:21-22; *al-ʿAnkabūt* 29:47 and several other verses.
51. *Al-Sajdah* 32:3; *Yūnus* 10:37; *Banī Isrā'īl* 17:88; *Yūnus* 10:16, and 38; *Hūd* 11:13-14 and *al-Ṭūr* 52:33-34.
52. Al-*Naḥl* 16:103; *al-Shuʿarā'* 26:195; *Fuṣṣilat* 41:44; *Yūsuf* 12:2; *al-Raʿd* 13:27; *Ṭā Hā* 20:112; *al-Zumar* 39-28; *al-Shūrā* 42:7; *al-Zukhruf* 43:3.
53. On the piecemeal revelation of the Qur'ān see *al-Furqān* 25:32; Why it was sent down to the Prophet Muḥammad, *al-Zukhruf* 43:31. The above-quoted verses answer also why it was revealed in Arabic, not some other language. On the myths in the Qur'ān see *al-Anʿām* 6:25; *al-Anfāl* 8:31; *al-Naḥl* 16:24; *al-Mu'minūn* 23:83; *al-Furqān* 25:5; *al-Naml* 27:68; *al-Aḥqāf* 46:17 *al-Qalam* 68:15 and *al-Muṭaffifīn* 83:13.
54. On the Prophet's pre-Prophetic life see *Yūnus* 10:16; On the glad tidings about him by earlier Messengers, al-*Ṣaff* 61:61, which records Prophet Abraham's tiding about his advent; On his genuine Messengership, *Āl ʿImrān* 3:144; *al-Aḥzāb* 33:40; *Muḥammad* 47:2; *al-Fatḥ* 48:29 and many other verses.

55. *Al-Anbiyā'* 21:3 and 7-8; *al-Furqān* 25:7-8; *Yūsuf* 12:109; *al-Ra'd* 13:38; *Yūnus* 10:2; *al-Taghābun* 64:5-6; *Banī Isrā'īl* 17:94-95; *al-Aḥqāf* 46:9; *Ṣād* 38:8 and *al-Zukhruf* 43:31-32.
56. Ibn Hishām 1, 420-421.
57. *Al-Ḥujurāt* 49:13; *al-Munāfiqūn* 63:8.
58. *Ḥujjatullāh al-Bālighah* 2, 204.

CHAPTER 6

1. Ibn Hishām 1, 131, 135-136; 142-144 and 198; see also the article 'Banū 'Abd Manāf. Aẓīm-Tar Muttaḥidah Khāndān-i Risālat'.
2. Ibn Hishām, Balādhurī and Ibn Sa'd.
3. Ibn Hishām 2, 31-34.
4. Ibn Hishām 1, 425.
5. Ibn Hishām 1, 427-428; Suhaylī 4, 59-64; Balādhurī 1, 237-238; Shiblī 1, 252-254; Mawdūdī 2, 686-687.
6. Ibn Hishām 1, 425.
7. Al-Suhaylī; Shiblī; Mawdūdī 2, 686.
8. Mawdūdī, *Sīrat* 2, 687-688 on the authority of Abū Nu'aym, al-Ḥākim and al-Bayhaqī. Al-Suhaylī has related this report at length; Shiblī 1, 253-254.
9. Mawdūdī, *Sīrat* 2, 688-689 on the authority of al-Wāqidi; al-Suhaylī 4, 62-63.
10. Balādhurī 1, 239, 243, 254, 266-267 and 525
11. Balādhurī 1, 243 and 333.
12. Balādhurī 1, 239, 245, 252, 271 and 288.
13. Ibn Sa'd 3, 579.
14. Balādhurī 1, 239, 247, 302, 323 and 380.
15. Balādhurī 1, 239.
16. Balādhurī 107, 248-249, 252-253, 333, 338; Ibn Hishām 1, 423-428.
17. *Fatḥ al-Bārī* 7, 273-278; Bukhārī, 'Kitāb Manāqib al-Anṣār'.
18. Ibn Hishām 2, 38-39; al-Suhaylī 4, 43-45 and 70; Ibn Sa'd 1, 219; Balādhurī 1, 237-240.
19. Ibn Sa'd 1, 218-219.
20. Ibn Sa'd 1, 221.
21. Ibn Sa'd 3, 492-493.

22. Ibn Saʿd 3,621-622; Bukhārī, 'Kitāb al-Maghāzī', *Fatḥ al-Bārī* 7, 407-411; *Ṣaḥīḥ Ta'rīkh al-Islām wa al-Muslimīn*, 898.
23. Ibn Saʿd 3, 578-579)
24. Bukhārī, 'Kitāb al-Adab', Ḥadīth No. 6137; *Fatḥ al-Bārī* 10, 653-656; Muslim, 'Kitāb al-Wuḍū''; *Ṣaḥīḥ Ta'rīkh al-Islām*, 694.
25. *Ta'rīkh al-Islām wa al-Muslimīn* 877-882; Ibn Saʿd 3, 574.
26. Ibn Hishām 2, 38, *Fatḥ al-Bārī* 7, 273-278; al-Suhaylī 4, 43-45; Shiblī 1, 262-263; Ibn Saʿd 1, 218-219; Balādhurī 1, 239-240 and Ibn Kathīr 3, 148-150.
27. Ibn Hishām 2, 39-42; al-Suhaylī 4, 71-74; Ibn Saʿd 1, 218-219; Balādhurī 1, 239-240; Ibn Kathīr 3, 150-166.
28. Ibn Hishām 2, 40-42; al-Suhaylī 4, 73-74; Ibn Saʿd 1, 219-220; Balādhurī 1, 239; Ibn Kathīr 3, 148-151 and 158-166; Mawdūdī, *Sīrat* 2, 695-697.
29. Ibn Hishām 2, 50-51 and 63; al-Suhaylī 4, 74-75; Ibn Saʿd 1, 221-223; Balādhurī 1, 240-255; Ibn Kathīr 3, 158-166; Shiblī 1, 264-265.
30. Ibn Hishām 2, 55 on authority of al-ʿAbbās ibn al-Khazrajī.
31. Ibn Hishām 2, 64-75.
32. Ibn Saʿd 1, 221.
33. Ibn Saʿd 1, 222.
34. *Fatḥ al-Bārī* 7, 217-221; Ibn Ḥajar, *al-Iṣābah*; Ibn al-Athīr, *Usd al-Ghābah,* Ibn Kathīr 3, 34.
35. *Al-Iṣābah*; *Musnad* of Imām Aḥmad; *Ṣaḥīḥ Muslim*; Ibn Kathīr 3, 33-37.
36. Ibn Kathīr 3, 36; *al-Iṣābah.*
37. Ibn ʿAbd al-Barr, *al-Istīʿāb*; *al-Iṣābah.*
38. Bukhārī, 'Kitābat Bad' al-Waḥy'; *Fatḥ al-Bārī* 12, 441-450; al-Suhaylī 2, 406; Muslim, 'Bāb Bad' al-Waḥy'.
39. Ibn Isḥāq/Ibn Hishām; Ibn Kathīr 3, 66, *Fatḥ al-Bārī* 7, 237.
40. Bukhārī, 'Kitāb Manāqib al-Anṣār'. Ḥadīth No. 3900; *Fatḥ al-Bārī*, 7, 282 and 285-286.
41. *Fatḥ al-Bārī* 7, 285-286.
42. *Fatḥ al-Bārī* 7, 281-285; Muslim, 'Kitāb al-Faḍā'il' Ibn Kathīr 3, 168-169.
43. Ibn Saʿd 1, 226; Balādhurī 1, 257-258.
44. Ibn Kathīr 3, 36 on the authority of *Ṣaḥīḥ Muslim.*
45. Ibn Isḥāq/Ibn Hishām 1, 468-470; Ibn Kathīr 3, 169; al-Suhaylī 4, 148-149; Balādhurī 1, 258-259; Bukhārī 'Kitāb Manāqib al-Anṣār';

Fatḥ al-Bārī 7, 324-326 regarding the earliest migrants – *Musnad*, Ibn Maktūm and Abū Salamah.
46. Ṭabarī 2, 369; Ibn Saʿd 1, 226.
47. Al-Tirmidhī; al-Ḥākim 3, 7; *Musnad* of Aḥmad; Ibn Kathīr 3, 305-306 and 221-222.
48. 'Kitāb Manāqib al-Anṣār'; *Fatḥ al-Bārī* 7, 327.
49. Bukhārī; *Fatḥ al-Bārī* 7, 327-328.

CHAPTER 7

1. *Fatḥ al-Bārī* 7, 281-324; Bukhārī 'Kitāb Manāqib al-Anṣār'.
2. For a detailed discussion see *ʿAhd-i Nabawī mayn Tanẓīm-i Riyāsat wa Ḥukūmat*, Chapter 1.
3. See the works on *sīrah* by Shiblī, Kāndhlawī and Mawdūdī.
4. See *ʿAhd-i Nabawī* Chapter 2.
5. Ibn Saʿd 4, 94-100.
6. Bukhārī, 'Kitāb al-Shurūṭ', Ḥadīth Nos. 2731-2732; *Fatḥ al-Bārī* 5, 403-406 and 422.
7. ʿUrwah ibn al-Zubayr, *Maghāzī Rasūl Allāh*, Urdu translation by Muhammad Saeedur Rahman Alvi, Idārah Thaqāfat-i Islāmiyyah, Lahore, 1990, p. 197 does not cite this incident. See also Balādhurī 1, 220-221; Ibn Kathīr 4, 168-169 for the reports provided by Ibn Isḥāq/Ibn Hishām and Bukhārī.
8. Balādhurī 1, 219-220 and 362; al-Suhaylī 6, 463-464; *Fatḥ al-Bārī* 5, 422; Ibn Kathīr 4, 169; Mawdūdī, *Sīrat* 2, 718. Reports indicate that he had a companion during his captivity.
9. Bukhārī, 'Kitāb al-Shurūṭ'; *Fatḥ al-Bārī* 5, 407-408 and 427-431; 'Kitāb al-Maghāzī'; *Fatḥ al-Bārī* 7, 566; Balādhurī 1, 211, 220-221; Ibn Hishām 3, 372; al-Suhaylī 6, 469-471 and 492.
10. Bukhārī 1, 208; Ibn Saʿd 4, 130-131.
11. Ibn Hishām 2, 85-88; al-Suhaylī 4, 170-171; Balādhurī, 1, 208-209; Ibn Saʿd 4, 129-131; Ibn Kathīr 3, 172.
12. Ibn Hishām 2, 85-88; al-Suhaylī 4, 171-172; Balādhurī 1, 215-220.
13. Ibn Saʿd 4, 191.
14. Balādhurī 1, 220; Ibn Saʿd 4, 191; Ibn Kathīr 3, 172.
15. Ibn Hishām 2, 652-655; al-Suhaylī 5, 163; Ibn Saʿd 8, 131.

16. Ibn Hishām 2, 469-470; al-Suhaylī 4, 148.
17. Ibn Hishām 3, 375; al-Suhaylī 6, 472-474; Ibn Sa'd 8, 230; Bukhārī, 'Kitāb al-Maghāzī', Bāb Ghazwat al-Ḥudaybīyah, Ḥadīth Nos 4180-4181; *Fatḥ al-Bārī* 7, 566-567; 'Kitāb al-Shurūṭ' Ḥadīth Nos. 2711-2712; *Fatḥ al-Bārī* 5, 383-384.
18. Bukhārī, 'Kitāb Manāqib al-Anṣār', *Fatḥ al-Bārī*, 7, 236-237; Balādhurī 1, 222-223.
19. Ibn Sa'd 4, 139.
20. Balādhurī 1, 216-217.
21. Ibn Hishām; al-Suhaylī 3, 211-212 and 232-233; Ibn Kathīr 3, 90-91.
22. Ibn Kathīr 3, 91.
23. The Qur'ān, *al-Nisā'* 4:75.
24. Ibn Kathīr, *Tafsīr al-Qur'ān al-'Aẓīm*, Muṣṭafā al-Bābī, Cairo, n.d. 1, 525.
25. *Fatḥ al-Bārī* 8, 321-323.
26. *Bayān al-Qur'ān*, 1, 134.
27. *Tafhīm al-Qur'ān* 1, 372.
28. The Qur'ān, *al-Nisā'* 4:75.
29. *Tadabbur-i Qur'ān*, Faran Foundation, Lahore, 1983, 2, 636.
30. Ibn Hishām 2, 283.
31. 'Kitāb al-Tafsīr', *Sūrah al-Nisā'*, Chapter 19.
32. *Fatḥ al-Bārī* 8, 232.
33. See also *tafsīr* works of Thānwī, Mawdūdī and Iṣlāḥī.
34. Ibn Sa'd 4, 10.
35. Ibn Hishām 1, 446; Ibn Sa'd 4, 10; Ṭabarī 2, 461.
36. Ibn Sa'd 4, 10-12; Ṭabarī 2, 448-450.
37. Ibn Sa'd 4, 12-14; Balādhurī 1, 301 and Ibn Kathīr 1, 328.
38. Balādhurī 1, 313-314.
39. Ibn Sa'd 4, 16-17.
40. Ibn Sa'd 4, 17
41. Ibn Sa'd 4, 17-18.
42. Ibn Sa'd 4, 18-20; Balādhurī 1, 355.
43. Balādhurī 1, 355.
44. Ibn Isḥāq/Ibn Hishām; al-Suhaylī 3, 365; Ibn Kathīr 3, 79-80.
45. Ibn Sa'd 4, 138-139.
46. Ibn Sa'd 4, 252-254.
47. Ibn Sa'd 4, 252-385.

48. See also Ibn Kathīr 4, 236-240.
49. Al-Zubayrī, *Kitāb Nasab Quraysh* 124-126; *al-Iṣābah* 1, 112 and 6, 113. *Usd al-Ghābah* 4, 384; Ibn Sa'd 4, 40; *al-Istīʿāb*3, 1416; Syed Suleman Nadvi, *Shiblī's Sīrat al-Nabī* 1, 467.
50. Ibn Hishām 3, 372; *Fatḥ al-Bārī*; al-Suhaylī 6, 468; Shiblī 1, 459; Kāndhalawī 2, 366.
51. Ibn Hishām 2, 476; Balādhurī 1, 210-211; Ibn Saʿd 4, 129, 131 and 191-192.
52. Balādhurī 1, 219-220.
53. Ibn Hishām 2, 673-674; Balādhurī 1, 220; Ibn Saʿd 4, 132-133.
54. Ibn Hishām 2, 372-374; al-Suhaylī 6, 463-464; Balādhurī 1, 211 and 219; Ibn Kathīr 4, 176-177.
55. Balādhurī 1, 220.
56. The Qur'ān, *al-Zumar* 39: 53-55.
57. Ibn Hishām 1m 475-476; al-Suhaylī 4, 171-172 and 4, 191.
58. *Fatḥ al-Bārī* 8, 232.
59. Ibn Hishām 2, 77-78; al-Suhaylī 4, 148.
60. Ibn Hishām 2, 296-299.
61. Bukhārī, 'Kitāb al-Īmān'; *Fatḥ al-Bārī*, 171-178.
62. *Tadabbur* 2, 236.

CONCLUSION

1. *Ḥujjatullāh al-Bālighah* 1, 124-125.
2. The Qur'ān, *al-ʿAnkabūt* 29:69.
3. The Qur'ān, *al-Qaṣaṣ 28:70*

Index